The Complete Mason Jar Cookbook

Quick, Easy and Delicious Mason Jar Meal Recipes For for Breakfast, Lunch and Dinner

BY: FAYE C. BRACEY

TABLE OF CONTENTS

RECIPES

1. Caprese Pasta Salad

Prep Time: 15 mins

Cook Time: 10 mins

Total Time: 25 mins

Servings: 4

Ingredients:

- 8 **oz**s fusilli or penne pasta
- 1 **cup of** cherry tomatoes, halved
- 1 **cup of** fresh mozzarella balls, halved
- 1/4 **cup of** fresh basil leaves, torn
- 2 **tbsp** extra-virgin olive oil
- 1 **tbsp** balsamic vinegar
- 1 garlic clove, **chop-up**
- Salt and pepper **as needed**

Instructions:

1. Pasta **Must** be cooked as directed on the **box/pkg up to** it is al dente. To end cooking, drain and rinse with cold water. Place aside.
2. The cooked pasta, cherry tomatoes, mozzarella balls, and torn basil leaves **Must** all be **combine**d in a big bowl.
3. **Combine** the olive oil, balsamic vinegar, garlic powder, salt, and pepper in a **mini** bowl.
4. After adding the dressing, gently toss the pasta **Mixture** to incorporate.
5. Serve right away or chill for a few **hrs** before serving to **let** the flavors to mingle.

Nutrition (per serving):
Cals: 350, Fat: 17g, **Carb**s: 36g, Protein: 12g
Fiber: 3g

2. Chicken Caesar Salad

Prep Time: 20 mins

Cook Time: 20 mins

Total Time: 40 mins

Servings: 2

Ingredients:

- 2 boneless, skinless chicken breasts
- Salt and pepper **as needed**
- 2 **tbsp** olive oil
- 4 **cups of** romaine lettuce, **chop-up**
- 1/4 **cup of finely grated** Parmesan cheese
- 1/2 **cup of** croutons
- Caesar dressing (store-bought or homemade)

Instructions:

1. Chicken breasts **Must** be salted and peppered.
2. Olive oil **Must** be heated to a medium-high temperature in a big skillet. When the chicken breasts are fully cooked, add them and grill them for roughly 6-7 **min**s on **every** side.
3. Before slicing, take the chicken out of the skillet and let it rest for a while.
4. **Combine** the romaine lettuce, croutons, and **finely grated** Parmesan cheese in a big bowl.
5. **Split** chicken **Must** be added to the bowl along with Caesar dressing.
6. **Combine** everything **up to** it is completely covered in dressing.
7. Serve right away as a satisfying and tasty Caesar salad.

Nutrition (per serving):
Cals: 420, Fat: 24g
Carbs: 12g
Protein: 40g, Fiber: 3g

3. Mason Jar Ramen Noodles

Prep Time: 15 mins

Cook Time: 10 mins

Total Time: 25 mins

Servings: 1

Ingredients:

- 1 pack of instant ramen noodles (discard the seasoning packet if desired)
- 1/2 **cup of** cooked and shredded chicken or tofu
- 1/4 **cup of split** carrots
- 1/4 **cup of split** bell peppers
- 1/4 **cup of** baby spinach
- 1 green onion, **split**
- 1 **tbsp** soy sauce
- 1 **tbsp** sesame oil
- 1 **tsp** sriracha (**non-compulsory**)
- 1 boiled egg, halved (**non-compulsory**)
- Sesame seeds for garnish (**non-compulsory**)

Instructions:

1. Ramen noodles **Must** be prepared as directed on the packaging. Drain, then set apart.
2. Layer the cooked, shredded chicken or tofu, **split** carrots, **split** bell peppers, baby spinach, and green onions in a mason jar or other microwave-safe container.
3. **Combine** the soy sauce, sesame oil, and sriracha (if using) in a **mini** bowl. Over the piled ingredients in the mason jar, pour the sauce.
4. **Up to** you are ready to eat, place the mason jar's lid in the refrigerator.
5. When you're ready to eat the ramen, cover the contents of the mason jar with boiling water **up to** everything is covered.

6. To **let** the flavors to merge, tightly close the lid and leave it alone for 3–4 **min**s.
7. If preferred, garnish with a halved boiled egg and sesame seeds after opening the jar and thoroughly stirring the contents.
8. Enjoy your delicious and easy Mason jar ramen!

Nutrition (per serving):
Cals: 450, Fat: 20g, **Carb**s: 40g

Protein: 25g, Fiber: 5g

4.Rainbow Fruit Parfait

Prep Time: 15 **min**s

Total Time: 15 **min**s

Servings: 2

Ingredients:
- 1 **cup of** Greek yogurt
- 1 **tbsp** honey
- 1 **tsp** vanilla extract
- 1 **cup of** strawberries, diced
- 1 **cup of** mandarin oranges, drained
- 1 **cup of** pineapple chunks, drained
- 1 **cup of** kiwi, **peel off** and diced
- 1 **cup of** blueberries
- 1/4 **cup of** granola

Instructions:
1. Greek yogurt, honey, and vanilla essence **Must** all be thoroughly blended in a **mini** basin.
2. Layer the diced strawberries, mandarin oranges, chunks of pineapple, diced kiwi, and blueberries in serving glasses or bowls.
3. **Every** glass of fruit **Must** have a coating of the Greek yogurt **Mixture** on top.
4. Till the glasses are full, keep adding yogurt and fruit layers.
5. Granola can be sprinkled on top of **every** parfait to add crunch and taste.
6. Serve right away or quickly cool in the refrigerator before serving.

Nutrition (per serving):
Cals: 250, Fat: 3g, **Carb**s: 50g

Protein: 10g, Fiber: 8g

5.Blueberry Almond Chia Pudding

Prep Time: 5 **min**s

Total Time: 4 **hr**s (includes chilling time)

Servings: 2

Ingredients:
- 1 **cup of** almond milk
- 1/4 **cup of** chia seeds
- 1 **tbsp** honey or maple syrup
- 1/2 **tsp** vanilla extract
- 1/2 **cup of** fresh blueberries
- 2 **tbsp split** almonds

Instructions:
1. Almond milk, chia seeds, honey (or maple syrup), and vanilla essence **Must** all be thoroughly blended in a bowl.
2. **Let** the **Mixture** to rest for approximately 5 **min**s, then whisk it once more to avoid clumping.
3. To help the chia seeds absorb the liquid and take on the consistency of pudding, cover the bowl and place it in the refrigerator for at least 4 **hr**s or overnight.
4. Give the chia pudding a vigorous swirl after it has thickened.
5. Layer the chia pudding, fresh blueberries, and **split** almonds in serving glasses or bowls.
6. Continue layering the ingredients **up to** all are utilized, and then top with a scattering of blueberries and **split** almonds.
7. Serve right away or store in the fridge **up to** you're ready to eat.

Nutrition (per serving):
Cals: 220, Fat: 10g, **Carb**s: 27g

Protein: 6g, Fiber: 11g

5. Overnight Oats with Combined Berries

Prep Time: 10 **min**s

Total Time: 8 **hr**s 10 **min**s (including overnight chilling)

Servings: 2

Ingredients:
- 1 **cup of** rolled oats
- 1 **cup of** milk (dairy or plant-based)
- 1 **tbsp** chia seeds
- 1 **tbsp** honey or maple syrup
- 1/2 **tsp** vanilla extract
- 1/2 **cup of combined** berries (blueberries, strawberries, raspberries)
- 1 **tbsp split** almonds (**non-compulsory**)

Instructions:
1. Rolling oats, milk, chia seeds, honey, maple syrup, and vanilla essence **Must** all be **combine**d in a dish or jar.
2. Add half of the **combined** berries to the **Mixture** after thoroughly combining.
3. Place the dish or jar in the fridge for at least eight **hr**s or overnight.
4. Give the oats a thorough stir in the morning. To achieve the required consistency, add more milk if the **Mixture** is too thick.
5. The leftover **combined** berries and **split** almonds (if used) **Must** be sprinkled on top of the overnight oats.

6. Enjoy your tasty and nourishing Overnight Oats with **Combined** Berries chilled.

Nutrition (per serving):
Cals: 320 kcal, **Carb**s: 52g, Protein: 9g
Fat: 9g, Fiber: 8g

6.Southwest Quinoa Salad

Prep Time: 15 **min**s
Cook Time: 20 **min**s
Total Time: 35 **min**s
Servings: 4

Ingredients:
- 1 **cup of** quinoa, rinsed
- 2 **cups of** water or vegetable broth
- 1 can (15 oz) black beans, drained and rinsed
- 1 **cup of** corn kernels (fresh, **refrigerate**, or canned)
- 1 red bell pepper, diced
- 1/2 **cup of** cherry tomatoes, halved
- 1/4 **cup of chop-up** fresh cilantro
- 1 avocado, diced
- 1/4 **cup of** lime juice
- 2 **tbsp** olive oil
- 1 **tsp** ground cumin
- Salt and pepper **as needed**

Instructions:
1. Bring the quinoa, water, and/or vegetable broth to a boil in a medium saucepan. Once the quinoa is cooked and the liquid has been absorbed, lower the heat to low, cover the pan, and simmer for 15 to 20 **min**s.
2. Cooked quinoa, black beans, corn, **split** red bell pepper, cherry tomatoes, and cilantro **Must** all be **combine**d in a big bowl.
3. To create the dressing, **combine** the lime juice, cumin powder, olive oil, salt, and pepper in a separate **mini** bowl.
4. When everything is thoroughly incorporated, drizzle the dressing over the quinoa **Mixture**.
5. Fold the cubed avocado in gently.
6. Southwest Quinoa Salad is best served cold or at room temperature.

Nutrition (per serving):
Cals: 350 kcal, **Carb**s: 49g, Protein: 10g
Fat: 14g, Fiber: 11g

7. Lemon Herb Roasted Vegetables

Prep Time: 15 **min**s
Cook Time: 25 **min**s
Total Time: 40 **min**s
Servings: 4

Ingredients:
- 1 zucchini, **split**
- 1 yellow squash, **split**
- 1 red bell pepper, **slice** into strips
- 1 yellow bell pepper, **slice** into strips
- 1 red onion, **slice** into wedges
- 1 **cup of** cherry tomatoes
- 3 **tbsp** olive oil
- 2 cloves garlic, **chop-up**
- Zest of 1 lemon
- 2 **tbsp** lemon juice
- 1 **tsp** dried thyme
- 1 **tsp** dried rosemary
- Salt and pepper **as needed**

Instructions:
1. Turn on the oven to 425 °F (220 °C).
2. **Split** zucchini, yellow squash, red and yellow bell peppers, red onion, and cherry tomatoes **Must** all be **combine**d in a sizable **combining** dish.
3. **Combine** the olive oil, **chop-up** garlic, lemon zest, lemon juice, dried thyme, dried rosemary, salt, and pepper in a separate **mini** bowl.
4. When the vegetables are thoroughly coated, pour the dressing over them and **combine**.
5. On a baking sheet, arrange the vegetables in a single layer.
6. The veggies **Must** be roasted in the preheated oven for 20 to 25 **min**s, stirring once halfway through, or **up to** they are soft and just beginning to brown.
7. Serve the Lemon Herb Roasted Vegetables as a tasty and eye-catching side dish after taking them out of the oven.

Nutrition (per serving):
Cals: 170 kcal, **Carb**s: 12g, Protein: 2g, Fat: 14g
Fiber: 4g

8. Tex-Mex Taco Salad

Prep Time: 20 **min**s
Cook Time: 10 **min**s
Total Time: 30 **min**s
Servings: 4

Ingredients:
- 1 lb ground beef or turkey
- 1 **tbsp** olive oil
- 1 packet taco seasoning **combine**
- 1/2 **cup of** water
- 4 **cups of chop-up** lettuce (romaine or iceberg)

- 1 **cup of** cherry tomatoes, halved
- 1 **cup of** black beans, drained and rinsed
- 1 **cup of** corn kernels (fresh, **refrigerate**, or canned)
- 1/2 **cup of** shredded cheddar cheese
- 1/4 **cup of chop-up** green onions
- 1/4 **cup of split** black olives
- 1/4 **cup of chop-up** fresh cilantro
- 1 avocado, diced
- 1/2 **cup of** sour cream (**non-compulsory**)
- Salsa for serving (**non-compulsory**)

Instructions:

1. Olive oil **Must** be heated in a sizable skillet over medium heat. Cook the ground beef or turkey, breaking it up with a spoon as it cooks, **up to** it is browned and well done.
2. Add the water and taco seasoning **combine** and stir. The sauce will thicken after a few **min**s of simmering.
3. Place the **chop-up** lettuce, cherry tomatoes, black beans, corn, shredded cheddar cheese, green onions, black olive slices, and cilantro in a **Big** salad dish.
4. Add **chop-up** avocado and cooked taco meat to the salad as a garnish.
5. Serve the dish with salsa on the side and some sour cream drizzled on top, if preferred.
6. To enjoy the Tex-Mex Taco Salad, **combine** everything right before eating.

Nutrition (per serving):
Cals: 480 kcal, **Carb**s: 28g, Protein: 29g
Fat: 30g, Fiber: 9g

9. Layered Greek Salad

Prep Time: 20 **min**s
Total Time: 20 **min**s
Servings: 4

Ingredients:

- 2 **cups of chop-up** Romaine lettuce
- 1 **cup of chop-up** cucumber
- 1 **cup of** cherry tomatoes, halved
- 1/2 **cup of split** red onion
- 1/2 **cup of** Kalamata olives, pitted
- 1/2 **cup of cut up** feta cheese
- 1/4 **cup of chop-up** fresh parsley
- 1/4 **cup of** extra-virgin olive oil
- 2 **tbsp** red wine vinegar
- 1 **tsp** dried oregano
- Salt and pepper **as needed**

Instructions:

1. Half of the **chop-up** Romaine lettuce **Must** be layered in a sizable, transparent serving bowl or trifle dish.
2. After that, incorporate half of the diced cucumber, cherry tomatoes, red onion slices, Kalamata olives, feta cheese **cut up**s, and fresh parsley.
3. Over the salad, drizzle the remaining extra-virgin olive oil and red wine vinegar.
4. Add salt, pepper, and half of the dried oregano.
5. With the remaining ingredients, repeat the stacking procedure.
6. Layered Greek Salad **Must** be covered and kept in the fridge **up to** ready to serve.
7. Toss the salad gently just before serving to **combine** the layers, or let your guests do so at the table.

Nutrition (per serving):
Cals: 230 kcal, **Carb**s: 9g, Protein: 5g, Fat: 20g
Fiber: 3g

10.Pesto Chicken and Tomato Pasta

Prep Time: 15 **min**s
Cook Time: 15 **min**s
Total Time: 30 **min**s
Servings: 4

Ingredients:

- 8 oz (225g) pasta of your choice
- 2 boneless, skinless chicken breasts, cooked and diced
- 1 **cup of** cherry tomatoes, halved
- 1/4 **cup of** pesto sauce
- 1/4 **cup of finely grated** Parmesan cheese
- Salt and pepper **as needed**
- Fresh basil leaves for garnish

Instructions:

1. Pasta **Must** be cooked as directed on the **box/pkg up to** it is al dente. Drain, then set apart.
2. **Combine** the cooked pasta, chicken, cherry tomatoes, and pesto sauce in a sizable **combining** bowl. Till everything is completely coated, toss.
3. **As needed**, add salt and pepper to the food.
4. Fresh basil leaves **Must** be used as a garnish, then top with **finely grated** Parmesan cheese.
5. Serve right away and delight in!

Nutrition (per serving):
Cals: 450 kcal, Protein: 30g, Fat: 15g, **Carb**s: 45g, Fiber: 3g

11.Mason Jar Cobb Salad

Prep Time: 20 mins

Cook Time: 0 mins

Total Time: 20 mins

Servings: 2

Ingredients:

- 1 **cup of chop-up** romaine lettuce
- 1 **cup of** diced cooked chicken breast
- 1/2 **cup of** cherry tomatoes, halved
- 1/2 **cup of** diced cucumber
- 1/2 **cup of cut up** blue cheese
- 2 hard-boiled eggs, **chop-up**
- 4 slices cooked bacon, **cut up**
- 1/4 **cup of** ranch dressing

Instructions:

1. Ranch dressing, cherry tomatoes, diced cucumber, **chop-up** romaine lettuce, diced chicken breast, **chop-up** hard-boiled eggs, **cut up** blue cheese, and **cut up** bacon **Must** be layered in two mason jars.
2. Prior to serving, seal the jars and place them in the refrigerator.
3. When it's time to dine, shake the mason jars to incorporate the ingredients and dressing, or add everything to a big salad bowl and toss it all together.
4. Enjoy your convenient and delicious Cobb salad in a jar!

Nutrition (per serving):

Cals: 480 kcal, Protein: 32g, Fat: 34g, **Carb**s: 12g, Fiber: 3g

12.Thai Peanut Noodles

Prep Time: 15 mins

Cook Time: 10 mins

Total Time: 25 mins

Servings: 4

Ingredients:

- 8 oz (225g) rice noodles
- 1/4 **cup of** peanut butter
- 3 tbsp soy sauce
- 1 tbsp sesame oil
- 1 tbsp honey or maple syrup
- 1 tsp **finely grated** ginger
- 2 cloves garlic, **chop-up**
- 1/4 **cup of** hot water
- 1 **cup of** shredded carrots
- 1 **cup of** shredded purple cabbage
- 1 red bell pepper, thinly **split**
- 2 green onions, **split**
- 1/4 **cup of chop-up** peanuts (**non-compulsory**)
- Lime wedges for serving
- Fresh cilantro for garnish

Instructions:

1. Rice noodles **Must** be prepared as directed on the **box/pkg up to** they are al dente. Drain, then set apart.
2. To create the sauce, **combine** the boiling water, peanut butter, soy sauce, sesame oil, honey (or maple syrup), **finely grated** ginger, and **chop-up** garlic in a bowl.
3. The cooked noodles, shredded carrots, shredded purple cabbage, **split** red bell pepper, and **split** green onions **Must** all be **combine**d in a sizable **combining** dish.
4. Over the noodles and vegetables, drizzle the peanut sauce. **Combine** everything and toss **up to** evenly coated.
5. Add fresh cilantro and **chop-up** peanuts as a garnish.
6. Lime wedges **Must** be served alongside.

Nutrition (per serving):

Cals: 420 kcal, Protein: 10g, Fat: 12g, **Carb**s: 70g, Fiber: 5g

13.Apple Cinnamon Overnight Oats

Prep Time: 10 mins

Cook Time: 0 mins

Total Time: 8 hrs 10 mins (including overnight soaking)

Servings: 2

Ingredients:

- 1 **cup of** rolled oats
- 1 **cup of** almond milk (or any milk of your choice)
- 1/2 **cup of** Greek yogurt
- 1 apple, **finely grated** or **lightly chop-up**
- 1 tbsp honey or maple syrup
- 1/2 tsp ground cinnamon
- 1/4 **cup of chop-up** nuts (e.g., almonds, walnuts, or pecans)
- 1/4 **cup of** dried cranberries or raisins (**non-compulsory**)

Instructions:

1. Rolling oats, almond milk, Greek yogurt, **finely grated** apple, honey (or maple syrup), and ground cinnamon are **combine**d in a **combining** basin. **Combine** thoroughly.
2. In two jars or other airtight containers with lids, divide the **Mixture**.
3. To let the oats soak and soften, cover the containers and place them in the refrigerator for at least 8 **hr**s or overnight.
4. Give the oats a good toss in the morning and, if like, top with **chop-up** nuts, raisins, or dried cranberries.
5. Take pleasure in your savory and nourishing Apple Cinnamon Overnight Oats!

Cals: 350 kcal, Protein: 10g, Fat: 10g, **Carb**s: 55g, Fiber: 8g

14.Mediterranean Couscous Salad

Prep Time: 15 **min**s

Cook Time: 10 **min**s

Total Time: 25 **min**s

Servings: 4

Ingredients:

- 1 **cup of** couscous
- 1 1/4 **cups of** vegetable broth or water
- 1 **cup of** cherry tomatoes, halved
- 1 cucumber, diced
- 1/2 red onion, **lightly chop-up**
- 1/2 **cup of cut up** feta cheese
- 1/4 **cup of** Kalamata olives, pitted and halved
- 1/4 **cup of chop-up** fresh parsley
- 2 tbsp extra-virgin olive oil
- 2 tbsp lemon juice
- Salt and pepper **as needed**

Instructions:

1. Bring the water or vegetable broth to a boil in a saucepan. The couscous is then added, the pan is covered, and the heat is turned off. **Let** the couscous to absorb the liquid for about five **min**s. Use a fork to fluff it.
2. Cooked couscous, **split** cucumber, **lightly chop-up** red onion, feta cheese, and halved Kalamata olives **Must** all be **combine**d in a **Big combining** dish.
3. To make the dressing, **combine** the extra-virgin olive oil and lemon juice in a separate **mini** bowl.
4. The couscous **Mixture Must** be well-coated once the dressing has been added.
5. Garnish with fresh parsley that has been **slice** and season with salt and pepper to suit.
6. Serve refrigerated or at room temperature.

Nutrition (per serving):

Cals: 320 kcal, Protein: 9g, Fat: 14g, **Carb**s: 40g

Fiber: 4g

15.Shrimp and Avocado Salad

Prep Time: 20 **min**s

Cook Time: 5 **min**s

Total Time: 25 **min**s

Servings: 2

Ingredients:

- 8 oz (225g) cooked shrimp, **peel off** and deveined
- 1 avocado, diced
- 1 **cup of** cherry tomatoes, halved
- 1/4 **cup of** diced red onion
- 1/4 **cup of chop-up** cucumber
- 2 tbsp **chop-up** fresh cilantro
- 2 tbsp olive oil
- 1 tbsp lime juice
- 1 clove garlic, **chop-up**
- Salt and pepper **as needed**
- **Non-compulsory**: chop-up jalapeno for added heat

Instructions:

1. The cooked shrimp, diced avocado, cherry tomatoes, red onion, cucumber, and fresh cilantro **Must** all be **combine**d in a sizable **combining** dish.
2. To prepare the dressing, **combine** the olive oil, lime juice, garlic that has been **chop-up**, salt, and pepper in a **mini** bowl.
3. Over the shrimp and avocado combination, drizzle the dressing. Gently blend by tossing.
4. If you want to give the salad some heat, add some **split** jalapenos.
5. Enjoy your reviving Shrimp and Avocado Salad right away!

Nutrition (per serving):

Cals: 380 kcal, Protein: 20g, Fat: 25g

Carbs: 18g, Fiber: 9g

16.Antipasto Pasta Salad

Prep Time: 15 **min**s

Cook Time: 10 **min**s

Total Time: 25 **min**s

Servings: 4

Ingredients:

- 8 **oz**s rotini pasta
- 1 **cup of** cherry tomatoes, halved
- 1 **cup of** mozzarella cheese balls
- 1/2 **cup of split** pepperoni
- 1/2 **cup of split** black olives
- 1/4 **cup of split** red onions
- 1/4 **cup of split** banana peppers
- 1/4 **cup of chop-up** fresh basil
- 2 **tbsp** balsamic vinegar
- 2 **tbsp** extra-virgin olive oil
- Salt and pepper **as needed**

Instructions:

1. Rotini pasta **Must** be prepared per the directions on the **box/pkg**. Let it cool and then drain.

2. Cooked spaghetti, cherry tomatoes, mozzarella cheese balls, pepperoni, black olives, red onions, banana peppers, and fresh basil **Must** all be **combine**d in a sizable **combining** dish.
3. **Combine** the balsamic vinegar, extra virgin olive oil, salt, and pepper in a **mini** bowl.
4. When the pasta salad is thoroughly covered, drizzle the dressing over it and toss to **combine**.
5. To **let** the flavors to mingle, serve right away or place in the fridge for a few **hr**s.

Nutrition (per serving):
Cals: 380 kcal, **Carb**s: 37g, Protein: 15g
Fat: 20g, Fiber: 3g

17.Mason Jar Veggie Stir-Fry

Prep Time: 15 **min**s
Cook Time: 15 **min**s
Total Time: 30 **min**s
Servings: 2

Ingredients:
- 1 **cup of** broccoli florets
- 1 **cup of split** bell peppers (assorted colors)
- 1 **cup of split** carrots
- 1 **cup of** snow peas
- 1/2 **cup of split** mushrooms
- 1 **tbsp** vegetable oil
- 2 **tbsp** soy sauce
- 1 **tbsp** hoisin sauce
- 1 **tsp** sesame oil
- 1/2 **tsp finely grated** fresh ginger
- 1 clove garlic, **chop-up**
- 2 green onions, **chop-up**
- 1 **tbsp** sesame seeds (**non-compulsory**)

Instructions:
1. In a sizable skillet or wok, warm the vegetable oil over medium-high heat.
2. To the skillet, add the broccoli, bell peppers, carrots, snow peas, and mushrooms. Vegetables **Must** be stir-fried for 5-7 **min**s, or **up to** they are crisp-tender.
3. **Combine** the soy sauce, hoisin sauce, sesame oil, **finely grated** ginger, and **chop-up** garlic in a **mini** bowl.
4. The stir-fried vegetables **Must** be evenly coated once the sauce has been added.
5. Take the stir-fry off the heat and give it a moment to cool.
6. Layer the stir-fried vegetables and **lightly chop-up** green onions in two mason jars.
7. Sesame seeds can be added for texture and taste if desired.

8. Before serving, refrigerate the mason jars that have been sealed. Shake the jar before pouring the food onto a plate or dish to eat.

Nutrition (per serving):
Cals: 220 kcal, **Carb**s: 25g, Protein: 6g
Fat: 12g, Fiber: 7g

18.Berry Cheesecake Parfait

Prep Time: 20 **min**s
Cook Time: No cooking required
Total Time: 20 **min**s
Servings: 4

Ingredients:
- 1 **cup of** graham cracker crumbs
- 2 **tbsp** unsalted butter, **dilute**
- 8 **oz**s cream cheese, **melted**
- 1/2 **cup of** powdered sugar
- 1 **tsp** vanilla extract
- 1 **cup of** whipped cream or whipped topping
- 1 **cup of** fresh **combined** berries (strawberries, blueberries, raspberries)

Instructions:
1. Graham cracker crumbs and **dilute** butter **Must** be **combined** together in a **mini** bowl **up to** the crumbs are thoroughly covered.
2. Beat the **melted** cream cheese **up to** it is creamy and smooth in a different bowl.
3. As you continue to whip the cream cheese, add the powdered sugar and vanilla extract.
4. Whipping cream or other whipped topping **Must** be gently incorporated into the cream cheese **Mixture** to create a light cheesecake filling.
5. Create layers in serving glasses or mason jars by first layering the graham cracker crumbs, then the cheesecake filling, and finally the **combined** berries.
6. Continue layering **up to** you r**every** the top, then add a garnish of a final layer of berries.
7. Before serving, place in the refrigerator for at least an **hr** to enable the flavors to mingle.

Nutrition (per serving):
Cals: 350 kcal, **Carb**s: 25g, Protein: 5g
Fat: 26g, Fiber: 3g

19.Mexican Street Corn Salad

Prep Time: 15 **min**s
Cook Time: 10 **min**s
Total Time: 25 **min**s
Servings: 6

Ingredients:

- 4 **cups of** cooked corn kernels (fresh, canned, or **refrigerate** and thawed)
- 1/2 **cup of** mayonnaise
- 1/2 **cup of** sour cream
- 1/2 **cup of** cut up cotija cheese (or feta cheese)
- 1/4 **cup of chop-up** fresh cilantro
- 1/4 **cup of chop-up** green onions
- 1 garlic clove, **chop-up**
- 1 jalapeño pepper, seeds **take out**d and **lightly chop-up** (**non-compulsory**)
- 1 **tbsp** lime juice
- 1 **tsp** chili powder
- Salt and pepper **as needed**

Instructions:

1. The cooked corn kernels, mayonnaise, sour cream, cotija cheese, cilantro, green onions, **chop-up** garlic, and diced jalapenos (if using) **Must** all be **combined** together in a sizable bowl.
2. Sprinkle salt, pepper, and chili powder over the **Mixture** after squeezing lime juice over it.
3. Toss everything together **up to** the dressing and spices are equally distributed throughout the corn.
4. If necessary, taste and adjust the seasoning.
5. Serve right away or keep chilled **up to** you're ready to.

Nutrition (per serving):
Cals: 250 kcal, **Carb**s: 20g, Protein: 6g
Fat: 18g, Fiber: 3g

20.Layered Sushi Salad

Prep Time: 20 **min**s
Cook Time: No cooking required
Total Time: 20 **min**s
Servings: 2

Ingredients:

- 2 **cups of** cooked sushi rice, cooled
- 1 avocado, **split**
- 1/2 **cup of** cucumber, julienned
- 1/2 **cup of** imitation crab meat, shredded
- 1 **tbsp** sesame seeds
- 2 **tbsp** soy sauce
- 1 **tbsp** rice vinegar
- 1 **tsp** sugar
- 1/2 **tsp** wasabi paste (**non-compulsory**)
- Pickled ginger and nori sheets for garnish (**non-compulsory**)

Instructions:

1. To make the dressing, **combine** the soy sauce, rice vinegar, sugar, and wasabi paste (if using).
2. Start arranging the sushi salad in two serving dishes or mason jars. Sushi rice **Must** be placed at the bottom to start.
3. Slices of avocado, julienned cucumber, and shredded imitation crab meat **Must** all be added in layers.
4. Sesame seeds **Must** be scattered on top of **every** layer.
5. Up till the top of the bowl or jar, repeat the layering process.
6. Just before serving, drizzle the salad with the dressing.
7. Pickled ginger and nori sheets can be used as garnish, if preferred.

Nutrition (per serving):
Cals: 420 kcal, **Carb**s: 60g, Protein: 9g
Fat: 16g, Fiber: 8g

21.Mason Jar Breakfast Burrito

Prep Time: 20 **min**s
Cook Time: 10 **min**s
Total Time: 30 **min**s
Servings: 2

Ingredients:

- 4 **Big** eggs
- 1/4 **cup of** milk
- 1/2 **cup of** diced bell peppers (assorted colors)
- 1/2 **cup of** diced onions
- 1/2 **cup of** cooked and **cut up** breakfast sausage
- 1/2 **cup of** shredded cheddar cheese
- 2 **Big** flour tortillas
- Salt and pepper **as needed**
- Salsa or hot sauce for serving (**non-compulsory**)

Instructions:

1. Whisk the eggs and milk together in a **combining** bowl. **As needed**, add salt and pepper to the food.
2. A nonstick skillet **Must** be heated to medium. The skillet will now contain the egg **Mixture**.
3. To the eggs, add the diced bell peppers and onions. Cook the eggs **up to** they are fully cooked and scrambled, stirring periodically.
4. For a little while, reheat the flour tortillas in the microwave or on a different skillet.
5. The scrambled eggs, cooked breakfast sausage, and shredded cheddar cheese **Must** be **slice up** between the two tortillas after they have been spread out.
6. To secure the fillings, roll the burritos up while tucking in the sides.
7. For simple transportation and storage, wrap

every burrito in foil or parchment paper before packing it into a mason jar.

8. If preferred, serve with salsa or hot sauce on the side.

Nutrition (per serving):

Cals: 450 kcal, **Carb**s: 30g, Protein: 20g

Fat: 28g, Fiber: 2g

22. Layered Ratatouille

Prep Time: 15 **min**s

Cook Time: 1 **hr**

Total Time: 1 **hr** 15 **min**s

Servings: 4

Ingredients:

- 1 **Big** eggplant, **split**
- 2 zucchinis, **split**
- 2 **Big** tomatoes, **split**
- 1 red bell pepper, **split**
- 1 yellow bell pepper, **split**
- 1/4 **cup of** olive oil
- 2 cloves garlic, **chop-up**
- 1 **tsp** dried thyme
- Salt and pepper **as needed**
- 1 **cup of finely grated** Parmesan cheese

Instructions:

1. Set the oven's temperature to 375°F (190°C). Olive oil **Must** be used to grease a baking pan.
2. In the baking dish, put the **split** vegetables in alternate layers, slightly overlapping **every** layer.
3. **Combine** the **chop-up** garlic, dry thyme, salt, and pepper in a **mini** bowl. Sprinkle half of the seasoning combination and drizzle half of the olive oil over the vegetables.
4. With the remaining vegetables, olive oil, and seasoning combination, repeat the layering.
5. Bake the dish for 45 **min**s with the foil covering.
6. After taking off the foil, cover with **finely grated** Parmesan cheese and bake for an additional 15 **min**s, or **up to** the cheese is bubbling and brown.
7. Before serving, let it cool a little.

NUTRITION INFO (per serving):

Cals: 220 kcal, **Carb**s: 15g, Protein: 9g

Fat: 15g, Fiber: 7g, Sugar: 9g

23. Key Lime Pie Parfait

Prep Time: 20 **min**s

Cook Time: 10 **min**s

Total Time: 30 **min**s

Servings: 2

Ingredients:

- 1 **cup of** graham cracker crumbs
- 4 **tbsp** unsalted butter, **dilute**
- 1/4 **cup of** granulated sugar
- 1 **cup of** heavy cream
- 1/2 **cup of** sweetened condensed milk
- 1/4 **cup of** key lime juice
- 1 **tbsp** lime zest
- Lime slices and mint leaves for garnish

Instructions:

1. Graham cracker crumbs, **dilute** butter, and granulated sugar **Must** all be thoroughly **combined** in a basin.
2. Whip the heavy cream to stiff peaks in a separate dish.
3. The whipped cream **Must** be delicately incorporated with the sweetened condensed milk, key lime juice, and lime zest.
4. The graham cracker **Mixture** and the key lime cream **Mixture Must** be alternately layered in serving glasses.
5. Layer the ingredients **up to** you r**every** the rim of the glasses, then top with a layer of key lime cream.
6. Lime slices and mint leaves are used as a garnish.
7. Before serving, place in the fridge for at least one **hr**.

NUTRITION INFO (per serving):

Cals: 550 kcal, **Carb**s: 45g, Protein: 6g

Fat: 38g, Fiber: 1g, Sugar: 32g

24. Layered Chickpea Salad

Prep Time: 20 **min**s

Cook Time: 0 **min**s

Total Time: 20 **min**s

Servings: 4

Ingredients:

- 2 cans (15 **oz**s **every**) chickpeas, drained and rinsed
- 1 **cup of** cherry tomatoes, halved
- 1 cucumber, diced
- 1 red bell pepper, diced
- 1/2 red onion, thinly **split**
- 1/4 **cup of** fresh parsley, **chop-up**
- 1/4 **cup of** feta cheese, **cut up**
- 1/4 **cup of** black olives, pitted and **split**
- 3 **tbsp** extra-virgin olive oil
- 2 **tbsp** red wine vinegar
- Salt and pepper **as needed**

Instructions:

1. Chickpeas, cherry tomatoes, cucumber, red bell pepper, red onion, and fresh parsley **Must** all be **combine**d in a sizable **combining** dish.
2. Add red wine vinegar and olive oil, then toss everything together **up to** everything is thoroughly coated.
3. Depending on your taste, add salt and pepper to the dish.
4. Layer the feta cheese and black olives with the chickpea salad in individual serving glasses or bowls.
5. Layers **Must** be repeated **up to** all the components have been used.
6. Serve right away or keep chilled **up to** you're ready to.

Nutrition (per serving):

Cals: 280 kcal, **Carb**s: 32g, Protein: 9g

Fat: 14g, Fiber: 8g

25.Lemon Raspberry Chia Pudding

Prep Time: 10 **min**s

Cook Time: 0 **min**s

Total Time: 4 **hr**s 10 **min**s (including chilling time)

Servings: 2

Ingredients:

- 1 **cup of** unsweetened almond milk (or any other plant-based milk)
- 1/4 **cup of** chia seeds
- 2 **tbsp** maple syrup
- 1 **tsp** lemon zest
- 1/2 **tsp** vanilla extract
- 1/2 **cup of** fresh raspberries
- Lemon slices and more raspberries for garnish (**non-compulsory**)

Instructions:

1. Almond milk, chia seeds, maple syrup, lemon zest, and vanilla essence **Must** all be thoroughly blended in a bowl.
2. **Let** the **Mixture** to rest for approximately 5 **min**s, then whisk it once more to avoid clumping.
3. Let the chia pudding thicken and set in the refrigerator for at least 4 **hr**s or overnight.
4. Give the pudding a thorough stir when it has cold and set.
5. Layer fresh raspberries and chia pudding in serving **cups of** or bowls.
6. Add extra raspberries and lemon slices as a garnish, if desired.
7. Offer cold.

Nutrition (per serving):

Cals: 210 kcal, **Carb**s: 26g, Protein: 5g

Fat: 10g, Fiber: 12g

26.Buffalo Chicken Pasta Salad

Prep Time: 15 **min**s

Cook Time: 10 **min**s

Total Time: 25 **min**s

Servings: 6

Ingredients:

- 8 **oz**s rotini or penne pasta
- 2 **cups of** cooked chicken breast, shredded or diced
- 1/2 **cup of** buffalo sauce (adjust to your spice preference)
- 1/3 **cup of** ranch dressing
- 1/2 **cup of** celery, diced
- 1/2 **cup of** carrots, shredded
- 1/4 **cup of** red onion, **lightly chop-up**
- 1/4 **cup of** fresh cilantro or parsley, **chop-up** (**non-compulsory** for garnish)
- Salt and pepper **as needed**

Instructions:

1. Pasta **Must** be cooked as directed on the **box/pkg up to** it is al dente. To chill the pasta, drain and rinse under cold water.
2. **Combine** cooked pasta, diced chicken, buffalo sauce, and ranch dressing in a big bowl.
3. Add the celery, carrots, and red onion, all diced. Blend thoroughly.
4. **As needed**, add salt and pepper to the food.
5. If preferred, garnish with fresh cilantro or parsley.
6. Serve right away or keep chilled **up to** you're ready to.

Nutrition (per serving):

Cals: 320 kcal, **Carb**s: 29g, Protein: 22g

Fat: 12g, Fiber: 2g

27.Tiramisu Parfait

Prep Time: 20 **min**s

Cook Time: 0 **min**s

Total Time: 20 **min**s

Servings: 4

Ingredients:

- 1 **cup of** mascarpone cheese
- 1/2 **cup of** heavy cream
- 1/4 **cup of** powdered sugar
- 1 **tsp** vanilla extract
- 1 **cup of** brewed coffee, cooled
- 2 **tbsp** coffee liqueur (**non-compulsory**)
- 16-20 ladyfinger cookies
- Cocoa powder for dusting

Instructions:

1. Mascarpone cheese, heavy cream, powdered sugar, and vanilla extract **Must** be thoroughly blended and creamy in a **combining** dish.
2. Coffee liqueur (if using) and freshly made coffee **Must** be **combine**d in a separate sh**let** dish.
3. **Every** ladyfinger **Must** be briefly dipped into the coffee **Mixture** to moisten them, but not to sop them up.
4. Place the tiramisu parfaits in serving glasses or dessert **cups of** and begin layering. Lay down a layer of wet ladyfingers first.
5. Place a layer of the mascarpone **Mixture** on top next.
6. Up till the glass's top, keep adding layers, finishing with a layer of mascarpone.
7. For decoration, sprinkle some chocolate powder over the top.
8. Before serving, place the parfaits in the refrigerator for at least an **hr** to let the flavors to mingle.

Nutrition (per serving):
Cals: 450 kcal, **Carb**s: 24g, Protein: 6g
Fat: 36g, Fiber: 1g

28.Mediterranean Quinoa Bowl

Prep Time: 15 **min**s
Cook Time: 20 **min**s
Total Time: 35 **min**s
Servings: 4

Ingredients:

- 1 **cup of** quinoa, rinsed and drained
- 2 **cups of** vegetable broth or water
- 1 can (15 **oz**s) chickpeas, drained and rinsed
- 1 **cup of** cherry tomatoes, halved
- 1 cucumber, diced
- 1/4 **cup of** Kalamata olives, pitted and **split**
- 1/4 **cup of cut up** feta cheese
- 1/4 **cup of** fresh parsley, **chop-up**
- 1/4 **cup of** lemon juice
- 2 **tbsp** extra-virgin olive oil
- 1 **tsp** dried oregano
- Salt and pepper **as needed**

Instructions:

1. Quinoa and vegetable broth (or water) **Must** be **combine**d in a medium saucepan and heated to a rolling boil.
2. Turn down the heat to low, cover the pan, and simmer the quinoa for 15 to 20 **min**s, or **up to** it is cooked and the liquid has been absorbed.
3. Cooked quinoa, chickpeas, cherry tomatoes, cucumber, Kalamata olives, **cut up** feta cheese,

and **chop-up** parsley **Must** all be **combine**d in a sizable **combining** dish.
4. To make the dressing, **combine** the lemon juice, olive oil, dried oregano, salt, and pepper in a **mini** bowl.
5. The quinoa **Mixture Must** be well-coated once the dressing has been added.
6. Serve the quinoa salad with Mediterranean flavors in **mini** bowls or on plates.

Nutrition (per serving):
Cals: 350 kcal, **Carb**s: 42g, Protein: 11g
Fat: 16g, Fiber: 8g

29.Mason Jar Taco Dip

Prep Time: 15 **min**s
Cook Time: 0 **min**s
Total Time: 15 **min**s
Servings: 6

Ingredients:

- 1 can (15 **oz**s) refried beans
- 1 **cup of** guacamole (homemade or store-bought)
- 1 **cup of** sour cream
- 1 packet taco seasoning **combine**
- 1 **cup of** shredded cheddar cheese
- 1 **cup of** diced tomatoes
- 1/2 **cup of split** black olives
- 1/4 **cup of chop-up** green onions
- Tortilla chips for serving

Instructions:

1. **Combine** the sour cream and taco seasoning thoroughly in a **mini** basin.
2. Start by adding a layer of refried beans to the bottom of **every** mason jar before assembling the mason jar taco dip.
3. Guacamole and taco-flavored sour cream **Must** next be added in layers.
4. Shredded cheddar cheese, diced tomatoes, **split** black olives, and **lightly chop-up** green onions **Must** be placed on top of **every** container.
5. Before serving, cover the lids of the mason jars and place them in the refrigerator.
6. Offer tortilla chips for dipping while serving, and savor the mouthwatering combinations of tastes.

Nutrition (per serving):
Cals: 280 kcal, **Carb**s: 16g, Protein: 8g
Fat: 20g, Fiber: 6g

30.Veggie Sushi Mason Jar:

Prep Time: 20 **min**s
Cook Time: 0 **min**s
Total Time: 20 **min**s

Servings: 2

Ingredients:

- 1 **cup of** sushi rice, cooked and cooled
- 2 **tbsp** rice vinegar
- 1 **tbsp** sugar
- 1/2 **tsp** salt
- 1 carrot, julienned
- 1 cucumber, julienned
- 1 avocado, **split**
- 2 sheets nori (seaweed), **slice** into **mini** pieces
- 2 **tbsp** soy sauce
- 1 **tbsp** sesame seeds

Instructions:

1. **Combine** rice vinegar, sugar, and salt in a **mini** bowl. Gently whisk this **Mixture** into the cooked sushi rice after adding it.
2. Layer the seasoned sushi rice, carrot, cucumber, avocado, and nori sheets in **every** mason jar.
3. Sesame seeds **Must** be added along with soy sauce.
4. Before serving, seal the Mason jars and place them in the refrigerator.

Nutrition (per serving):

Cals: 320 kcal, Fat: 8g, **Carb**s: 60g

Fiber: 6g, Protein: 6g

31.Mason Jar Chicken Pot Pie

Prep Time: 20 **min**s

Cook Time: 30 **min**s

Total Time: 50 **min**s

Servings: 2

Ingredients:

- 1 **cup of** cooked chicken, diced
- 1 **cup of refrigerate combined** vegetables (carrots, peas, corn)
- 1/2 **cup of** diced potatoes
- 1/3 **cup of** diced onions
- 1/3 **cup of** diced celery
- 2 cloves garlic, **chop-up**
- 2 **tbsp** butter
- 2 **tbsp** all-purpose flour
- 1 **cup of** chicken broth
- 1/2 **cup of** milk
- 1/2 **tsp** dried thyme
- Salt and pepper **as needed**
- 1 sheet pre-made pie crust, **slice** into circles to fit the jar tops

Instructions:

1. Melt the butter in a pan over medium heat. Add the celery, onions, and garlic. Cook for softening.

2. The flour **Must** be stirred in and cooked for 1-2 **min**s, or **up to** a roux develops.
3. Stir in the milk and chicken broth gradually. Bring to a simmer, then cook for a while to thicken.
4. Add the potatoes, dry thyme, cubed chicken, **combined** vegetables, and salt and pepper. Stir thoroughly and cook the vegetables **up to** they are tender.
5. Set the oven's temperature to 375°F (190°C).
6. Pour roughly 3/4 of the chicken **Mixture** into **every** mason jar.
7. **Every** jar **Must** have a circle of pre-made pie crust on top.
8. The jars **Must** be baked for 20 to 25 **min**s, or **up to** the crust is golden brown, on a baking sheet.

Nutrition (per serving):

Cals: XX kcal **Carb**s: XX g Protein: XX g Fat: XX g Fiber: XX g

32.Layered Fruit Salad

Prep Time: 15 **min**s

Total Time: 15 **min**s

Servings: 4

Ingredients:

- 2 **cups of combined** fresh fruits (strawberries, blueberries, kiwi, grapes, etc.)
- 1 **cup of** Greek yogurt
- 2 **tbsp** honey
- 1/4 **cup of** granola

Instructions:

1. Fruits **Must** be washed and prepared as needed (**split**, halved, or left whole).
2. Greek yogurt and honey **Must** be thoroughly blended in a bowl.
3. Beginning with the fruit and yogurt combination, layer individual serving jars or glasses. Layer fruit first, then yogurt, and repeat the process **up to** the jar is full.
4. Add some granola to the top of **every** jar for some extra crunch.
5. Serve right away or keep chilled **up to** you're ready to.

33.Spinach and Feta Pasta Salad

Prep Time: 10 **min**s

Cook Time: 10 **min**s

Total Time: 20 **min**s

Servings: 2

Ingredients:

- 6 **oz**s (170g) pasta (bowtie, penne, or fusilli)
- 2 **cups of** fresh baby spinach
- 1/2 **cup of cut up** feta cheese
- 1/4 **cup of** cherry tomatoes, halved
- 2 **tbsp** olive oil
- 1 **tbsp** balsamic vinegar
- 1 **tsp** Dijon mustard
- Salt and pepper **as needed**

Instructions:

1. Pasta **Must** be cooked as directed on the **box/pkg up to** it is al dente. Drain, then leave to cool.
2. To make the dressing, **combine** the olive oil, balsamic vinegar, Dijon mustard, salt, and pepper in a **mini** bowl.
3. Layer the cooked spaghetti, fresh baby spinach, cherry tomatoes, and feta cheese **cut ups** in a mason jar or serving bowl.
4. Dressing **Must** be drizzled over the top layer.
5. Refrigerate **up to** ready to serve by sealing the container or covering the serving bowl.
6. Before serving, shake or toss the jar/bowl to **combine** the contents and dressing.

34.Chia Seed and Mango Delight

Prep Time: 5 **min**s (**+** soaking time)

Total Time: 5 **min**s (**+** soaking time)

Servings: 2

Ingredients:

- 1/4 **cup of** chia seeds
- 1 **cup of** unsweetened almond milk (or any preferred milk)
- 1 ripe mango, diced
- 1 **tbsp** honey (**non-compulsory**)
- 1/4 **tsp** vanilla extract
- **Split** almonds or shredded coconut for topping (**non-compulsory**)

Instructions:

1. Chia seeds, almond milk, honey (if used), and vanilla essence **Must** all be **combine**d in a mason jar or other airtight container.
2. Stir thoroughly to distribute the chia seeds evenly.
3. To give the chia seeds time to soak and expand, cover the jar or container and place it in the refrigerator for at least 2 **hr**s or overnight.
4. Give the **Mixture** a thorough swirl just before serving to help break up any clumps that may have developed.
5. In serving jars, layer the chia seed **Mixture** with the diced mango.

6. If desired, garnish with **chop-up** almonds or shredded coconut.
7. As a delightful and healthful dessert or choice for breakfast, serve cold.

35.Mason Jar Eggs Benedict

Prep Time: 15 **min**s

Cook Time: 15 **min**s

Total Time: 30 **min**s

Servings: 2

Ingredients:

- 4 **Big** eggs
- 2 English muffins, split and toasted
- 4 slices Canadian bacon or ham
- Hollandaise sauce:
- 3 **Big** egg yolks
- 1 **tbsp** lemon juice
- 1/2 **cup of** unsalted butter, **dilute**
- Salt and cayenne pepper **as needed**

Instructions:

1. To make the Hollandaise sauce, **combine** the egg yolks and lemon juice in a heatproof bowl and whisk **up to** the liquid is light in color and slightly thickened.
2. When the sauce is smooth and thickened, set the bowl over a saucepan of simmering water (double boiler) and continue whisking while gradually adding the **dilute** butter.
3. Add salt and a dash of cayenne pepper **as needed**. Warm up the sauce on a low heat setting.
4. To poach eggs:
5. Water **Must** be added to a pot and heated to a slow simmer.
6. **Every** egg **Must** be cracked into a different little bowl or ramekin.
7. One at a time, carefully slip the eggs into the middle of the gentle vortex you've created in the simmering water.
8. For a runny yolk, poach the eggs for 3–4 **min**s; for a firmer yolk, poach for longer.
9. The poached eggs **Must** be taken out of the water with a slotted spoon and dried on paper towels.
10. Put the Mason jar together. Benedict eggs:
11. Place a poached egg, a slice of ham or Canadian bacon, and half an English muffin in **every** mason jar.
12. Over the poached eggs, generously spoon Hollandaise sauce.
13. Serve right away and delight in!

36.Layered Caprese Salad

Prep Time: 10 **min**s

Total Time: 10 **min**s

Servings: 2

Ingredients:

- 1 **cup of** cherry tomatoes, halved
- 1 **cup of** fresh mozzarella balls (or diced mozzarella)
- Fresh basil leaves
- Balsamic glaze
- Extra virgin olive oil
- Salt and pepper **as needed**

Instructions:

1. Layer the cherry tomatoes in halves, then the fresh mozzarella balls, then the fresh basil leaves in a mason jar or transparent glass.
2. Continue layering **up to** the jar is full, then add a layer of tomatoes and a few basil leaves to the top to complete the dish.
3. drizzle with extra virgin olive oil and balsamic glaze.
4. **As needed**, add a touch of salt and pepper.
5. Serve right away or keep chilled **up to** you're ready to. If the tastes are given a little time to mingle, the result will be lovely.

37.Pevery Melba Parfait

Prep Time: 15 **min**s

Cook Time: 0 **min**s

Total Time: 15 **min**s

Servings: 2

Ingredients:

- 2 **cups of** Greek yogurt
- 2 **cups of** fresh or **refrigerate** peveryes, diced
- 1/2 **cup of** raspberry sauce or puree
- 1/4 **cup of** granola
- Fresh raspberries for garnish (**non-compulsory**)
- Fresh mint leaves for garnish (**non-compulsory**)

Instructions:

1. Start by adding 1/4 **cup of** of Greek yogurt to the bottom of **every** serving glass or parfait dish.
2. To the yogurt, add a layer of diced peveryes.
3. Over the peveryes, drizzle some raspberry sauce or puree.
4. One **tbsp** of granola **Must** be added to the sauce.
5. Continue layering **up to** the glass is full, then top it off with a dollop of Greek yogurt.
6. If preferred, garnish with mint leaves and fresh raspberries.
7. Serve right away or keep chilled **up to** you're ready to.

Nutrition (per serving):

Cals: 250 kcal, Protein: 15g, Fat: 5g, **Carb**s: 40g

Fiber: 5g

38.Mason Jar Egg Fried Rice

Prep Time: 10 **min**s

Cook Time: 15 **min**s

Total Time: 25 **min**s

Servings: 2

Ingredients:

- 2 **cups of** cooked rice, preferably chilled
- 2 eggs, lightly beaten
- 1 **cup of combined** vegetables (carrots, peas, corn, etc.)
- 2 **tbsp** soy sauce
- 1 **tbsp** vegetable oil
- 2 green onions, **chop-up** (for garnish)
- Sesame seeds (for garnish)

Instructions:

1. Heat the vegetable oil over medium-high heat in a big skillet or wok.
2. Stir-fry the **combined** vegetables for a short while, **up to** they are soft.
3. Pour the beaten eggs on the other side of the skillet after pushing the vegetables to one side.
4. The eggs **Must** be well scrambled before being **combine**d with the veggies.
5. Stir-fry the vegetables, eggs, and cold cooked rice in the skillet with the other ingredients.
6. Stir-fry the rice **Mixture** while adding soy sauce **up to** everything is thoroughly incorporated and cooked.
7. Take it off the fire and give it a **min** to cool.
8. Place the fried rice in mason jars and top with sesame seeds and **lightly chop-up** green onions.
9. Put the jar lids on tightly and either keep in the refrigerator or consume right away.

Nutrition (per serving):)

Cals: 380 kcal, Protein: 12g, Fat: 8g, **Carb**s: 65g

Fiber: 5g

39.Layered Taco Salad

Prep Time: 20 **min**s

Cook Time: 10 **min**s

Total Time: 30 **min**s

Servings: 4

- 1 **lb** ground beef or turkey
- 1 packet taco seasoning **combine**
- 1 **cup of** cherry tomatoes, halved
- 1 **cup of** black beans, cooked and drained
- 1 **cup of** corn kernels (fresh, canned, or **refrigerate**)
- 1 **cup of** shredded cheddar cheese
- 1 **cup of** shredded lettuce
- 1/2 **cup of** diced red onion
- 1/2 **cup of** diced bell peppers (any color)
- 1/2 **cup of split** black olives
- 1/2 **cup of** salsa
- 1/2 **cup of** sour cream
- Tortilla chips for serving

Instructions:

1. Cook the ground beef or turkey in a pan over medium heat **up to** browned. **Take out** any extra fat.
2. In accordance with the directions on the **box/pkg**, add the taco seasoning **combine** to the cooked meat. It **Must** simmer for a few **min**s before being placed aside to cool.
3. Start layering the ingredients in a **Big** bowl or in **mini** serving bowls as follows:
4. diced lettuce
5. seasoned and prepared beef
6. Brown beans
7. corn grain
8. Plum tomatoes
9. **slice** up a red onion
10. Bell peppers, diced
11. cheddar cheese **cut up**s
12. black olives, **split**
13. Sour cream and salsa are added to the top of **every** salad.
14. With tortilla chips on the side, serve right away.

Nutrition (per serving):
Cals: 420 kcal, Protein: 25g, Fat: 20g, **Carb**s: 35g, Fiber: 8g

40.Chocolate Peanut Butter Delight

Prep Time: 20 **min**s

Cook Time: 0 **min**s

Total Time: 20 **min**s

Servings: 6

Ingredients:

- 1 1/2 **cups of** chocolate cookie crumbs
- 1/2 **cup of** unsalted butter, **dilute**
- 1 **cup of** cream cheese, **melted**
- 1 **cup of** creamy peanut butter
- 1 **cup of** powdered sugar
- 1 **tsp** vanilla extract

- 1 **cup of** heavy cream
- 1/4 **cup of** chocolate sauce
- 1/4 **cup of chop-up** peanuts (**non-compulsory**)

Instructions:

1. **Cut up** chocolate cookie and **dilute** butter in a **combining** basin and stir to coat the crumbs evenly.
2. To create the crust, press the ingredients into the bottom of a 9x9-inch baking dish or a serving dish of a comparable size.
3. Cream cheese, peanut butter, powdered sugar, and vanilla extract **Must** be thoroughly blended in a separate basin.
4. Whip the heavy cream **up to** firm peaks form in a separate bowl.
5. Once the whipped cream is entirely **combined**, gently fold it into the peanut butter **Mixture**.
6. In the baking dish, cover the chocolate cookie crust with the peanut butter filling.
7. Add some chocolate sauce to the dessert's top.
8. To add more crunch and flavor, you might top the dish with **chop-up** peanuts.
9. Before serving, place the dessert in the refrigerator for at least 2 **hr**s to **let** it set.
10. Enjoy while serving chilled!

Nutrition (per serving):
Cals: 580 kcal, Protein: 11g, Fat: 43g, **Carb**s: 42g, Fiber: 3g

41.Mason Jar Spinach and Artichoke Dip

Prep Time: 15 **min**s

Cook Time: 25 **min**s

Total Time: 40 **min**s

Servings: 4

Ingredients:

- 1 **cup of refrigerate chop-up** spinach, thawed and drained
- 1 **cup of** canned artichoke hearts, **chop-up**
- 1 **cup of** cream cheese, **melted**
- 1/2 **cup of** mayonnaise
- 1 **cup of** shredded mozzarella cheese
- 1/2 **cup of finely grated** Parmesan cheese
- 1 clove garlic, **chop-up**
- 1/2 **tsp** onion powder
- Salt and pepper **as needed**
- Tortilla chips or pita bread for serving

Instructions:

1. Set the oven's temperature to 350°F (175°C).
2. Cream cheese, mayonnaise, mozzarella cheese, Parmesan cheese that has been shredded, **chop-up** garlic, onion powder, salt, and pepper **Must** all be **combin**ed in a **combining** bowl. Stir thoroughly to **combine**.

3. To equally distribute the **chop-up** spinach and artichoke hearts, gently fold them into the **Mixture**.
4. Fill the mason jars with the dip **Mixture up to** they are about three-quarters full.
5. Bake the jars in the preheated oven for about 25 **min**s, or **up to** they are hot and bubbling. Place the jars on a baking sheet.
6. Before serving, take it out of the oven and **let** it cool somewhat.
7. Serve pita bread or tortilla chips alongside the spinach and artichoke dip.

Nutrition (per serving):
Cals: 380 kcal, Protein: 10g, Fat: 32g, **Carb**s: 12g, Fiber: 2g

42.Raspberry Chocolate Mousse:

Prep Time: 20 **min**s

Cook Time: 0 **min**s

Total Time: 20 **min**s

Servings: 4

Ingredients:
- 1 **cup of** fresh raspberries
- 1/4 **cup of** sugar
- 1 **cup of** heavy cream
- 1/2 **cup of** semisweet chocolate chips
- 1 **tsp** vanilla extract

Instructions:
1. The fresh raspberries and sugar **Must** be blended or processed **up to** smooth.
2. Whip the heavy cream **up to** firm peaks form in a separate bowl.
3. In a bowl suitable for the microwave, melt the chocolate chips for 30 seconds at a time **up to** smooth.
4. Gently **combine** the whipped cream with the raspberry puree and **dilute** chocolate.
5. Add the vanilla extract and stir.
6. Four mason jars or serving dishes **Must** receive the mousse.
7. Before serving, place in the fridge for at least one **hr**.
8. If preferred, garnish with fresh raspberries and chocolate shavings.

Nutrition (per serving):
Cals: 320 kcal, Fat: 24g, **Carb**s: 28g
Protein: 3g

43.Mason Jar Chicken Alfredo:

Prep Time: 15 **min**s

Cook Time: 25 **min**s

Total Time: 40 **min**s

Servings: 2

Ingredients:
- 1 **cup of** cooked chicken breast, diced
- 8 oz fettuccine pasta
- 1 **cup of** heavy cream
- 1/2 **cup of finely grated** Parmesan cheese
- 2 **tbsp** unsalted butter
- 2 cloves garlic, **chop-up**
- Salt and pepper **as needed**
- Fresh parsley for garnish

Instructions:
1. To prepare the fettuccine pasta, follow the directions on the **box/pkg**. Drain, then set apart.
2. Melt the butter in a saucepan over medium heat. When aromatic, add the **chop-up** garlic and stir for one to two **min**s.
3. Add the heavy cream and Parmesan cheese, then turn the heat down to low. Cook while continuously stirring **up to** the sauce thickens.
4. Stir the sauce while adding the cooked chicken, **up to** it is thoroughly warm. **As needed**, add salt and pepper to the food.
5. Layer the cooked fettuccine pasta and the chicken Alfredo sauce in mason jars.
6. Add fresh parsley as a garnish.

Nutrition (per serving):
Cals: 750 kcal, Fat: 45g, **Carb**s: 50g
Protein: 40g

44.Layered Ratatouille Quinoa Bowl:

Prep Time: 20 **min**s

Cook Time: 35 **min**s

Total Time: 55 **min**s

Servings: 4

Ingredients:
- 1 **cup of** quinoa, rinsed
- 2 **cups of** vegetable broth
- 1 eggplant, **split** into rounds
- 1 zucchini, **split** into rounds
- 1 yellow squash, **split** into rounds
- 1 red bell pepper, **split** into strips
- 1 yellow bell pepper, **split** into strips
- 1 can (14 oz) diced tomatoes, drained
- 2 cloves garlic, **chop-up**
- 2 **tbsp** olive oil
- 1 **tsp** dried thyme
- 1 **tsp** dried oregano
- Salt and pepper **as needed**
- Fresh basil for garnish

Instructions:

1. Bring the vegetable broth to a boil in a saucepan. Add the rinsed quinoa, lower the heat to a simmer, cover the pot, and cook the quinoa for 15 to 20 **min**s, or **up to** it is tender and the liquid has been absorbed.
2. Set the oven's temperature to 375°F (190°C).
3. **Split** eggplant, zucchini, yellow squash, red, and yellow bell peppers **Must** be **combine**d with olive oil, **chop-up** garlic, dried thyme, dried oregano, salt, and pepper in a **Big** bowl.
4. Place the seasoned vegetables on a baking sheet in a single layer. For about 15 **min**s, or **up to** tender, roast in the preheated oven.
5. Vegetables that have been roasted and cooked quinoa **Must** be layered in serving dishes or mason jars.
6. Add diced, drained tomatoes on top.
7. Fresh basil is a good garnish.

Nutrition (per serving):
Cals: 350 kcal, Fat: 10g, **Carb**s: 56g
Protein: 12g

45. Lemon Blueberry Chia Pudding:

Prep Time: 10 **min**s

Cook Time: 0 **min**s

Total Time: 4 **hr**s 10 **min**s (includes chilling time)

Servings: 2

Ingredients:

- 1 **cup of** unsweetened almond milk (or any other milk of your choice)
- 1/4 **cup of** chia seeds
- 2 **tbsp** maple syrup (or honey)
- 1 **tsp** lemon zest
- 1 **tbsp** lemon juice
- 1/2 **cup of** fresh blueberries
- Lemon slices and additional blueberries for garnish

Instructions:

1. Almond milk, chia seeds, maple syrup, lemon zest, and lemon juice **Must** all be thoroughly blended in a **combining** dish.
2. Fold in the fresh blueberries gently.
3. To enable the chia seeds to absorb the liquid and develop a pudding-like consistency, cover the bowl and place in the refrigerator for at least 4 **hr**s or overnight.
4. To distribute the ingredients equally, give the chia pudding a stir just before serving.
5. Pour the lemon blueberry chia pudding into bowls or mason jars for serving.

6. Lemon slices and more blueberries are used as a garnish.

Nutrition (per serving):
Cals: 220 kcal, Fat: 9g, **Carb**s: 32g
Protein: 6g

46. Layered Mexican Rice and Beans

Prep Time: 15 **min**s

Cook Time: 30 **min**s

Total Time: 45 **min**s

Servings: 4

Ingredients:

- 1 **cup of** long-grain white rice
- 1 can (15 oz) black beans, drained and rinsed
- 1 **cup of** salsa
- 1 **cup of** shredded cheddar cheese
- 1 **cup of** guacamole
- 1 **cup of** sour cream
- 1 **cup of** diced tomatoes
- 1/2 **cup of chop-up** cilantro
- 1 lime, **slice** into wedges
- Salt and pepper **as needed**

Instructions:

1. The rice **Must** be prepared as directed on the packaging.
2. The black beans **Must** be warmed in a skillet over medium heat. **As needed**, add salt and pepper to the food.
3. Layer the following ingredients in a glass dish or individual serving glasses: cooked rice, black beans, salsa, shredded cheddar cheese, guacamole, sour cream, diced tomatoes, and cilantro.
4. Serve with lime juice added on top.

NUTRITION INFO (per serving):
Cals: 450, Fat: 18g, **Carb**s: 57g
Protein: 18g, Fiber: 10g

47. Pumpkin Spice Overnight Oats

Prep Time: 10 **min**s

Total Time: 8 **hr**s (overnight soaking)

Servings: 2

Ingredients:

- 1 **cup of** rolled oats
- 1 **cup of** almond milk (or any milk of your choice)
- 1/2 **cup of** pumpkin puree
- 2 **tbsp** maple syrup
- 1 **tsp** pumpkin spice **combine** (or a combination of cinnamon, nutmeg, ginger, and cloves)
- 1/4 **cup of chop-up** nuts (e.g., pecans or walnuts)

- 2 **tbsp** dried cranberries or raisins

Instructions:

1. Rolling oats, almond milk, pumpkin puree, maple syrup, and pumpkin spice **combine Must** all be thoroughly blended in a dish or jar.
2. Place the dish or jar in the fridge for at least eight **hr**s or overnight.
3. Give the **Mixture** a brisk toss in the morning. To get the appropriate consistency, add more milk if it's too thick.
4. Before serving, sprinkle **chop-up** nuts, dried cranberries, or raisins on top of the overnight oats.

NUTRITION INFO (per serving):
Cals: 320, Fat: 10g, **Carb**s: 52g

Protein: 8g, Fiber: 9g

48.Mason Jar Quiche Lorraine

Prep Time: 15 **min**s

Cook Time: 30 **min**s

Total Time: 45 **min**s

Servings: 4

Ingredients:

- 1 pre-made pie crust (store-bought or homemade)
- 1 **cup of** diced ham
- 1 **cup of** shredded Swiss cheese
- 4 **Big** eggs
- 1 **cup of** half-and-half or whole milk
- 1/2 **tsp** salt
- 1/4 **tsp** black pepper
- 1/4 **tsp** ground nutmeg
- 1 **tbsp chop-up** fresh chives

Instructions:

1. Set your oven's temperature to 375°F (190°C).
2. The pie dough **Must** be rolled out and **slice** into circles that fit the bottoms of the mason jars. Insert the rings of crust into the jars.
3. Distribute the Swiss cheese and diced ham among the jars.
4. **Combine** the eggs, half-and-half (or milk), salt, black pepper, and ground nutmeg in a **combining** bowl.
5. Covering the ham and cheese with the egg **Mixture**, pour it into the mason jars.
6. The quiches **Must** be set and somewhat brown on top after about 30 **min**s of baking in the preheated oven with the jars on a baking sheet.
7. Before serving, take them out of the oven, cover with **chop-up** chives, and **let** them cool somewhat.

NUTRITION INFO (per serving):
Cals: 420, Fat: 28g, **Carb**s: 22g

Protein: 20g, Fiber: 1g

49.Layered Waldorf Salad

Prep Time: 20 **min**s

Total Time: 20 **min**s

Servings: 4

Ingredients:

- 4 **cups of combined** salad greens (e.g., lettuce, spinach, arugula)
- 1 **cup of** diced apples (use a **combine** of sweet and tart apples)
- 1 **cup of** red seedless grapes, halved
- 1/2 **cup of chop-up** celery
- 1/2 **cup of chop-up** walnuts or pecans
- 1/4 **cup of cut up** blue cheese (**non-compulsory**)
- 1/4 **cup of** plain Greek yogurt
- 2 **tbsp** mayonnaise
- 1 **tbsp** honey
- 1 **tbsp** lemon juice
- Salt and pepper **as needed**

Instructions:

1. **Combine** the **combined** salad greens, diced apples, grapes, celery, almonds, and **cut up** blue cheese (if using) in a big bowl.
2. To prepare the dressing, **combine** the Greek yogurt, mayonnaise, honey, lemon juice, salt, and pepper in a separate **mini** bowl.
3. A big glass bowl or individual serving glasses can be used to arrange the salad ingredients. Drizzle the dressing in between **every** layer.
4. If desired, add more nuts, grapes, and blue cheese on the top.

NUTRITION INFO (per serving):
Cals: 280, Fat: 18g, **Carb**s: 24g

Protein: 7g, Fiber: 4g

50.Tuna Niçoise Salad

Prep Time: 15 **min**s

Cook Time: 10 **min**s

Total Time: 25 **min**s

Servings: 2

Ingredients:

- 2 **cups of combined** salad greens
- 2 (5 oz) cans of tuna, drained
- 1 **cup of** cherry tomatoes, halved
- 1/2 **cup of** boiled and **split** potatoes
- 1/4 **cup of split** black olives
- 1/4 **cup of** blanched green beans

- 2 hard-boiled eggs, quartered
- 2 **tbsp** extra-virgin olive oil
- 1 **tbsp** red wine vinegar
- 1 **tsp** Dijon mustard
- 1 **tbsp chop-up** fresh parsley
- Salt and pepper **as needed**

Instructions:

1. Place the **combined** salad greens in a big salad bowl.
2. Add tuna, cherry tomatoes, **split** potatoes, black olives, blanched green beans, and quartered hard-boiled eggs to the greens as garnish.
3. To create the dressing, **combine** the extra virgin olive oil, red wine vinegar, Dijon mustard, parsley that has been **chop-up**, salt, and pepper in a **mini** bowl.
4. Over the salad, drizzle the dressing, and toss just enough to **combine**.

NUTRITION INFO (per serving):
Cals: 460, **Fat**: 24g, **Carb**s: 25g

Protein: 36g, Fiber: 6g

51.Mason Jar Buffalo Cauliflower Salad:

Prep Time: 15 **min**s

Cook Time: 25 **min**s

Total Time: 40 **min**s

Servings: 2

Ingredients:

- 1 **mini** head cauliflower, **chop-up** into florets
- 2 **tbsp** olive oil
- 2 **tbsp** hot sauce (adjust to your spice preference)
- 1 **tsp** garlic powder
- Salt and pepper **as needed**
- 1 **cup of** cherry tomatoes, halved
- 1/2 **cup of** shredded carrots
- 1/4 **cup of** diced red onion
- 2 **cups of combined** greens
- 1/4 **cup of cut up** blue cheese
- 1/4 **cup of** ranch dressing

Instructions:

1. Set the oven's temperature to 425°F (220°C).
2. Cauliflower florets **Must** be **combined** with olive oil, spicy sauce, garlic powder, salt, and pepper in a bowl.
3. On a baking sheet, spread out the cauliflower, and roast for 20 to 25 **min**s, or **up to** soft but still slightly crisp.
4. The roasted cauliflower, cherry tomatoes, shredded carrots, **split** red onion, **combined** greens, blue cheese, and ranch dressing **Must** be arranged in two Mason jars.

5. Before serving, seal the jars and place them in the refrigerator.

Nutrition (per serving):
Cals: 320 kcal, **Carb**s: 16g

Protein: 8g, Fat: 24g, Fiber: 4g

52.Layered Mediterranean Orzo Salad:

Prep Time: 15 **min**s

Cook Time: 10 **min**s

Total Time: 25 **min**s

Servings: 4

Ingredients:

- 1 **cup of** orzo pasta
- 1 **cup of** cherry tomatoes, halved
- 1 cucumber, diced
- 1/2 **cup of** Kalamata olives, pitted and halved
- 1/4 **cup of** red onion, thinly **split**
- 1/2 **cup of cut up** feta cheese
- 1/4 **cup of chop-up** fresh parsley
- 2 **tbsp** lemon juice
- 2 **tbsp** olive oil
- Salt and pepper **as needed**

Instructions:

1. To prepare the orzo pasta, follow the directions on the **box/pkg**. Let it cool and then drain.
2. To create the dressing, **combine** the lemon juice, olive oil, salt, and pepper in a **mini** bowl.
3. Prepared orzo, cherry tomatoes, cucumber, Kalamata olives, red onion, feta cheese, and **chop-up** parsley **Must** be arranged in four Mason jars.
4. Open the jars, then drizzle the dressing over **every** salad.
5. Keep chilled **up to** you're ready to serve. Give the jar a thorough shake before serving to **combine** the ingredients and dressing.

Nutrition (per serving):
Cals: 290 kcal, **Carb**s: 35g, Protein: 8g

Fat: 14g, Fiber: 3g

53.Banana Cream Pie Parfait:

Prep Time: 20 **min**s

Total Time: 20 **min**s

Servings: 2

Ingredients:

- 2 ripe bananas, mashed
- 1 **cup of** vanilla yogurt
- 1/2 **cup of** granola
- 1/4 **cup of** whipped cream
- 1/4 **cup of** crushed graham crackers
- 1 **tbsp** honey

Instructions:

1. The mashed bananas and honey **Must** be thoroughly blended in a **mini** bowl.
2. Place the banana-honey **Mixture**, vanilla yogurt, granola, whipped cream, and broken graham crackers in two Mason jars.
3. Till the jars are full, keep adding layers.
4. Graham cracker crumbs and whipped cream **Must** be added as garnish.
5. Serve right now or keep chilled **up to** you're ready to eat.

Nutrition (per serving):

Cals: 320 kcal, **Carb**s: 58g, Protein: 7g

Fat: 9g, Fiber: 4g

54.Mason Jar Taco Soup:

Prep Time: 15 **min**s

Cook Time: 25 **min**s

Total Time: 40 **min**s

Servings: 4

Ingredients:

- 1 **lb** ground beef or turkey
- 1 **mini** onion, diced
- 1 bell pepper, diced
- 1 can (15 oz) diced tomatoes
- 1 can (15 oz) black beans, drained and rinsed
- 1 can (15 oz) corn, drained
- 1 packet taco seasoning **combine**
- 2 **cups of** beef or chicken broth
- 1 **cup of** shredded cheddar cheese
- 1/4 **cup of chop-up** fresh cilantro
- Tortilla chips (**non-compulsory**, for serving)

Instructions:

1. Cook the ground beef or turkey in a **Big** skillet over medium heat. **Take out** any extra fat.
2. The bell pepper and onion dice **Must** be added to the skillet and cooked **up to** tender.
3. Add the broth, black beans, corn, taco seasoning **combine**, and diced tomatoes. 10 **min**s **Must** pass while stirring occasionally.
4. Layer the taco soup **Mixture**, shredded cheddar cheese, and cilantro in four Mason jars.
5. Before serving, seal the jars and place them in the refrigerator.

6. To prepare the soup for serving, microwave it in the jar or pour it into a dish and top with tortilla chips.

Nutrition (per serving):

Cals: 420 kcal, **Carb**s: 30g, Protein: 30g

Fat: 20g, Fiber: 7g

55.Layered Pancake Breakfast:

Prep Time: 10 **min**s

Cook Time: 15 **min**s

Total Time: 25 **min**s

Servings: 2

Ingredients:

- 1 **cup of** pancake **combine**
- 3/4 **cup of** milk
- 1 **Big** egg
- 1 **tbsp** vegetable oil
- 1 **cup of** Greek yogurt
- 1 **cup of combined** berries (strawberries, blueberries, raspberries)
- 1 **tbsp** honey
- 1/4 **cup of chop-up** nuts (almonds, walnuts, or your choice)

Instructions:

1. Prepare the pancake **combine** in a bowl using the milk, egg, and vegetable oil recommended on the container.
2. To make **every** pancake, pour 1/4 **cup of** of the batter onto a nonstick skillet that has been preheated over medium heat. Cook **up to** surface bubbles appear, then turn and continue to cook the other side **up to** golden. Continue **up to** all of the batter has been used.
3. Place the cooked pancakes, Greek yogurt, **combined** berries, honey, and **chop-up** almonds in two Mason jars.
4. Before serving, seal the jars and place them in the refrigerator.
5. Simply crack open the jar and dig in with a spoon to enjoy.

Nutrition (per serving):

Cals: 540 kcal, **Carb**s: 70g, Protein: 19g

Fat: 22g, Fiber: 6g

56.Black Bean and Corn Salsa Salad

Prep Time: 15 **min**s

Cook Time: 0 **min**s

Total Time: 15 **min**s

Servings: 4

Ingredients:
- 1 can (15 oz) black beans, drained and rinsed
- 1 **cup of refrigerate** corn kernels, thawed
- 1 **cup of** diced tomatoes
- 1/2 **cup of** diced red onion
- 1/2 **cup of chop-up** fresh cilantro
- 1 jalapeño pepper, seeds **take out**d and **lightly chop-up**
- 2 **tbsp** lime juice
- 2 **tbsp** olive oil
- 1 **tsp** ground cumin
- Salt and pepper **as needed**

Instructions:
1. **Combine** the black beans, corn, tomatoes, red onion, cilantro, and jalapenos in a sizable **combining** basin.
2. **Combine** the lime juice, olive oil, ground cumin, salt, and pepper in a separate **mini** bowl.
3. The dressing **Must** be poured over the black bean **Mixture**, and everything **Must** be thoroughly **combined**.
4. To **let** the flavors to mingle, serve right away or place in the fridge for an **hr**. Enjoy with tortilla chips or as a cool side dish.

Nutrition (per serving):
Cals: 180 kcal, **Carb**s: 28g, Protein: 6g
Fat: 6g, Fiber: 7g

57.Vanilla Raspberry Delight

Prep Time: 20 **min**s

Cook Time: 10 **min**s

Total Time: 30 **min**s

Servings: 6

Ingredients:
- 1 **cup of** fresh raspberries
- 2 **cups of** vanilla yogurt
- 1 **tbsp** honey
- 1/2 **tsp** vanilla extract
- 1/4 **cup of** granola

Instructions:
1. Fresh raspberries **Must** be gently heated in a **mini** saucepan over low heat **up to** their juices are released. Raspberries are stirred and slightly mushed before being **take out**d from heat and **let**ed to cool.
2. Honey, vanilla extract, and vanilla yogurt are **combine**d in a **combining** basin. As soon as the honey is added, thoroughly **combine**.
3. Layer the yogurt **Mixture**, granola, and raspberry sauce in serving glasses or bowls.

4. Continue the layering and finish with a dab of raspberry sauce.
5. Before serving, place in the fridge for at least 10 **min**s. Take pleasure in the beautiful blending of flavors and textures!

Nutrition (per serving):
Cals: 150 kcal, **Carb**s: 28g, Protein: 6g
Fat: 2g, Fiber: 3g

58.Mason Jar Chicken Shawarma

Prep Time: 30 **min**s

Cook Time: 25 **min**s

Total Time: 55 **min**s

Servings: 2

Ingredients:
- 1 lb boneless, skinless chicken breasts, thinly **split**
- 2 **tbsp** olive oil
- 2 **tbsp** lemon juice
- 2 cloves garlic, **chop-up**
- 1 **tsp** ground cumin
- 1 **tsp** paprika
- 1/2 **tsp** ground coriander
- 1/4 **tsp** cayenne pepper (adjust to your spice preference)
- Salt and pepper **as needed**
- 1 **cup of** cooked quinoa
- 1 **cup of** cherry tomatoes, halved
- 1 **cup of** cucumber, diced
- 1/2 **cup of** diced red onion
- 1/4 **cup of chop-up** fresh parsley
- 1/4 **cup of chop-up** fresh mint
- 1/2 **cup of** hummus (store-bought or homemade)
- 2 pita bread, **slice** into wedges

Instructions:
1. Slices of chicken, olive oil, lemon juice, **chop-up** garlic, paprika, ground coriander, cayenne pepper, salt, and pepper are all **combine**d in a bowl. **Combine** thoroughly, then let it sit for at least 15 **min**s.
2. The marinated chicken **Must** be cooked through and slightly browned after being fried in a skillet over medium-high heat.
3. Put the cooked quinoa, cherry tomatoes, cucumber, red onion, **chop-up** parsley, and **chop-up** mint in two mason jars.
4. Add the cooked chicken shawarma to the top of **every** mason jar.
5. Pita bread wedges and hummus **Must** be served on the side.

Nutrition (per serving):
Cals: 560 kcal, **Carb**s: 43g, Protein: 45g

Fat: 23g, Fiber: 8g

59.Layered Asian Noodle Salad

Prep Time: 20 **min**s

Cook Time: 10 **min**s

Total Time: 30 **min**s

Servings: 4

Ingredients:

- 4 oz rice noodles
- 1 **cup of** shredded lettuce
- 1 **cup of** shredded carrots
- 1 **cup of** thinly **split** cucumber
- 1/2 **cup of** thinly **split** red bell pepper
- 1/4 **cup of chop-up** green onions
- 1/4 **cup of chop-up** cilantro
- 1/4 **cup of chop-up** peanuts
- 1 **tbsp** sesame seeds
- For the Dressing:
- 2 **tbsp** soy sauce
- 2 **tbsp** lime juice
- 1 **tbsp** rice vinegar
- 1 **tbsp** honey
- 1 **tbsp** sesame oil
- 1 clove garlic, **chop-up**
- 1 **tsp finely grated** ginger
- 1/4 **tsp** red pepper flakes (**non-compulsory**)
- Salt and pepper **as needed**

Instructions:

1. As directed on the packaging, prepare the rice noodles. To stop sticking, drain and rinse with cold water.
2. All the components for the dressing **Must** be thoroughly blended in a **mini** bowl.
3. Layer the lettuce, carrots, cucumber, red bell pepper, green onions, and cilantro in a sizable serving bowl.
4. Place the cooked rice noodles on top, then garnish the salad with the dressing.
5. Add **chop-up** peanuts and sesame seeds as a garnish.
6. Just before serving, **combine** everything.

Nutrition (per serving):
Cals: 240 kcal, **Carb**s: 38g

Protein: 6g, Fat: 8g, Fiber: 4g

60.Strawberry Shortcake Parfait

Prep Time: 15 **min**s

Cook Time: 20 **min**s

Total Time: 35 **min**s

Servings: 4

Ingredients:

- 1 **lb** fresh strawberries, hulled and **split**
- 2 **tbsp** granulated sugar
- 1 1/2 **cups of** whipped cream
- 1 **cup of cut up** shortcake or **lb** cake
- Fresh mint leaves for garnish (**non-compulsory**)

Instructions:

1. **Split** strawberries and sugar **Must** be **combine**d in a bowl and let to macerate for about 15 **min**s.
2. Layer whipped cream, macerated strawberries, and shortcake or **lb** cake crumbs in serving **cups of** or bowls.
3. Continue the layering, and then top it off with a dab of whipped cream.
4. If desired, garnish with fresh mint leaves.
5. The dessert **Must** be chilled in the refrigerator before serving.

Nutrition (per serving):
Cals: 280 kcal, **Carb**s: 38g, Protein: 2g

Fat: 14g, Fiber: 3g

61.Mason Jar Zucchini Lasagna

Prep Time: 20 **min**s

Cook Time: 40 **min**s

Total Time: 1 **hr**

Servings: 2

Ingredients:

- 1 **Big** zucchini, thinly **split**
- 1 **cup of** ricotta cheese
- 1 **cup of** marinara sauce
- 1 **cup of** shredded mozzarella cheese
- 1/4 **cup of finely grated** Parmesan cheese
- 1 **tbsp** olive oil
- 1 **tsp** dried oregano
- Salt and pepper **as needed**

Instructions:

1. Set the oven's temperature to 375°F (190°C).
2. Ricotta cheese, olive oil, dried oregano, salt, and pepper **Must** all be **combine**d in a **mini** bowl.
3. Marinara sauce, zucchini slices, ricotta **Mixture**, mozzarella cheese, and **finely grated** Parmesan **Must** be arranged in this order in a mason jar.
4. Up till the jar is full, keep adding layers; the final layer **Must** be mozzarella and Parmesan.
5. The mason jar **Must** be placed on a baking sheet, and it **Must** be baked for 40 **min**s, or **up to** the cheese is **dilute** and bubbling, in the preheated oven.
6. Before serving, let it cool a little.

Nutrition (per serving):
Cals: 380 kcal, Fat: 25g, **Carb**s: 12g

Protein: 28g

62. Layered Cobb Dip

Prep Time: 15 mins

Cook Time: 0 mins

Total Time: 15 mins

Servings: 6

Ingredients:

- 2 **cups of** shredded lettuce
- 1 **cup of** diced cooked chicken
- 1 **cup of** diced tomatoes
- 1/2 **cup of cut up** blue cheese
- 1/4 **cup of** diced red onion
- 1/4 **cup of** cooked and **cut up** bacon
- 1/4 **cup of** ranch dressing
- 1 **tbsp chop-up** chives

Instructions:

1. The bottom layer of the dish **Must** be lettuce that has been shred.
2. On top of the lettuce, layer **split** tomatoes after adding a layer of chicken.
3. Over the tomatoes, scatter the blue cheese **cut up**s and red onion dice.
4. Layer cooked, **cut up** bacon on top.
5. Ranch dressing **Must** be drizzled over the dish before adding the chives.
6. Serve right away with pita bread or tortilla chips for dipping.

Nutrition (per serving):

Cals: 240 kcal, **Fat**: 15g, **Carbs**: 10g

Protein: 18g

63. Watermelon Feta Salad

Prep Time: 15 mins

Cook Time: 0 mins

Total Time: 15 mins

Servings: 4

Ingredients:

- 4 **cups of** diced watermelon
- 1 **cup of cut up** feta cheese
- 1/2 **cup of** fresh mint leaves, **chop-up**
- 1/4 **cup of** balsamic glaze
- 1 **tbsp** extra-virgin olive oil

Instructions:

1. The diced watermelon, feta cheese, and **chop-up** mint leaves **Must** all be **combine**d in a big bowl.
2. Over the watermelon combination, drizzle the olive oil and balsamic glaze.
3. **Combine** the ingredients together by gently tossing them.
4. Serve chilled as a tasty and refreshing salad.

Nutrition (per serving):

Cals: 180 kcal, **Fat**: 8g, **Carbs**: 22g

Protein: 6g

64. Piña Colada Chia Pudding

Prep Time: 10 mins

Cook Time: 0 mins

Total Time: 4 hrs 10 mins (including chilling time)

Servings: 2

Ingredients:

- 1 **cup of** coconut milk
- 1/4 **cup of** chia seeds
- 1/2 **cup of** diced pineapple
- 2 **tbsp** shredded coconut
- 1 **tbsp** honey (or more **as needed**)
- 1/2 **tsp** pure vanilla extract

Instructions:

1. **Combine** the coconut milk, chia seeds, honey, and vanilla extract in a bowl.
2. **Let** the **Mixture** to rest for around 10 **min**s, stirring every so often to avoid clumps.
3. Add the **split** pineapple and coconut once the chia seeds have absorbed part of the liquid.
4. Once the **Mixture** has thickened and taken on the consistency of pudding, cover the bowl and place in the refrigerator for at least 4 **hr**s or overnight.
5. If desired, top the chilled Pia Colada Chia Pudding with more pineapple and shredded coconut.

Nutrition (per serving):

Cals: 270 kcal, **Fat**: 15g

Carbs: 30g

Protein: 6g

65. Mason Jar Lemon Herb Farro Salad

Prep Time: 15 mins

Cook Time: 25 mins

Total Time: 40 mins

Servings: 2

Ingredients:

- 1 **cup of** cooked farro
- 1/2 **cup of** cherry tomatoes, halved
- 1/4 **cup of chop-up** cucumber
- 1/4 **cup of cut up** feta cheese
- 2 **tbsp chop-up** fresh parsley
- 2 **tbsp** extra-virgin olive oil
- 1 **tbsp** lemon juice
- 1 clove garlic, **chop-up**
- Salt and pepper **as needed**

Instructions:

1. Cooked farro, diced cucumber, cherry tomatoes, feta cheese, and **chop-up** parsley **Must** all be **combine**d in a big bowl.
2. To create the dressing, **combine** the extra virgin olive oil, lemon juice, **chop-up** garlic, salt, and pepper in a separate **mini** bowl.
3. The farro **Mixture Must** be well coated once the dressing has been added.
4. Before serving, divide the salad among mason jars and put them in the fridge.
5. You can eat this salad cold or at room temperature.

Nutrition (per serving):

Cals: 360 kcal, Fat: 21g, **Carb**s: 35g

Protein: 8g

66.Layered BBQ Beans and Coleslaw

Prep Time: 20 **min**s

Cook Time: 40 **min**s

Total Time: 1 **hr**

Servings: 6

Ingredients:

- 2 **cups of** canned baked beans
- 1 **cup of** BBQ sauce
- 1 **cup of** coleslaw
- 1 **cup of** corn chips
- 1 **cup of** shredded cheddar cheese
- 1/2 **cup of** diced red onion
- 1/4 **cup of chop-up** fresh cilantro

Instructions:

1. Set the oven's temperature to 350°F (175°C).
2. Baked beans and BBQ sauce **Must** be **combine**d in a pan over medium heat. Cook for about 5 **min**s, or **up to** thoroughly heated.
3. Layer the ingredients in a trifle bowl or a big glass basin. Start with half of the corn chips, then distribute the remaining beans, coleslaw, shredded cheese, diced red onion, and cilantro.
4. One more time, arrange the ingredients, and then top with a scattering of **chop-up** cilantro.
5. Bake for 30-35 **min**s in a preheated oven, or **up to** the cheese is **dilute** and bubbling.
6. Serve hot and enjoy!

Nutrition (per serving):

Cals: 380 kcal, Fat: 16g, **Carb**s: 47g

Protein: 14g

67.Chocolate Cherry Cheesecake Parfait

Prep Time: 30 **min**s

Cook Time: No cook

Total Time: 30 **min**s

Servings: 4

Ingredients:

- 1 **cup of** chocolate cookies (crushed)
- 2 **cups of** cream cheese (**melted**)
- 1/2 **cup of** powdered sugar
- 1 **tsp** vanilla extract
- 1 **cup of** cherry pie filling
- 1/2 **cup of** whipped cream
- Chocolate shavings (for garnish)

Instructions:

1. **Combine** the **melted** cream cheese, powdered sugar, and vanilla extract thoroughly in a medium basin.
2. Create layers in serving glasses or dessert **cups of** by starting at the bottom with a scoop of crushed chocolate cookies.
3. The cream cheese **Mixture Must** next be layered on top of the cherry pie filling.
4. Continue layering **up to** the glasses are almost filled, then top with whipped cream.
5. Add chocolate shavings as a garnish.
6. Before serving, let the food cool for at least an **hr** in the refrigerator.
7. Enjoy the tasty parfait when chilled!

Nutrition (per serving):

Cals: 420 kcal, Fat: 25g, **Carb**s: 40g

Protein: 7g

68.Mason Jar Veggie Frittata

Prep Time: 15 **min**s

Cook Time: 25 **min**s

Total Time: 40 **min**s

Servings: 4

Ingredients:

- 6 **Big** eggs
- 1/4 **cup of** milk
- 1/2 **tsp** salt
- 1/4 **tsp** black pepper
- 1/2 **cup of** diced bell peppers
- 1/2 **cup of** diced tomatoes
- 1/4 **cup of chop-up** spinach
- 1/4 **cup of** shredded cheddar cheese
- 2 **tbsp chop-up** green onions
- Cooking spray

Instructions:

1. Set the oven's temperature to 375°F (190°C).
2. Eggs, milk, salt, and black pepper **Must** all be thoroughly blended in a bowl.
3. Add to the egg **Mixture** the diced bell peppers,

tomatoes, spinach, shredded cheddar cheese, and green onions.

4. To avoid sticking, coat the interior of four mason jars with cooking spray.
5. Fill **every** mason jar with an even layer of the egg and vegetable **Mixture**, **let**ing some space at the top for growth.
6. When the frittatas are set and the tops are faintly golden, place the mason jars on a baking sheet and bake in the preheated oven for 20 to 25 **min**s.
7. Before serving, take them out of the oven and **let** them to cool somewhat.
8. You may eat these frittatas warm or at room temperature.

Nutrition (per serving):
Cals: 180 kcal, Fat: 11g

Carbs: 7g

Protein: 14g

69.Layered Greek Dip

Prep Time: 20 **min**s

Cook Time: No cook

Total Time: 20 **min**s

Servings: 8

Ingredients:
- 1 **cup of** hummus
- 1 **cup of** Greek yogurt
- 1 cucumber (seeded and diced)
- 1 **cup of** cherry tomatoes (halved)
- 1/2 **cup of** pitted kalamata olives (**chop-up**)
- 1/2 **cup of cut up** feta cheese
- 1/4 **cup of chop-up** fresh dill
- 2 **tbsp** extra-virgin olive oil
- Pita bread or pita chips (for serving)

Instructions:
1. Spread the hummus thinly in a sh**let** serving dish or trifle bowl to serve as the base.
2. Greek yogurt **Must** then be spread on top of the hummus layer.
3. Over the yogurt layer, scatter the diced cucumber, **chop-up** cherry tomatoes, **chop-up** kalamata olives, and **cut up** feta cheese.
4. Extra virgin olive oil **Must** be drizzled on top, and fresh dill **Must** be diced as a garnish.
5. Pita chips or bread **Must** be provided for dipping.
6. Enjoy this layered Greek dip, which is tasty and refreshing.

Nutrition (per serving):
Cals: 180 kcal, Fat: 12g, **Carb**s: 10g

Protein: 8g

70.Mango Tango Salad

Prep Time: 15 **min**s

Cook Time: No cook

Total Time: 15 **min**s

Servings: 4

Ingredients:
- 2 ripe mangoes (**peel off**, pitted, and diced)
- 1 red bell pepper (diced)
- 1/2 red onion (thinly **split**)
- 1/4 **cup of chop-up** fresh cilantro
- 1 jalapeno (seeded and **lightly chop-up**)
- Juice of 1 lime
- Salt and pepper **as needed**
- **Combined** salad greens (**non-compulsory**, for serving)

Instructions:
1. The diced mangoes, diced red bell pepper, thinly **split** red onion, **chop-up** cilantro, and **lightly chop-up** jalapeno **Must** all be **combine**d in a big bowl.
2. Toss the salad lightly to **combine** all the ingredients after adding the lime juice.
3. **As needed**, add salt and pepper to the food.
4. For enhanced freshness and presentation, if preferred, serve the mango tango salad over a bed of **combined** salad greens.
5. Enjoy this energizing salad's vivid flavors!

Nutrition (per serving):
Cals: 120 kcal, Fat: 0.5g

Carbs: 30g

Protein: 2g

71.Layered Mediterranean Hummus Dip

Prep Time: 20 **min**s

Cook Time: 0 **min**s

Total Time: 20 **min**s

Servings: 8

Ingredients:
- 2 **cups of** hummus
- 1 **cup of** cucumber, diced
- 1 **cup of** cherry tomatoes, halved
- 1/2 **cup of** red onion, **lightly chop-up**
- 1/2 **cup of** Kalamata olives, pitted and **chop-up**
- 1/4 **cup of cut up** feta cheese
- 2 **tbsp** fresh parsley, **chop-up**
- 2 **tbsp** olive oil
- 1 **tbsp** lemon juice
- Salt and pepper **as needed**
- Pita chips or **split** vegetables for serving

Instructions:

1. To make the Mediterranean salad topper, **combine** the diced cucumber, cherry tomatoes, red onion, Kalamata olives, fresh parsley, olive oil, lemon juice, salt, and pepper in a **mini** bowl.
2. Spread a thin layer of hummus evenly across the bottom of a serving dish or a bowl made of clear glass.
3. Add the Mediterranean salad combination on top of the hummus.
4. Top the salad with some feta cheese **cut up**s.
5. Pita chips or **split** vegetables go well with the layered Mediterranean hummus dip.

Nutrition (per serving):

Cals: 210 kcal, Fat: 14g

Carbs: 17g, Fiber: 4g

Protein: 6g

72.Raspberry White Chocolate Parfait

Prep Time: 15 **min**s

Cook Time: 0 **min**s

Total Time: 15 **min**s

Servings: 4

Ingredients:

- 1 **cup of** fresh raspberries
- 2 **cups of** vanilla yogurt
- 1/2 **cup of** granola
- 1/2 **cup of** white chocolate chips

Instructions:

1. Layer the ingredients in four parfait glasses or serving glasses as follows:
2. At the bottom, place a few fresh raspberries.
3. Vanilla yogurt **Must** then be spread over the raspberries.
4. Add some granola on top of the yogurt layer.
5. Some white chocolate chips **Must** be added.
6. Till the glasses are full, keep adding layers.
7. Add some white chocolate chips and raspberries as a garnish on the top.
8. The Raspberry White Chocolate Parfait can be served right away or stored in the refrigerator **up to** needed.

Nutrition (per serving):

Cals: 320 kcal, Fat: 12g, **Carb**s: 44g

Fiber: 3g, Protein: 9g

73.Mason Jar Hawaiian Chicken Salad

Prep Time: 20 **min**s

Cook Time: 15 **min**s

Total Time: 35 **min**s

Servings: 2

Ingredients:

- 1 **cup of** cooked chicken breast, shredded or diced
- 1/2 **cup of** pineapple chunks
- 1/2 avocado, diced
- 1/4 **cup of** red bell pepper, diced
- 1/4 **cup of** cucumber, diced
- 2 **tbsp** red onion, **lightly chop-up**
- 2 **tbsp** macadamia nuts, **chop-up**
- 2 **tbsp** fresh cilantro, **chop-up**
- 2 **tbsp** mayonnaise
- 1 **tbsp** Greek yogurt
- 1 **tbsp** lime juice
- Salt and pepper **as needed**
- Lettuce leaves for serving

Instructions:

1. Chicken that has been shredded or diced, pineapple chunks, avocado, red bell pepper, cucumber, red onion, macadamia nuts, and fresh cilantro **Must** all be **combine**d in a bowl.
2. To make the dressing, **combine** the mayonnaise, Greek yogurt, lime juice, salt, and pepper in a separate **mini** bowl.
3. The chicken **Mixture Must** be well coated after the dressing has been added.
4. The Hawaiian Chicken Salad ought to be put into two Mason jars.
5. On a bed of lettuce leaves, dish up the Hawaiian chicken salad in a mason jar.

Nutrition (per serving):

Cals: 460 kcal, Fat: 32g

Carbs: 21g

Fiber: 7g, Protein: 24g

74.Layered Caprese Dip

Prep Time: 15 **min**s

Cook Time: 0 **min**s

Total Time: 15 **min**s

Servings: 6

Ingredients:

- 2 **cups of** fresh basil leaves
- 1 **cup of** cherry tomatoes, halved
- 8 **oz**s fresh mozzarella cheese, **split**
- 1/4 **cup of** balsamic glaze
- 2 **tbsp** extra-virgin olive oil
- Salt and pepper **as needed**
- Baguette slices or crackers for serving

Instructions:

1. A layer of fresh basil leaves **Must** be placed at the bottom of a serving dish or sh**let** bowl.

2. Over the basil layer, scatter the fresh mozzarella slices.
3. On top of the mozzarella, arrange cherry tomato halves.
4. Over the layers, drizzle extra-virgin olive oil and balsamic glaze.
5. Add salt and pepper according **as needed**.
6. Serve crackers or baguette slices alongside the layered caprese dip.

Nutrition (per serving):
Cals: 220 kcal, **Fat**: 16g, **Carb**s: 6g

Fiber: 1g, Protein: 12g

75.Waldorf Chicken Salad

Prep Time: 20 **min**s

Cook Time: 15 **min**s

Total Time: 35 **min**s

Servings: 4

Ingredients:
- 2 **cups of** cooked chicken breast, diced
- 1 **cup of** red seedless grapes, halved
- 1 **cup of** celery, diced
- 1/2 **cup of** walnuts, **chop-up**
- 1/2 **cup of** mayonnaise
- 1/4 **cup of** Greek yogurt
- 1 **tbsp** honey
- 1 **tbsp** lemon juice
- Salt and pepper **as needed**
- Lettuce leaves or sandwich bread for serving

Instructions:
1. **Combine** the diced chicken, grape halves, celery, and walnuts in a big bowl.
2. To make the dressing, **combine** the mayonnaise, Greek yogurt, honey, lemon juice, salt, and pepper in a separate **mini** bowl.
3. The chicken **Mixture Must** be well coated after the dressing has been added.
4. Use the Waldorf Chicken Salad as a sandwich filling or serve it on a bed of lettuce leaves.

Nutrition (per serving):
Cals: 450 kcal, **Fat**: 28g

Carbs: 20g, Fiber: 3g

Protein: 30g

76.Tiramisu Chia Pudding

Prep Time: 10 **min**s

Total Time: 4 **hr**s 10 **min**s

Servings: 2

Ingredients:
- 1 **cup of** unsweetened almond milk
- 1/4 **cup of** chia seeds
- 2 **tbsp** unsweetened cocoa powder
- 2 **tbsp** maple syrup
- 1 **tsp** instant coffee granules
- 1/2 **tsp** vanilla extract
- Ladyfinger cookies (**non-compulsory**, for layering)
- Cocoa powder or **finely grated** dark chocolate for topping

Instructions:
1. Almond milk, chia seeds, cocoa powder, maple syrup, instant coffee, and vanilla extract **Must** all be thoroughly blended in a **combining** dish.
2. **Let** the chia seeds to absorb the liquid and develop a pudding-like consistency by covering the bowl and placing it in the refrigerator for at least 4 **hr**s or overnight.
3. In serving glasses or jars, stack the chia pudding with ladyfinger biscuits (if using).
4. Add some cocoa powder or **finely grated** dark chocolate over top.

Nutrition (per serving):
Cals: 220 kcal, **Carb**s: 28g

Protein: 7g, Fat: 10g, Fiber: 12g

77.Mason Jar Cauliflower Rice Burrito Bowl

Prep Time: 15 **min**s

Cook Time: 15 **min**s

Total Time: 30 **min**s

Servings: 2

Ingredients:
- 2 **cups of** cauliflower rice
- 1 **cup of** cooked black beans
- 1 **cup of** cooked corn kernels
- 1 avocado, diced
- 1 **cup of** cherry tomatoes, halved
- 1/4 **cup of** diced red onion
- 1/4 **cup of chop-up** fresh cilantro
- 1 lime, juiced
- Salt and pepper **as needed**
- **Non-compulsory** toppings: salsa, Greek yogurt, shredded cheese

Instructions:
1. Cauliflower rice, black beans, corn, avocado, cherry tomatoes, red onion, and cilantro **Must** all be **combine**d in a big **combining** dish.
2. Give the **Mixture** a lime juice drizzle and toss to incorporate. **As needed**, add salt and pepper to the food.

3. In two mason jars, divide the burrito bowl **Mixture** equally.
4. If desired, top the burrito bowl with your preferred extra toppings, such as salsa, Greek yogurt, or shredded cheese.
5. Prior to serving, seal the Mason jars and place in the refrigerator.

Nutrition (per serving):
Cals: 350 kcal, **Carb**s: 50g, Protein: 15g
Fat: 14g, Fiber: 18g

78.Layered Tex-Mex Dip

Prep Time: 20 **min**s
Total Time: 20 **min**s
Servings: 6

Ingredients:
- 1 can (16 **oz**s) refried beans
- 1 **cup of** guacamole
- 1 **cup of** sour cream
- 1 **cup of** chunky salsa
- 1 **cup of** shredded cheddar cheese
- 1 **cup of** diced tomatoes
- 1/2 **cup of split** black olives
- 1/4 **cup of chop-up** green onions
- Tortilla chips, for serving

Instructions:
1. Refried beans **Must** be evenly distributed at the bottom of a clear glass dish or trifle bowl.
2. Guacamole, sour cream, chunky salsa, and finally more beans **Must** be layered on top of **every** other.
3. Diced tomatoes, black olives, and **chop-up** green onions **Must** be placed on top of the salsa layer, followed by shredded cheddar cheese.
4. If your dish is deep enough, repeat the layers; otherwise, just keep adding one layer of **every** component.
5. Tex-Mex dip **Must** be served with tortilla chips for scooping.

Nutrition (per serving):
Cals: 280 kcal, **Carb**s: 15g, Protein: 8g
Fat: 20g, Fiber: 5g

79.Peanut Butter Cup of Delight

Prep Time: 15 **min**s
Total Time: 2 **hr**s 15 **min**s
Servings: 8

Ingredients:
- 1 1/2 **cups of** crushed chocolate sandwich cookies
- 1/4 **cup of dilute** butter
- 1 **box/pkg** (8 **oz**s) cream cheese, **melted**
- 1 **cup of** creamy peanut butter
- 1 **cup of** powdered sugar
- 1 container (12 **oz**s) **refrigerate** whipped topping, thawed
- 20 mini peanut butter **cups of**, **chop-up**
- Chocolate syrup for drizzling

Instructions:
1. Crushed chocolate cookies and **dilute** butter **Must be combined** in a bowl **up to** the consistency of wet sand.
2. To create the crust, press the cookie **Mixture** firmly into the bottom of a 9x9-inch square baking dish.
3. Cream cheese, peanut butter, and powdered sugar **Must** be thoroughly blended in a different **combining** dish.
4. After the whipped topping has thawed, fold it in **up to** the **Mixture** is smooth and creamy.
5. Over the cookie crust in the baking dish, spread the peanut butter filling.
6. Then, spread chocolate syrup over the filling and top with **chop-up mini** peanut butter **cups of**.
7. Before serving, cover the dish and chill it for at least two **hr**s.

Nutrition (per serving):
Cals: 480 kcal, **Carb**s: 38g
Protein: 11g, Fat: 34g, Fiber: 3g

80.Mason Jar Pesto Zucchini Noodles

Prep Time: 15 **min**s
Total Time: 15 **min**s
Servings: 2

Ingredients:
- 2 **Big** zucchinis, spiralized into noodles
- 1/2 **cup of** cherry tomatoes, halved
- 1/4 **cup of** pitted black olives, **split**
- 2 **tbsp** store-bought or homemade pesto
- 2 **tbsp** pine nuts, toasted
- **Finely grated** Parmesan cheese for garnish (**non-compulsory**)

Instructions:
1. Utilizing a spiralizer or julienne peeler, create zucchini noodles.
2. Zucchini noodles, cherry tomatoes, and black olives **Must** all be **combined** in a big bowl.
3. When the noodles are completely covered in the

pesto sauce, add the pesto to the bowl and toss the contents together.
4. Put two mason jars' worth of pesto zucchini noodles in **every**.
5. Add toasted pine nuts and, if like, a little **finely grated** Parmesan cheese to the top of **every** jar.
6. Prior to serving, seal the Mason jars and place in the refrigerator.

Nutrition (per serving):
Cals: 220 kcal, **Carb**s: 12g

Protein: 6g, Fat: 18g, Fiber: 4g

81. Mason Jar Sushi Bowl

Prep Time: 20 **min**s

Cook Time: 0 **min**s

Total Time: 20 **min**s

Servings: 2

Ingredients:
- 1 **cup of** cooked sushi rice
- 1/2 **cup of** imitation crab meat, shredded
- 1/2 avocado, diced
- 1/2 cucumber, julienned
- 1 **tbsp** pickled ginger
- 1 **tbsp** soy sauce
- 1 **tbsp** rice vinegar
- 1 **tsp** sesame oil
- 1 **tsp** sesame seeds
- Nori seaweed sheets, **slice** into **mini** strips
- **Non-compulsory** toppings: wasabi, sriracha, and **split** green onions

Instructions:
1. **Combine** soy sauce, rice vinegar, sesame oil, and sesame seeds in a **mini** bowl. Place aside.
2. Place sushi rice at the bottom of **every** Mason jar before adding imitation crab meat, avocado, cucumber, and pickled ginger.
3. Over the top layer in **every** jar, pour the prepared sauce.
4. On the very top, add a few nori seaweed strips.
5. Before serving, place the Mason jars in the refrigerator and seal them.
6. When you're ready to eat, give the jar a gentle shake to **combine** the flavors, or dump everything into a bowl and stir it.
7. If desired, top with other ingredients and serve.

NUTRITION INFO (per serving):
Cals: 350 kcal, **Carb**s: 50g, Protein: 8g

Fat: 14g, Fiber: 6g

82. Layered Avocado and Shrimp Dip

Prep Time: 15 **min**s

Cook Time: 0 **min**s

Total Time: 15 **min**s

Servings: 4

Ingredients:
- 2 ripe avocados, **peel off** and mashed
- 1 **cup of** cooked shrimp, **chop-up**
- 1/2 **cup of** plain Greek yogurt
- 1/4 **cup of** mayonnaise
- 1/4 **cup of** diced red onion
- 1/4 **cup of** diced tomatoes
- 1/4 **cup of chop-up** fresh cilantro
- 1 **tbsp** lime juice
- 1 **tsp chop-up** garlic
- Salt and pepper **as needed**
- Tortilla chips or vegetable sticks for serving

Instructions:
1. Mash avocados and **combine** with lime juice, **chop-up** garlic, salt, and pepper in a **mini** bowl.
2. **Combine chop-up** shrimp, Greek yogurt, mayonnaise, tomatoes, cilantro, red onion, and in another bowl.
3. Place a layer of the avocado **Mixture** first, then a layer of the shrimp **Mixture**, in **every** Mason jar.
4. Up till the jar is full, keep adding layers, and then top it off with a layer of shrimp.
5. Before serving, place the Mason jars in the refrigerator and seal them.
6. Serve with vegetable sticks or tortilla chips.

NUTRITION INFO (per serving):
Cals: 250 kcal, **Carb**s: 9g, Protein: 12g

Fat: 19g, Fiber: 5g

83. Lemon Poppy Seed Chia Pudding

Prep Time: 5 **min**s

Cook Time: 0 **min**s

Total Time: 5 **min**s

Servings: 2

Ingredients:
- 1/4 **cup of** chia seeds
- 1 **cup of** almond milk (or any milk of your choice)
- 1 **tbsp** maple syrup (or honey)
- 1 **tbsp** lemon juice
- 1 **tsp** lemon zest
- 1 **tsp** poppy seeds
- Fresh berries for topping (e.g., blueberries, strawberries)

Instructions:
1. Chia seeds, almond milk, maple syrup, poppy seeds, lemon juice, and lemon zest **Must** all be **combine**d in a bowl.

2. To prevent clumping, let the **Mixture** settle for about 5 **min**s before stirring it once more.
3. The chia pudding **Mixture Must** be added to **every** Mason jar.
4. To help the pudding thicken, seal the Mason jars and place them in the refrigerator for at least two **hr**s or overnight.
5. Stir the pudding well before serving, then top with fresh berries.

NUTRITION INFO (per serving):
Cals: 180 kcal, **Carb**s: 22g, Protein: 5g

Fat: 9g, Fiber: 10g

84. Mason Jar Beef and Broccoli Stir-Fry

Prep Time: 15 **min**s

Cook Time: 15 **min**s

Total Time: 30 **min**s

Servings: 2

Ingredients:
- 1/2 lb (225g) beef steak, thinly **split**
- 2 **cups of** broccoli florets
- 1/4 **cup of** soy sauce
- 2 **tbsp** oyster sauce
- 2 **tbsp** hoisin sauce
- 1 **tbsp** vegetable oil
- 2 cloves garlic, **chop-up**
- 1 **tsp finely grated** ginger
- 1/2 **tsp** red pepper flakes (**non-compulsory**)
- Cooked rice or noodles for serving

Instructions:
1. **Combine** the soy sauce, oyster sauce, and hoisin sauce in a **mini** bowl. Place aside.
2. Vegetable oil **Must** be heated over medium-high heat in a skillet or wok.
3. Add red pepper flakes (if using), **finely grated** ginger, and **chop-up** garlic to the skillet. **Up to** aromatic, stir-fry for one **min**.
4. Cook the meat slices **up to** they are browned. The beef **Must** be taken out of the griddle and put aside.
5. Broccoli florets **Must** be stir-fried in the same skillet **up to** crisp-tender.
6. Pour the sauce over the meat and broccoli as you add the cooked steak back to the skillet. Everything **Must** be thoroughly coated in sauce after being **combine**d.
7. Place cooked rice or noodles on top of the beef and broccoli stir-fry in **every** Mason jar.
8. Refrigerate the Mason jars with their lids on **up to** you're ready to eat.
9. When you're ready to eat, either reheat the contents in the jar in the microwave or move them to a plate that can be heated in the microwave.

NUTRITION INFO (per serving, excluding rice or noodles):
Cals: 300 kcal, **Carb**s: 14g, Protein: 26g

Fat: 15g, Fiber: 3g

85. Layered Mexican Street Corn Dip

Prep Time: 20 **min**s

Cook Time: 10 **min**s

Total Time: 30 **min**s

Servings: 4

Ingredients:
- 4 **cups of** cooked corn kernels (fresh, canned, or **refrigerate**)
- 1/2 **cup of** mayonnaise
- 1/2 **cup of** sour cream
- 1/2 **cup of cut up** cotija cheese (or feta cheese)
- 1/4 **cup of chop-up** fresh cilantro
- 1/4 **cup of** lightly **chop-up** red onion
- 1 jalapeño pepper, seeds **take out**d and **lightly chop-up**
- 1 clove garlic, **chop-up**
- 1 **tbsp** lime juice
- 1 **tsp** chili powder
- Salt and pepper **as needed**
- Tortilla chips for serving

Instructions:
1. **Combine** mayonnaise, sour cream, cotija cheese, **chop-up** garlic, red onion, jalapenos, cilantro, lime juice, chili powder, salt, and pepper in a sizable bowl. To prepare the dressing, thoroughly stir.
2. Layer corn kernels and dressing in **every** Mason jar in alternating layers **up to** the jar is full.
3. Before serving, place the Mason jars in the refrigerator and seal them.
4. Tostito chips **Must** be provided for dipping.

NUTRITION INFO (per serving, excluding tortilla chips):
Cals: 350 kcal, **Carb**s: 25g

Protein: 7g, Fat: 25g, Fiber: 4g

86. Black Forest Parfait

Prep Time: 15 **min**s

Cook Time: 0 **min**s

Total Time: 15 **min**s

Servings: 4

Ingredients:

- 2 **cups of** Greek yogurt
- 1 **cup of** pitted cherries, **chop-up**
- 1/2 **cup of** chocolate shavings or mini chocolate chips
- 1/2 **cup of** granola
- 1 **tbsp** honey (**non-compulsory**)

Instructions:

1. Greek yogurt and honey, if using, **Must** be thoroughly **combined** in a bowl.
2. Start arranging the ingredients in four serving glasses or mason jars. Greek yogurt **Must** be the first layer, then cherries that have been diced, granola, and then chocolate shavings **Must** be added.
3. The layers **Must** be repeated **up to** the glasses are completely filled.
4. Add some cherries and chocolate shavings as a garnish on the top.
5. Serve right away or wait a few **hr**s and then chill.

NUTRITION INFO (per serving):

Cals: 250 kcal, **Carb**s: 35g, Protein: 12g

Fat: 7g, Fiber: 4g

87.Mason Jar Spinach and Mushroom Quiche

Prep Time: 20 **min**s

Cook Time: 25 **min**s

Total Time: 45 **min**s

Servings: 4

Ingredients:

- 4 **Big** eggs
- 1 **cup of** milk
- 1 **cup of** fresh spinach, **chop-up**
- 1 **cup of** mushrooms, **split**
- 1/2 **cup of** shredded cheddar cheese
- Salt and pepper **as needed**
- Cooking spray

Instructions:

1. Set your oven's temperature to 375°F (190°C).
2. Whisk the eggs and milk together in a **combining** bowl. Add salt and pepper **as needed**.
3. To avoid sticking, coat four 8-**oz** Mason jars with cooking spray.
4. Divide the **split** mushrooms and **chop-up** spinach among the mason jars.
5. The egg **Mixture Must** cover the vegetables to roughly 3/4 of the jars' capacity.

6. **Every** quiche **Must** have shredded cheddar cheese on it.
7. The quiches **Must** be set and the tops golden brown, then place them in the mason jars on a baking sheet and bake in the preheated oven for 20 to 25 **min**s.
8. Serve after taking them out of the oven and **let**ing them to cool somewhat.

NUTRITION INFO (per serving):

Cals: 200 kcal, **Carb**s: 6g, Protein: 14g

Fat: 13g, Fiber: 1g

88.Layered Buffalo Chicken Dip

Prep Time: 15 **min**s

Cook Time: 25 **min**s

Total Time: 40 **min**s

Servings: 6

Ingredients:

- 2 **cups of** cooked chicken, shredded
- 1 **cup of** buffalo sauce
- 8 **oz**s cream cheese, **melted**
- 1 **cup of** ranch dressing
- 1 **cup of** shredded cheddar cheese
- 1/2 **cup of cut up** blue cheese
- 1/4 **cup of chop-up** green onions
- Tortilla chips or celery sticks for serving

Instructions:

1. Turn on the oven to 350 °F (175 °C).
2. Shredded chicken and buffalo sauce **Must** be **combined** together in a bowl **up to** the chicken is thoroughly coated.
3. **Combine** the **melted** cream cheese and ranch dressing thoroughly in a another bowl.
4. Start arranging the ingredients in a baking dish or a transparent trifle dish. The cream cheese **Mixture Must** be the first layer, then buffalo chicken, shredded cheddar cheese, and then **cut up** blue cheese.
5. Continue layering **up to** all the ingredients have been utilized, and then top with a layer of blue cheese **cut up**s and shredded cheddar cheese.
6. Bake for about 25 **min**s in the preheated oven, or **up to** the cheese is **dilute** and bubbling and the dip is thoroughly cooked.
7. Before serving, scatter **chop-up** green onions over top.
8. Serve tortilla chips or celery sticks alongside the layered buffalo chicken dip.

NUTRITION INFO (per serving):

Cals: 380 kcal, **Carb**s: 3g, Protein: 18g

Fat: 33g, Fiber: 0g

89. Mango Coconut Rice Pudding

Prep Time: 5 **min**s

Cook Time: 25 **min**s

Total Time: 30 **min**s

Servings: 4

Ingredients:

- 1 **cup of** Arborio rice (or other short-grain rice)
- 2 **cups of** coconut milk
- 1 **cup of** water
- 1/4 **cup of** sugar (adjust **as needed**)
- 1 ripe mango, diced
- 1/4 **cup of** toasted coconut flakes
- 1/4 **tsp** vanilla extract
- Pinch of salt

Instructions:

1. Rice, coconut milk, water, sugar, vanilla essence, and a dash of salt **Must** all be **combine**d in a pan.
2. Over medium heat, bring the **Mixture** to a boil while stirring occasionally.
3. When the rice is soft and has soaked up the majority of the liquid, reduce the heat to low, cover the pan, and let the rice simmer for about 20 to 25 **min**s. To avoid sticking, stir every so while.
4. **Take out** the rice pudding from the pan and let it cool slightly once it r**every**es the proper consistency.
5. Put the rice pudding into mason jars or serving bowls.
6. Diced mango and toasted coconut flakes go on top of **every** serving.
7. Serve warm or chill for a few **hr**s before serving.

NUTRITION INFO (per serving):
Cals: 350 kcal, **Carb**s: 57g, Protein: 4g

Fat: 12g, Fiber: 2g

90. Mason Jar Ratatouille and Polenta

Prep Time: 20 **min**s

Cook Time: 40 **min**s

Total Time: 1 **hr**

Servings: 4

Ingredients:

- 1 **cup of** polenta
- 4 **cups of** water
- 2 **tbsp** olive oil
- 1 **mini** eggplant, diced
- 1 zucchini, diced
- 1 red bell pepper, diced
- 1 yellow bell pepper, diced
- 1 onion, **chop-up**
- 2 cloves garlic, **chop-up**
- 1 can (14 **oz**s) diced tomatoes
- 2 **tbsp** tomato paste
- 1 **tsp** dried basil
- 1 **tsp** dried oregano
- Salt and pepper **as needed**
- Fresh basil leaves for garnish

Instructions:

1. Bring the water to a boil in a saucepan. Pour the polenta in gradually while continuously whisking to prevent lumps.
2. The polenta **Must** simmer for 15 to 20 **min**s, stirring periodically, or **up to** it thickens and becomes creamy. **As needed**, add salt.
3. The olive oil **Must** be heated over medium heat in a different skillet.
4. To the skillet, add the **chop-up** garlic and onion, and cook **up to** the onion is transparent.
5. To the skillet, add the diced eggplant, zucchini, red pepper, and yellow pepper. The vegetables **Must** be sautéed for 5 to 7 **min**s **up to** they begin to soften.
6. Add salt, pepper, dried oregano, dried basil, and diced tomatoes to the sauce. **Let** the flavors to **combine** for an additional 10 **min**s of cooking.
7. To assemble, layer the polenta and ratatouille in mason jars, beginning with the polenta and moving to the ratatouille. Continue **up to** all of the jars are full.
8. Before serving, garnish with fresh basil leaves.

NUTRITION INFO (per serving):
Cals: 320 kcal, **Carb**s: 55g, Protein: 7g

Fat: 8g, Fiber: 9g

91. Layered Mediterranean Couscous Dip

Prep Time: 15 **min**s

Cook Time: 10 **min**s

Total Time: 25 **min**s

Servings: 6

Ingredients:

- 1 **cup of** cooked couscous
- 1 **cup of** hummus
- 1 **cup of** diced cucumber
- 1 **cup of** cherry tomatoes, halved
- 1/2 **cup of** diced red onion
- 1/4 **cup of chop-up** Kalamata olives
- 1/4 **cup of cut up** feta cheese
- 2 **tbsp chop-up** fresh parsley
- Pita chips or crackers, for serving

Instructions:

1. Spread a layer of cooked couscous in a uniform layer in a transparent glass serving dish.
2. Put a uniform layer of hummus on top of the couscous.
3. Over the hummus, arrange the **chop-up** cucumber, cherry tomatoes, and red onion.
4. On top, strew feta cheese **cut up**s and **chop-up** Kalamata olives.
5. Add **chop-up** parsley as a garnish.
6. Serve alongside crackers or pita chips for dipping.

Nutrition (per serving):

Cals: 230 kcal, **Carb**s: 32g, Protein: 8g

Fat: 8g, Fiber: 5g

92.Strawberry Cheesecake Parfait

Prep Time: 20 **min**s

Cook Time: 0 **min**s

Total Time: 20 **min**s

Servings: 4

Ingredients:

- 1 1/2 **cups of** graham cracker crumbs
- 1/4 **cup of dilute** butter
- 1 **cup of** cream cheese, **melted**
- 1/2 **cup of** powdered sugar
- 1 **tsp** vanilla extract
- 1 1/2 **cups of split** fresh strawberries
- Whipped cream, for topping

Instructions:

1. Graham cracker crumbs and **dilute** butter **Must** be thoroughly **combined** in a bowl.
2. Cream cheese, powdered sugar, and vanilla extract **Must** be thoroughly blended and creamy in a separate basin.
3. Repeat layering **up to** all of the serving **cups of** are filled with the graham cracker **Mixture**, cream cheese **Mixture**, and strawberries.
4. Add a spoonful of whipped cream to the top of **every** parfait.
5. Before serving, place in the fridge for at least one **hr**.

Nutrition (per serving):

Cals: 450 kcal, **Carb**s: 32g

Protein: 6g, Fat: 34g, Fiber: 2g

93.Mason Jar Teriyaki Tofu Noodles

Prep Time: 30 **min**s

Cook Time: 15 **min**s

Total Time: 45 **min**s

Servings: 2

Ingredients:

- 8 oz firm tofu, drained and cubed
- 1/4 **cup of** teriyaki sauce
- 4 oz rice noodles, cooked according to **box/pkg** instructions
- 1 **cup of** shredded carrots
- 1 **cup of** shredded purple cabbage
- 1/2 **cup of split** scallions
- 1 **tbsp** sesame seeds
- Fresh cilantro, for garnish

Instructions:

1. The tofu cubes **Must** be marinated in teriyaki sauce for 15 **min**s in a bowl.
2. Place the cooked rice noodles, marinated tofu, shredded carrots, shredded purple cabbage, and **split** scallions in mason jars or bowls.
3. With fresh cilantro as a garnish, top with sesame seeds.
4. For a cold noodle salad, cover and chill or serve right away.

Nutrition (per serving):

Cals: 380 kcal, **Carb**s: 52g

Protein: 16g, Fat: 12g, Fiber: 6g

94.Layered Greek Hummus Dip

Prep Time: 15 **min**s

Cook Time: 0 **min**s

Total Time: 15 **min**s

Servings: 8

Ingredients:

- 2 **cups of** hummus
- 1 **cup of** Greek yogurt
- 1 **cup of** diced cucumber
- 1 **cup of** halved cherry tomatoes
- 1/2 **cup of** diced red onion
- 1/4 **cup of chop-up** fresh dill
- 1/4 **cup of cut up** feta cheese
- Pita chips or **split** vegetables, for serving

Instructions:

1. Spread a thin layer of hummus in a serving plate made of clear glass.
2. Greek yogurt **Must** be spread evenly on top of the hummus.
3. Over the yogurt, arrange the **chop-up** cucumber, cherry tomatoes, and red onion.
4. On top, strew feta cheese **cut up**s and **chop-up** fresh dill.

5. Serve with **split** vegetables or pita chips for dipping.

Nutrition (per serving):
Cals: 180 kcal, **Carb**s: 14g

Protein: 9g, Fat: 10g, Fiber: 4g

95.Pesto Shrimp Pasta Salad

Prep Time: 20 **min**s

Cook Time: 10 **min**s

Total Time: 30 **min**s

Servings: 4

Ingredients:
- 8 oz pasta (such as penne or fusilli)
- 1 lb cooked shrimp, **peel off** and deveined
- 1 **cup of** cherry tomatoes, halved
- 1/2 **cup of split** black olives
- 1/4 **cup of chop-up** fresh basil
- 1/4 **cup of** pine nuts, toasted
- 1/2 **cup of** pesto sauce
- Salt and pepper **as needed**

Instructions:
1. Pasta **Must** be cooked as directed on the **box/pkg up to** it is al dente. Let it cool and then drain.
2. The cooked pasta, shrimp, cherry tomatoes, black olives, fresh basil, and toasted pine nuts **Must** all be **combine**d in a big bowl.
3. Then, add the pesto sauce and **combine** everything **up to** it is thoroughly coated.
4. **As needed**, add salt and pepper to the food.
5. Before serving, let the food cool for at least 30 **min**s in the refrigerator.

Nutrition (per serving):
Cals: 450 kcal, **Carb**s: 32g, Protein: 30g

Fat: 22g, Fiber: 3g

96.Mason Jar Bacon and Egg Breakfast

Prep Time: 10 **min**s

Cook Time: 15 **min**s

Total Time: 25 **min**s

Servings: 1

Ingredients:
- 2 **Big** eggs
- 2 slices of bacon, cooked and **cut up**
- 1/4 **cup of** shredded cheddar cheese
- 1/4 **cup of** diced tomatoes
- 1/4 **cup of** diced bell peppers
- 2 **tbsp chop-up** green onions
- Salt and pepper **as needed**

Instructions:
1. Salt and pepper the eggs and whisk them in a **mini** bowl.
2. Scramble the eggs in a nonstick skillet over medium heat **up to** they are fully done. Get rid of the heat.
3. Scrambled eggs, **cut up** bacon, shredded cheddar cheese, **split** tomatoes, diced bell peppers, and **chop-up** green onions **Must** all be placed in a mason jar.
4. Till the jar is full, keep adding layers.
5. When you're ready to eat or take it with you, seal the Mason jar and place it in the fridge.

Nutrition (per serving):
Cals: 350 kcal, Protein: 22g, **Carb**s: 5g

Fat: 26g, Fiber: 1g

97.Layered Antipasto Dip

Prep Time: 15 **min**s

Cook Time: 0 **min**s

Total Time: 15 **min**s

Servings: 6-8

Ingredients:
- 1 **cup of** hummus
- 1 **cup of** ricotta cheese
- 1 **cup of** diced tomatoes
- 1 **cup of** diced cucumbers
- 1 **cup of chop-up** marinated artichoke hearts
- 1/2 **cup of split** black olives
- 1/2 **cup of** diced red onions
- 1/2 **cup of** diced roasted red peppers
- 1/4 **cup of chop-up** fresh basil
- 1/4 **cup of** balsamic glaze
- Salt and pepper **as needed**

Instructions:
1. Starting at the bottom of a clear glass bowl or trifle dish, spread an even layer of hummus.
2. The ricotta cheese is layered over the hummus.
3. Diced tomatoes, cucumbers, marinated artichoke hearts, black olives, red onions, and roasted red peppers are added as additional layers.
4. Depending on the size of your dish, repeat the layers as necessary.
5. Fresh basil that has been **chop-up** and balsamic glaze **Must** be drizzled over the dip.
6. Serve with breadsticks, veggie sticks, or pita chips for dipping.

Nutrition (per serving, based on 6 servings):
Cals: 220 kcal, Protein: 9g, **Carb**s: 16g

Fat: 14g, Fiber: 4g

98.Pevery Melba Cheesecake Parfait

Prep Time: 30 **min**s

Cook Time: 10 **min**s

Total Time: 40 **min**s

Servings: 4

Ingredients:

- 1 **cup of** graham cracker crumbs
- 2 **tbsp dilute** butter
- 8 oz cream cheese, **melted**
- 1/2 **cup of** powdered sugar
- 1 **tsp** vanilla extract
- 1 **cup of** whipped cream
- 2 p**every**es, **peel off** and diced
- 1 **cup of** fresh raspberries

Instructions:

1. Graham cracker crumbs and **dilute** butter **Must** be thoroughly **combined** in a bowl.
2. Cream the **melted** cream cheese, powdered sugar, and vanilla extract together **up to** smooth in a separate dish.
3. Till the whipped cream is completely inte**finely grated**, gently fold it into the cream cheese **Mixture**.
4. Layer the graham cracker **Mixture**, the cream cheese **Mixture**, diced p**every**es, and fresh raspberries in serving glasses or mason jars.
5. When finished, add a layer of fresh raspberries on top and continue layering as desired.
6. Before serving, the parfaits **Must** be chilled for at least an **hr**.

Nutrition (per serving):

Cals: 390 kcal, Protein: 6g, **Carb**s: 28g

Fat: 29g, Fiber: 3g

99.Mason Jar BBQ Pulled Pork Salad

Prep Time: 15 **min**s

Cook Time: 6-8 **hr**s (slow cooker) or 2-3 **hr**s (oven)

Total Time: Varies

Servings: 2

Ingredients:

- 1 **lb** pork **Must**er or pork butt
- 1 **cup of** BBQ sauce
- 1/4 **cup of** apple cider vinegar
- 1 **tbsp** brown sugar
- 1 **tsp** paprika
- 1/2 **tsp** garlic powder
- Salt and pepper **as needed**
- 2 **cups of** shredded lettuce
- 1/2 **cup of** corn kernels
- 1/2 **cup of** black beans, rinsed and drained
- 1/4 **cup of** diced red onions
- 1/4 **cup of** diced tomatoes

- 1/4 **cup of** shredded cheddar cheese
- 1/4 **cup of** ranch dressing

Instructions:

1. Cook the pork **Must**er or butt with the BBQ sauce, apple cider vinegar, brown sugar, paprika, garlic powder, salt, and pepper in a slow cooker or oven **up to** the meat is fork-tender and simple to shred.
2. When the pork is finished cooking, shred it with two forks and **combine** it with the remaining BBQ sauce.
3. Shredded lettuce, BBQ pulled pork, corn, black beans, diced red onions, diced tomatoes, and shredded cheddar cheese **Must** be layered in mason jars.
4. Ranch dressing **Must** be drizzled on top of the salad.
5. Mason jars **Must** be sealed and kept chilled **up to** serving time.

Nutrition (per serving):

Cals: 650 kcal, Protein: 30g, **Carb**s: 45g

Fat: 40g, Fiber: 7g

100.Layered Tex-Mex Breakfast

Prep Time: 20 **min**s

Cook Time: 15 **min**s

Total Time: 35 **min**s

Servings: 2

Ingredients:

- 4 **Big** eggs
- 1 **tbsp** milk
- Salt and pepper **as needed**
- 1/2 **cup of** cooked and seasoned ground turkey or beef
- 1/2 **cup of** black beans, rinsed and drained
- 1/2 **cup of** diced tomatoes
- 1/2 **cup of** diced bell peppers (assorted colors)
- 1/4 **cup of split** black olives
- 1/4 **cup of chop-up** fresh cilantro
- 1/2 **cup of** shredded cheddar cheese
- Salsa and sour cream (**non-compulsory**, for serving)

Instructions:

1. **Combine** the eggs, milk, salt, and pepper in a bowl.
2. The eggs **Must** be scrambled in a nonstick skillet **up to** done to your preference. Get rid of the heat.
3. Start layering the scrambled eggs, cooked mince beef or turkey, black beans, diced tomatoes, diced bell peppers, **split** black olives, **chop-up**

cilantro, and shredded cheddar cheese in two transparent glasses or mason jars.

4. Till the jars are full, keep adding layers.
5. Before serving, you can add salsa and sour cream to the breakfast as desired.

Nutrition (per serving):
Cals: 400 kcal, Protein: 25g, **Carb**s: 20g
Fat: 25g, Fiber: 6g

101.Lemon Raspberry Mousse

Prep Time: 20 **min**s

Cook Time: 0 **min**s

Total Time: 20 **min**s

Servings: 4

Ingredients:
- 1 **cup of** heavy cream
- 1/4 **cup of** powdered sugar
- 1 **tsp** lemon zest
- 1 **tbsp** fresh lemon juice
- 1 **cup of** fresh raspberries
- 1/4 **cup of** crushed graham crackers (for garnish)

Instructions:
1. Whip the heavy cream in a sizable **combining** bowl **up to** soft peaks form.
2. Whip the whipped cream **up to** stiff peaks form, then add the powdered sugar, lemon juice, and zest gradually.
3. Fresh raspberries **Must** be gently incorporated while being careful not to over**combine**.
4. Put a spoonful of the lemon-raspberry mousse in **every** serving glass or bowl.
5. Sprinkle some crushed graham crackers on top of **every** plate as a garnish.
6. To enable the flavors to mingle, place in the refrigerator for at least an **hr** before serving.

Nutrition (per serving):
Cals: 280 kcal, **Carb**s: 16g, Protein: 2g
Fat: 24g, Fiber: 3g

102.Mason Jar Chicken Enchilada Bowl

Prep Time: 15 **min**s

Cook Time: 20 **min**s

Total Time: 35 **min**s

Servings: 2

Ingredients:
- 1 **cup of** cooked and shredded chicken breast
- 1 **cup of** cooked brown rice
- 1 **cup of** black beans, drained and rinsed
- 1/2 **cup of** corn kernels (fresh, **refrigerate**, or canned)
- 1/2 **cup of** diced tomatoes
- 1/4 **cup of** diced red onion
- 1/4 **cup of chop-up** fresh cilantro
- 1/2 **cup of** enchilada sauce
- 1/2 **cup of** shredded cheddar cheese
- **Split** avocado (for garnish)

Instructions:
1. **Combine** the shredded chicken, cooked brown rice, black beans, corn, diced tomatoes, red onion, and cilantro in a sizable **combining** dish.
2. As you pour the enchilada sauce over the **Mixture**, toss it to evenly distribute it.
3. Divide the **Mixture** between two dishes or Mason jars.
4. Avocado slices and cheddar cheese slices **Must** be added to **every** bowl.
5. The bowls can **optionally** be heated in the oven or microwave **up to** the cheese is **dilute** and bubbling.
6. Enjoy your Mason jar chicken enchilada bowl while it's still hot!

Nutrition (per serving):
Cals: 550 kcal, **Carb**s: 54g, Protein: 30g
Fat: 24g, Fiber: 10g

103.Layered S'mores Dip

Prep Time: 10 **min**s

Cook Time: 5 **min**s

Total Time: 15 **min**s

Servings: 6

Ingredients:
- 1 **cup of** chocolate chips
- 1 **cup of** mini marshm**let**s
- 1 **cup of** graham cracker crumbs
- Fresh strawberries and bananas (for dipping)

Instructions:
1. Turn on the oven to 350 °F (175 °C).
2. Start by layering half of the chocolate chips in an oven-safe dish.
3. On top of the chocolate chips, sprinkle the remaining half of the **mini** marshm**let**s.
4. The marshm**let** layer **Must** be covered with half of the graham cracker crumbs.
5. With the remaining marshm**let**s, chocolate chips, and graham cracker crumbs, repeat the layering.
6. Bake the dish in the hot oven for around 5 **min**s, or **up to** the marshm**let**s are just beginning to brown.
7. Take it out of the oven, then let it to cool a little.
8. Fresh strawberries and bananas are served alongside the tiered s'mores dip as dipping options.

Nutrition (per serving):

Cals: 250 kcal

Carbs: 40g, Protein: 3g, Fat: 10g

Fiber: 2g

104.Tuna and Avocado Poke Bowl

Prep Time: 20 **min**s

Cook Time: 0 **min**s

Total Time: 20 **min**s

Servings: 2

Ingredients:

- 1 **cup of** sushi rice, cooked and seasoned with rice vinegar
- 2 (6-**oz**) sushi-grade tuna steaks, diced
- 1 avocado, diced
- 1/4 **cup of split** cucumber
- 1/4 **cup of** shredded carrots
- 1/4 **cup of** thinly **split** radishes
- 2 **tbsp** soy sauce
- 1 **tbsp** sesame oil
- 1 **tbsp** sesame seeds
- **Split** green onions (for garnish)

Instructions:

1. Tuna dice, soy sauce, sesame oil, and sesame seeds **Must** all be **combine**d in a **combining** dish. Till the tuna is completely covered in the marinade, toss.
2. Start by placing a layer of sushi rice at the bottom of **every** serving bowl.
3. On top of the rice, scatter the tuna that has been marinated, **chop-up** avocado, cucumber, shredded carrots, and thinly **split** radishes.
4. Add **split** green onions as a garnish.
5. Enjoy the Tuna and Avocado Poke Bowl right away!

Nutrition (per serving):

Cals: 450 kcal, **Carb**s: 30g

Protein: 30g, Fat: 24g, Fiber: 8g

105.Mason Jar Ratatouille Quinoa Bowl

Prep Time: 15 **min**s

Cook Time: 25 **min**s

Total Time: 40 **min**s

Servings: 2

Ingredients:

- 1 **cup of** quinoa, rinsed
- 2 **cups of** vegetable broth or water
- 1 **cup of** diced eggplant
- 1 **cup of** diced zucchini
- 1 **cup of** diced bell peppers (red, yellow, or green)

- 1 **cup of** cherry tomatoes, halved
- 1/4 **cup of** diced red onion
- 2 cloves garlic, **chop-up**
- 2 **tbsp** olive oil
- 1 **tsp** dried oregano
- Salt and pepper **as needed**
- Fresh basil leaves (for garnish)

Instructions:

1. Bring the water or vegetable broth to a boil in a saucepan. To cook the quinoa and **let** the liquid to be absorbed, add the quinoa, lower the heat to low, cover the pan, and simmer for 15 to 20 **min**s.
2. Olive oil **Must** be heated in a different pan over medium heat. Sauté the **chop-up** garlic **up to** fragrant after adding it.
3. The pan **Must** now contain the diced eggplant, zucchini, bell peppers, and red onion. The vegetables **Must** be cooked for 8 to 10 **min**s **up to** they are soft.
4. Add the cherry tomatoes, **slice** in half, and the dry oregano. Cook the tomatoes for a further 2 to 3 **min**s, or **up to** they start to soften.
5. **As needed**, add salt and pepper to the food.
6. Layer the cooked quinoa and the ratatouille **Mixture** in **every** mason jar or bowl.
7. Fresh basil leaves are a nice garnish.
8. The Mason Jar Ratatouille Quinoa Bowl can be served hot or cold.

Nutrition (per serving):

Cals: 400 kcal, **Carb**s: 55g

Protein: 11g, Fat: 16g, Fiber: 10g

106.Layered Buffalo Cauliflower Dip

Prep Time: 15 **min**s

Cook Time: 30 **min**s

Total Time: 45 **min**s

Servings: 6

Ingredients:

- 1 medium cauliflower, **slice** into florets
- 1 **cup of** buffalo sauce
- 1 **cup of** Greek yogurt
- 1 **cup of** shredded cheddar cheese
- 1/2 **cup of** blue cheese **cut up**s
- 1/4 **cup of chop-up** green onions
- 1/4 **cup of** diced celery
- 1 **tbsp** olive oil
- Salt and pepper **as needed**
- Tortilla chips or vegetable sticks, for serving

Instructions:

1. Turn on the oven to 400 °F (200 °C).

2. Cauliflower florets **Must** be **combined** with olive oil, salt, and pepper in a big basin.
3. On a baking sheet, spread the cauliflower and roast for 25 to 30 **min**s, or **up to** it is soft but still slightly crispy.
4. **Combine** the Greek yogurt and buffalo sauce thoroughly in a another bowl.
5. Start by layering the roasted cauliflower, the buffalo sauce combination, the shredded cheddar cheese, the blue cheese **cut up**s, the **split** celery, and the green onions.
6. Continue layering **up to** all of the ingredients are utilized, and then top with a layer of **cut up** blue cheese and cheddar cheese.
7. Before serving, cover and chill for at least an **hr**.
8. With tortilla chips or vegetable sticks, serve the Layered Buffalo Cauliflower Dip.

Nutrition (per serving):
Cals: 250 kcal, **Carb**s: 10g, Protein: 15g

Fat: 18g, Fiber: 3g, Sugar: 5g

107. Raspberry Lemonade Chia Pudding

Prep Time: 10 **min**s

Total Time: 4 **hr**s (including chilling time)

Servings: 4

Ingredients:
- 1 **cup of** fresh or **refrigerate** raspberries
- 2 **cups of** almond milk (or any other milk of your choice)
- 1/2 **cup of** chia seeds
- 1/4 **cup of** lemon juice
- 2 **tbsp** honey or maple syrup (adjust **as needed**)
- Lemon zest, for garnish (**non-compulsory**)

Instructions:
1. The raspberries **Must** be pureed in a blender **up to** smooth.
2. The raspberry puree, almond milk, chia seeds, lemon juice, honey, and/or maple syrup **Must** all be **combine**d in a sizable **combining** basin.
3. Stir thoroughly to distribute the chia seeds evenly.
4. To enable the chia seeds to en**Big** and take on the consistency of pudding, cover the bowl and place in the refrigerator for at least 4 **hr**s or overnight.
5. Give the **Mixture** a vigorous toss before serving and, if necessary, adjust the sweetness.
6. If desired, add lemon zest as a garnish.

Nutrition (per serving):
Cals: 180 kcal, **Carb**s: 20g, Protein: 5g

Fat: 9g, Fiber: 10g, Sugar: 8g

108. Mason Jar Thai Green Curry Noodles

Prep Time: 20 **min**s

Cook Time: 15 **min**s

Total Time: 35 **min**s

Servings: 2

Ingredients:
- 4 oz rice noodles
- 1 **cup of** coconut milk
- 2 **tbsp** Thai green curry paste
- 1 **tbsp** soy sauce
- 1 **tbsp** brown sugar
- 1 **cup of combined** vegetables (bell peppers, carrots, snow peas, etc.)
- 1/2 **cup of** firm tofu, cubed
- Fresh cilantro and lime wedges for garnish (**non-compulsory**)

Instructions:
1. Cook the rice noodles according to the **box/pkg** after which drain and set away.
2. The coconut milk **Must** be heated to a simmer in a medium saucepan over a medium heat.
3. Brown sugar, soy sauce, and Thai green curry paste **Must** all be added at this point and **combine**d thoroughly.
4. **Mixture** of vegetables and cubed tofu **Must** be added to the pan and cooked **up to** the tofu is heated through and the vegetables are soft.
5. Rice noodles **Must** be **slice up** between two serving bowls or Mason jars.
6. Over the noodles in **every** container, pour the Thai green curry sauce.
7. If preferred, garnish with lime wedges and fresh cilantro.

Nutrition (per serving):
Cals: 420 kcal, **Carb**s: 57g, Protein: 9g

Fat: 18g, Fiber: 4g, Sugar: 7g

109. Layered Mediterranean Pasta Salad

Prep Time: 20 **min**s

Cook Time: 10 **min**s

Total Time: 30 **min**s

Servings: 6

Ingredients:
- 8 oz rotini pasta (or any other pasta shape you prefer)
- 1 **cup of** cherry tomatoes, halved
- 1 **cup of** cucumber, diced
- 1 **cup of** bell peppers (**combine** of red and green), diced
- 1/2 **cup of** red onion, thinly **split**

- 1/2 **cup of** Kalamata olives, pitted and halved
- 1/2 **cup of** feta cheese, **cut up**
- 1/4 **cup of** fresh parsley, **chop-up**
- 1/4 **cup of** extra-virgin olive oil
- 2 **tbsp** red wine vinegar
- 1 clove garlic, **chop-up**
- Salt and pepper **as needed**

Instructions:

1. Pasta **Must** be cooked as directed on the **box/pkg up to** it is al dente. To halt the cooking process, drain and rinse under cold water.
2. Put the cooked pasta, Kalamata olives, red onion, bell peppers, cherry tomatoes, feta cheese, and fresh parsley in a big bowl.
3. To create the dressing, **combine** the extra virgin olive oil, red wine vinegar, **chop-up** garlic, salt, and pepper in a separate **mini** bowl.
4. When the pasta salad is thoroughly covered, pour the dressing over it and **combine**.
5. To **let** the flavors to mingle, either serve right away or place in the refrigerator for a few **hr**s.

Nutrition (per serving):
Cals: 320 kcal, **Carb**s: 35g, Protein: 8g

Fat: 16g, Fiber: 3g, Sugar: 4g

110. Spinach and Artichoke Dip Pasta

Prep Time: 10 **min**s

Cook Time: 20 **min**s

Total Time: 30 **min**s

Servings: 4

Ingredients:

8 oz penne pasta (or any pasta of your choice)

2 **cups of** fresh baby spinach, **chop-up**

1 can artichoke hearts, drained and **chop-up**

1 **cup of** Alfredo sauce

1/2 **cup of finely grated** Parmesan cheese

1/4 **cup of** cream cheese

2 cloves garlic, **chop-up**

1 **tbsp** olive oil

Salt and pepper **as needed**

Red pepper flakes for added spice (**non-compulsory**)

Instructions:

1. Pasta **Must** be cooked as directed on the **box/pkg up to** it is al dente. Drain, then set apart.
2. Olive oil **Must** be heated in a sizable skillet over medium heat. Add the **chop-up** garlic and cook **up to** fragrant, about 1 **min**.
3. To the skillet, add the **chop-up** artichoke hearts and spinach. Cook the artichokes and spinach **up to** they are well heated.

4. Add the cream cheese, **finely grated** Parmesan cheese, and Alfredo sauce after lowering the heat. Cook **up to** the sauce is creamy and the cheeses are **dilute**.
5. When the pasta is thoroughly coated with the spinach and artichoke sauce, add the cooked spaghetti to the skillet and toss to **combine**.
6. **As needed**, add salt and pepper to the food. Red pepper flakes can also be used if you like things hot.
7. Pasta with Spinach and Artichoke Dip **Must** be served right away, with additional Parmesan cheese on top if preferred.

Nutrition (per serving):
Cals: 480 kcal, **Carb**s: 50g, Protein: 14g

Fat: 25g, Fiber: 4g, Sugar: 3g

111. Vanilla Berry Chia Pudding

Prep Time: 10 **min**s

Cook Time: 0 **min**s

Total Time: 10 **min**s

Servings: 2

Ingredients:

- 1 **cup of** almond milk (or any milk of your choice)
- 1/4 **cup of** chia seeds
- 1 **tbsp** maple syrup (adjust **as needed**)
- 1 **tsp** vanilla extract
- Assorted berries (strawberries, blueberries, raspberries) for topping

Instructions:

1. Almond milk, chia seeds, maple syrup, and vanilla extract **Must** all be **combine**d in a **combining** bowl.
2. To make sure the chia seeds are dispersed equally, stir thoroughly.
3. **Let** the **Mixture** to thicken in the refrigerator for at least an **hr** or overnight.
4. Give it a thorough toss before serving, then divide the pudding among serving jars.
5. Enjoy! Add some fresh berries on top.

Nutrition (per serving):
Cals: 180 kcal, **Carb**s: 20g, Protein: 4g

Fat: 10g, Fiber: 8g

112. Mason Jar Buffalo Chicken Mac and Cheese

Prep Time: 15 **min**s

Cook Time: 20 **min**s

Total Time: 35 **min**s

Servings: 2

Ingredients:

- 1 **cup of** uncooked macaroni
- 1 **cup of** cooked chicken, shredded
- 1/2 **cup of** buffalo sauce
- 1/2 **cup of** cheddar cheese, shredded
- 1/2 **cup of** mozzarella cheese, shredded
- 1/4 **cup of** blue cheese, **cut up** (**non-compulsory**)
- 1/4 **cup of** diced green onions (**non-compulsory**)

Instructions:

1. The macaroni **Must** be prepared as directed on the **box/pkg**, drained, and set aside.
2. Buffalo sauce and cooked, shredded chicken **Must** be **combine**d in a pan and heated through over medium heat.
3. Cooked macaroni, buffalo chicken, cheddar cheese, mozzarella cheese, and blue cheese (if used) **Must** be placed in **every** mason jar.
4. When the jars are full, continue layering **up to** there is a layer of cheese on top.
5. The mason jars **Must** be placed to the broiler for two to three **min**s, or **up to** the cheese is **dilute** and bubbling.
6. If preferred, garnish with diced green onions and serve hot.

Nutrition (per serving):
Cals: 650 kcal, **Carb**s: 45g, Protein: 35g

Fat: 35g, Fiber: 2g

113.Layered Breakfast Burrito Dip

Prep Time: 20 **min**s

Cook Time: 10 **min**s

Total Time: 30 **min**s

Servings: 6

Ingredients:

- 1 **tbsp** olive oil
- 1/2 **cup of** diced onions
- 1/2 **cup of** diced bell peppers (any color)
- 1 **cup of** cooked and **cut up** breakfast sausage
- 1 can (15 oz) refried beans
- 1 packet taco seasoning **combine**
- 1 **cup of** guacamole
- 1 **cup of** sour cream
- 1 **cup of** salsa
- 1 **cup of** shredded cheddar cheese
- 1/4 **cup of split** black olives
- 1/4 **cup of chop-up** fresh cilantro
- Tortilla chips for serving

Instructions:

1. Olive oil **Must** be heated at a medium-low temperature in a skillet before softening the bell peppers and onions.

2. As soon as the taco seasoning **combine** and cooked morning sausage are added to the skillet, toss to thoroughly blend and heat everything.
3. Spread the refried beans as the first layer in a trifle dish or big glass bowl. Next, layer the sausage **Mixture**, guacamole, sour cream, salsa, shredded cheese, black olives, and cilantro.
4. Continue layering the ingredients **up to** all are utilized, then top with a garnish of cilantro and black olives.
5. Tostito chips **Must** be provided for dipping.

Nutrition (per serving):
Cals: 380 kcal, **Carb**s: 20g, Protein: 15g

Fat: 28g, Fiber: 5g

114.Shrimp and Mango Salad

Prep Time: 15 **min**s

Cook Time: 5 **min**s

Total Time: 20 **min**s

Servings: 4

Ingredients:

- 1 **lb** shrimp, **peel off** and deveined
- 2 ripe mangoes, **peel off** and diced
- 1/4 **cup of** red onion, **lightly chop-up**
- 1/4 **cup of** fresh cilantro, **chop-up**
- 1 jalapeño, seeds **take out**d and **lightly chop-up**
- 2 **tbsp** lime juice
- 1 **tbsp** olive oil
- Salt and pepper **as needed**
- **Combined** salad greens for serving

Instructions:

1. The shrimp **Must** be cooked in a kettle of boiling water for two to three **min**s, or **up to** they turn pink and opaque. Drain and **let** cooling.
2. The cooked shrimp, diced mangos, red onion, cilantro, and jalapeo **Must** all be **combine**d in a sizable **combining** dish.
3. Olive oil and lime juice **Must** be drizzled over the salad and gently **combined** together.
4. **As needed**, add salt and pepper to the dish.
5. Over a bed of **combined** salad greens, plate the shrimp and mango salad.

Nutrition (per serving):
Cals: 220 kcal, **Carb**s: 18g, Protein: 18g

Fat: 8g, Fiber: 3g

115.Mason Jar Teriyaki Salmon Noodles

Prep Time: 15 **min**s

Cook Time: 15 **min**s

Total Time: 30 **min**s

Servings: 2

Ingredients:

- 2 salmon fillets
- 1/4 **cup of** teriyaki sauce
- 2 packs instant ramen noodles
- 2 **cups of** broccoli florets
- 1 carrot, julienned
- 1 **tbsp** sesame oil
- 1 **tbsp** sesame seeds (**non-compulsory**)
- **Split** green onions for garnish

Instructions:

1. Set the oven's temperature to 400°F (200°C). Salmon fillets **Must** be placed on a baking pan and covered with teriyaki sauce.
2. The salmon **Must** be baked in the preheated oven for 12 to 15 **min**s, or **up to** fully done.
3. Cook the instant ramen noodles per the directions on the **box/pkg** while the salmon bakes. Drain, then set apart.
4. Broccoli and carrots that have been thinly **split Must** be sautéed in sesame oil **up to** tender-crisp.
5. Layer the prepared ramen noodles, sautéed veggies, and baked teriyaki salmon in **every** mason jar.
6. If desired, add sesame seeds and thinly **split** green onions as a garnish.

Nutrition (per serving):

Cals: 550 kcal, **Carb**s: 45g, Protein: 35g

Fat: 25g, Fiber: 6g

116.Mason Jar Cobb Salad Wrap

Prep Time: 20 **min**s

Cook Time: 0 **min**s

Total Time: 20 **min**s

Servings: 2

Ingredients:

- 1 **cup of** cooked chicken, diced
- 1/2 **cup of** cherry tomatoes, halved
- 1/2 **cup of** cucumber, diced
- 1/2 **cup of** avocado, diced
- 1/4 **cup of** red onion, thinly **split**
- 1/4 **cup of cut up** feta cheese
- 2 **cups of combined** salad greens
- 1/4 **cup of** balsamic vinaigrette dressing
- 2 **Big** whole wheat tortillas

Instructions:

1. **Combine** the chicken, feta cheese, red onion, cucumber, cherry tomatoes, and avocado in a bowl.
2. Divide the salad greens between two mason jars that you have.

3. **Every** jar's greens are covered with a layer of the chicken and vegetable combination.
4. Over the layers, drizzle the balsamic vinaigrette dressing.
5. The whole wheat tortillas **Must** be rolled up and set on top of the salad layers in the jars.
6. **Up to** you're ready to serve, seal the jars and keep them in the refrigerator.
7. Shake the jar to **combine** the salad and dressing before serving, then either pour the **Mixture** onto a dish or eat it straight from the container.

Nutrition (per serving):

Cals: 380 kcal, Fat: 20g, **Carb**s: 30g

Protein: 22g, Fiber: 6g

117.Layered Rainbow Veggie Dip

Prep Time: 15 **min**s

Cook Time: 0 **min**s

Total Time: 15 **min**s

Servings: 6

Ingredients:

- 1 **cup of** hummus
- 1 **cup of** Greek yogurt
- 1 **cup of** red bell pepper, diced
- 1 **cup of** yellow bell pepper, diced
- 1 **cup of** cucumber, diced
- 1 **cup of** cherry tomatoes, halved
- 1/2 **cup of** red onion, **lightly chop-up**
- 1/4 **cup of** fresh parsley, **chop-up**
- 1/4 **cup of** black olives, **split**

Instructions:

1. Greek yogurt and hummus **Must** be thoroughly blended in a **mini** bowl.
2. Layer the following ingredients in a clear serving bowl or trifle bowl: hummus **Mixture**, red and yellow bell peppers, cucumber, cherry tomatoes, red onion, parsley, and black olives.
3. Up **up to** all the components have been used, repeat the layering process, concluding with a layer of black olives on top.
4. For dipping, serve with tortilla chips, pita chips, or **split** vegetables.

Nutrition (per serving):

Cals: 180 kcal, Fat: 10g, **Carb**s: 18g

Protein: 8g, Fiber: 6g

118.Blueberry Cheesecake Parfait

Prep Time: 20 **min**s

Cook Time: 10 **min**s

Total Time: 30 **min**s

Servings: 4

Ingredients:

- 1 **cup of** graham cracker crumbs
- 1/4 **cup of** unsalted butter, **dilute**
- 1 **cup of** cream cheese, **melted**
- 1/2 **cup of** powdered sugar
- 1 **tsp** vanilla extract
- 1 **cup of** heavy cream
- 1 **cup of** blueberries

Instructions:

1. Graham cracker crumbs and **dilute** butter **Must** be thoroughly **combined** in a bowl.
2. Cream cheese, powdered sugar, and vanilla extract **Must** be thoroughly **combined** in a another basin.
3. Whip the heavy cream **up to** firm peaks form in a separate bowl.
4. To make the cheesecake filling, gently incorporate the whipped cream into the cream cheese **Mixture**.
5. Start assembling the dessert in four serving glasses or mason jars. Graham cracker crumbs **Must** be the first layer, then cheesecake filling, and finally blueberries.
6. Continue layering **up to** the glasses are full, then add a layer of blueberries on top to complete the look.
7. Before serving, place in the fridge for at least one **hr**.

Nutrition (per serving):
Cals: 450 kcal, Fat: 35g, **Carb**s: 30g

Protein: 5g, Fiber: 2g

119.Mason Jar Beef and Broccoli Quinoa Bowl

Prep Time: 15 **min**s

Cook Time: 25 **min**s

Total Time: 40 **min**s

Servings: 2

Ingredients:

- 1/2 **cup of** quinoa, rinsed
- 1 **cup of** beef steak, thinly **split**
- 1 **cup of** broccoli florets
- 1/4 **cup of** soy sauce
- 2 **tbsp** hoisin sauce
- 1 **tbsp** olive oil
- 2 green onions, **chop-up**
- 1 **tsp** sesame seeds (**non-compulsory**)

Instructions:

1. Quinoa **Must** be prepared per the directions on the **box/pkg** and kept aside.

2. Heat the olive oil over medium-high heat in a skillet or wok.
3. When the beef is cooked to your preference, add it and stir-fry it briefly.
4. When the broccoli florets are tender-crisp, add them to the skillet and stir-fry for an additional two to three **min**s.
5. Stirring to ensure that everything is properly coated, add the hoisin and soy sauce to the beef and broccoli.
6. Divide the cooked quinoa, meat, and broccoli between the two mason jars.
7. Add some sesame seeds (if using) and **split** green onions on top.
8. Prior to serving, seal the jars and place them in the refrigerator.
9. Use the microwave to reheat the jar's contents before serving, or simply eat it cold.

Nutrition (per serving):
Cals: 420 kcal, Fat: 16g, **Carb**s: 34g

Protein: 30g, Fiber: 5g

120.Layered Black Bean Salsa Dip

Prep Time: 15 **min**s

Cook Time: 0 **min**s

Total Time: 15 **min**s

Servings: 8

Ingredients:

- 1 can (15 oz) black beans, drained and rinsed
- 1 **cup of** salsa (choose your preferred level of spiciness)
- 1 **cup of** guacamole
- 1 **cup of** sour cream
- 1 **cup of** shredded cheddar cheese
- 1 **cup of** diced tomatoes
- 1/2 **cup of split** black olives
- 1/4 **cup of chop-up** fresh cilantro

Instructions:

1. Layer the dip ingredients in a clear serving bowl or trifle bowl starting with the black beans, salsa, guacamole, sour cream, cheddar cheese, **chop-up** tomatoes, black olives, and fresh cilantro.
2. Up **up to** all the ingredients have been used, repeat the layering process, concluding with a layer of fresh cilantro on top.
3. Serve with dipping chips like tortilla or pita chips or veggie sticks.

Nutrition (per serving):
Cals: 240 kcal, Fat: 16g, **Carb**s: 17g

Protein: 8g, Fiber: 5g

121.Layered Mediterranean Mezze Dip:

Prep Time: 20 **min**s

Cook Time: 0 **min**s

Total Time: 20 **min**s

Servings: 6-8

Ingredients:

- 1 **cup of** hummus
- 1 **cup of** Greek yogurt
- 1 **cup of** cucumber, dIced
- 1 **cup of** cherry tomatoes, halved
- 1/2 **cup of** Kalamata olives, pitted and **split**
- 1/4 **cup of** red onion, **lightly chop-up**
- 1/4 **cup of** feta cheese, **cut up**
- 2 **tbsp** fresh parsley, **chop-up**
- 2 **tbsp** lemon juice
- Salt and pepper **as needed**
- Pita bread or crackers for serving

Instructions:

1. Spread an even layer of hummus at the bottom of a transparent serving dish or trifle bowl.
2. Greek yogurt **Must** be spread evenly on top of the hummus.
3. Over the yogurt layer, scatter the diced cucumber, **chop-up** red onion, cherry tomato halves, and **split** olives.
4. Season the vegetables **as needed** with salt and pepper and a drizzle of lemon juice.
5. Top with feta cheese **cut up**s and parsley sprigs.
6. Serve alongside crackers or pita bread for dipping.

Nutrition (per serving):

Cals: 180 kcal, Fat: 10g, **Carb**s: 18g

Protein: 8g

122.Chocolate Mint Delight:

Prep Time: 15 **min**s

Cook Time: 5 **min**s

Total Time: 20 **min**s

Servings: 4

Ingredients:

- 1 **cup of** semi-sweet chocolate chips
- 1/2 **cup of** heavy cream
- 1 **tsp** peppermint extract
- 1 **tbsp** powdered sugar
- 1/4 **cup of** crushed peppermint candies or candy canes

Instructions:

1. The heavy cream and semi-sweet chocolate chips **Must** be put in a bowl that can go in the microwave.
2. **up to** the chocolate is **dilute** and smooth, stir in between 30-second bursts of microwave.

3. Add the powdered sugar and peppermint extract and **combine** thoroughly.
4. The chocolate **Mixture Must** be poured into individual bowls or glasses for serving.
5. Set in the refrigerator for at least an **hr**.
6. Sprinkle the crushed peppermint candies over top just before serving.

Nutrition (per serving):

Cals: 320 kcal, Fat: 22g, **Carb**s: 30g

Protein: 4g

123.Mason Jar Ratatouille Pasta Salad:

Prep Time: 20 **min**s

Cook Time: 15 **min**s

Total Time: 35 **min**s

Servings: 4

Ingredients:

- 8 **oz**s fusilli pasta (or any other pasta of your choice)
- 1 **mini** eggplant, diced
- 1 **mini** zucchini, diced
- 1 red bell pepper, diced
- 1 yellow bell pepper, diced
- 1 **cup of** cherry tomatoes, halved
- 3 **tbsp** olive oil
- 2 cloves garlic, **chop-up**
- 1 **tsp** dried oregano
- 1/2 **tsp** dried thyme
- Salt and pepper **as needed**
- 1/4 **cup of** fresh basil leaves, torn
- 1/4 **cup of** cut up feta cheese (**non-compulsory**)

Instructions:

1. Pasta **Must** be cooked as directed on the **box/pkg up to** it is al dente. Drain, then set apart.
2. Olive oil **Must** be heated in a sizable skillet over medium heat. Add the **chop-up** garlic and cook **up to** fragrant, about 1 **min**.
3. To the skillet, add the diced eggplant, zucchini, red pepper, and yellow pepper. Add salt, pepper, dried thyme, and oregano to season. Cook the vegetables **up to** they are soft, stirring periodically.
4. In a sizable **combining** bowl, **combine** the cooked pasta and the sautéed vegetables. Toss to evenly **combine** everything.
5. On top of the pasta salad, layer the half cherry tomatoes, torn basil leaves, and four mason jars.
6. Before sealing the jars, top with **cut up** feta cheese if desired.
7. For a delectable and reviving pasta salad, serve right away or put in the fridge.

Nutrition (per serving):
Cals: 380 kcal, Fat: 14g

Carbs: 55g

Protein: 10g

124.Layered BBQ Chicken Dip:

Prep Time: 15 **min**s

Cook Time: 25 **min**s

Total Time: 40 **min**s

Servings: 6-8

Ingredients:

- 2 **cups of** cooked and shredded chicken (rotisserie chicken works well)
- 1 **cup of** barbecue sauce
- 8 **oz**s cream cheese, **melted**
- 1 **cup of** sour cream
- 1 **cup of** shredded cheddar cheese
- 1/4 **cup of chop-up** green onions
- 1 **tbsp** olive oil
- Salt and pepper **as needed**
- Tortilla chips or crackers for serving

Instructions:

1. Set the oven's temperature to 350°F (175°C).
2. Olive oil **Must** be heated in a medium saucepan at a medium heat. When the chicken is heated through, add the chicken shreds and continue to sauté.
3. Stir well after adding the barbecue sauce to the chicken and **let**ing it to cook for five **min**s.
4. **Combine** the **melted** cream cheese and sour cream thoroughly in a another bowl.
5. Layer half of the cream cheese and sour cream **Mixture** at the bottom of an oven-safe dish or a deep pie plate.
6. Half of the BBQ chicken **Mixture** and half of the shredded cheddar cheese **Must** then be added.
7. With the remaining ingredients, repeat the layers.
8. Bake for about 20 **min**s, or **up to** the cheese is **dilute** and bubbling, in the preheated oven.
9. Before serving, garnish with **lightly split** green onions.
10. Serve with crackers or tortilla chips for dipping.

Nutrition (per serving):
Cals: 320 kcal, Fat: 20g

Carbs: 18g

Protein: 18g

125.Apple Cinnamon Chia Pudding:

Prep Time: 10 **min**s

Cook Time: 0 **min**s (+ chilling time)

Total Time: 4 **hr**s 10 **min**s

Servings: 2

Ingredients:

- 1 **cup of** unsweetened almond milk (or any other milk of your choice)
- 1/4 **cup of** chia seeds
- 1 **tbsp** pure maple syrup (adjust **as needed**)
- 1/2 **tsp** ground cinnamon
- 1/2 **tsp** vanilla extract
- 1 medium apple, diced
- 2 **tbsp chop-up** walnuts or almonds (**non-compulsory**)

Instructions:

1. Almond milk, chia seeds, maple syrup, cinnamon powder, and vanilla essence **Must** all be **combine**d in a **combining** dish. To make sure the chia seeds are dispersed equally, stir thoroughly.
2. For at least 4 **hr**s or overnight, cover the bowl and place in the refrigerator. Chia seeds will take up the liquid and produce a consistency similar to pudding.
3. Chia pudding **Must** be stirred to **take out** any clumps before serving.
4. Pour the chia pudding into bowls or serving glasses.
5. Add diced apples and **chop-up** almonds or walnuts on top.
6. For added taste, top with a **mini** amount of ground cinnamon.

Nutrition (per serving):
Cals: 220 kcal, Fat: 10g, **Carb**s: 27g

Protein: 6g

126.Mason Jar Mediterranean Falafel Salad

Prep Time: 20 **min**s

Cook Time: 15 **min**s

Total Time: 35 **min**s

Servings: 2

Ingredients:

- 1 **cup of** cooked falafel, **cut up**
- 1 **cup of** cherry tomatoes, halved
- 1 cucumber, diced
- 1/4 **cup of** red onion, thinly **split**
- 1/4 **cup of** Kalamata olives, pitted and halved
- 1/4 **cup of** feta cheese, **cut up**
- 2 **tbsp** fresh parsley, **chop-up**
- 2 **tbsp** olive oil
- 2 **tbsp** lemon juice
- Salt and pepper **as needed**

Instructions:

1. To make the dressing, **combine** the olive oil, lemon juice, salt, and pepper in a **mini** bowl.
2. Place a layer of the **cut up** falafel, cherry tomatoes, cucumber, red onion, olives, feta cheese, parsley, and cherry tomatoes in **every** Mason jar.
3. Over the salad in **every** jar, drizzle the dressing.
4. Prior to serving, seal the jars and place them in the refrigerator.
5. Shake the container to disperse the dressing when it's time to eat, then pour it into a bowl and dig in.

Nutrition (per serving):

Cals: 380 kcal, Protein: 12g, Fat: 25g

Carbs: 28g

Fiber: 6g

127. Layered Mexican Layer Dip

Prep Time: 15 **min**s

Cook Time: 0 **min**s

Total Time: 15 **min**s

Servings: 6

Ingredients:

- 1 can (16 **oz**s) refried beans
- 1 packet taco seasoning **combine**
- 1 **cup of** guacamole
- 1 **cup of** sour cream
- 1 **cup of** salsa
- 1 **cup of** shredded cheddar cheese
- 1 **cup of chop-up** tomatoes
- 1/2 **cup of split** black olives
- 1/2 **cup of chop-up** green onions
- Tortilla chips (for serving)

Instructions:

1. **Combine** the taco seasoning **combine** and refried beans thoroughly in a medium basin.
2. Layer the following ingredients in the following order in a trifle dish or a transparent serving dish:
3. Beans refried with taco spice
4. Guacamole
5. soured milk
6. Salsa
7. cheddar cheese **cut up**s
8. **slice**-up tomatoes
9. black olives, **split**
10. green onions, **chop-up**
11. With tortilla chips for dipping, serve right away.

Nutrition (per serving):

Cals: 280 kcal, Protein: 8g, Fat: 18g

Carbs: 21g, Fiber: 6g

128. Pina Colada Parfait

Prep Time: 15 **min**s

Cook Time: 0 **min**s

Total Time: 15 **min**s

Servings: 4

Ingredients:

- 2 **cups of** pineapple chunks, fresh or canned (drained)
- 1 **cup of** coconut cream
- 1 **cup of** Greek yogurt
- 1/4 **cup of** shredded coconut
- 1/4 **cup of** granola

Instructions:

1. To prepare pineapple puree, purée the pineapple pieces in a blender **up to** they are completely smooth.
2. Greek yogurt and coconut cream **Must** be thoroughly **combined** in a bowl.
3. Place the following ingredients in the following order in serving glasses or parfait **cups of**:
4. Pureed pineapple
5. coconut yogurt concoction
6. Granola with coconut shavings
7. Till the glasses are full, keep adding layers.
8. Add more shredded coconut as a garnish.
9. Serve right away or keep chilled **up to** you're ready to.

Nutrition (per serving):

Cals: 220 kcal, Protein: 5g, Fat: 14g

Carbs: 19g, Fiber: 3g

129. Mason Jar Thai Peanut Tofu Noodles

Prep Time: 25 **min**s

Cook Time: 10 **min**s

Total Time: 35 **min**s

Servings: 2

Ingredients:

- 4 **oz**s rice noodles, cooked according to **box/pkg** instructions
- 1/2 **cup of** firm tofu, cubed
- 1/4 **cup of** shredded carrots
- 1/4 **cup of** red bell pepper, julienned
- 1/4 **cup of** cucumber, julienned
- 2 **tbsp chop-up** peanuts
- 2 **tbsp chop-up** cilantro
- 2 **tbsp chop-up** green onions
- 2 **tbsp** soy sauce
- 2 **tbsp** lime juice
- 1 **tbsp** peanut butter
- 1 **tbsp** water

- 1 **tsp** sesame oil
- 1 **tsp** sriracha sauce (**non-compulsory**)

Instructions:
1. To prepare the dressing, **combine** the soy sauce, lime juice, peanut butter, water, sesame oil, and sriracha sauce (if using) in a **mini** bowl.
2. Place cooked rice noodles, tofu, shredded carrots, red bell pepper, cucumber, **chop-up** peanuts, cilantro, and green onions in a layer in **every** Mason jar.
3. Over the ingredients in **every** jar, pour the dressing.
4. Prior to serving, seal the jars and place them in the refrigerator.
5. Shake the container to disperse the dressing when it's time to eat, then pour it into a bowl and dig in.

Nutrition (per serving):
Cals: 380 kcal, Protein: 15g, Fat: 15g

Carbs: 50g, Fiber: 5g

130.Layered Caprese Pasta Dip

Prep Time: 20 **min**s

Cook Time: 10 **min**s

Total Time: 30 **min**s

Servings: 8

Ingredients:
- 8 **oz**s penne pasta, cooked and drained
- 1 **cup of** cherry tomatoes, halved
- 1 **cup of** fresh mozzarella balls, halved
- 1/2 **cup of** fresh basil leaves, torn
- 1/4 **cup of** balsamic glaze
- 1/4 **cup of** extra-virgin olive oil
- Salt and pepper **as needed**

Instructions:
1. **Combine** the cooked penne pasta, cherry tomatoes, fresh mozzarella, and torn basil leaves in a big bowl.
2. Over the pasta **Mixture**, drizzle extra virgin olive oil and balsamic glaze.
3. Add salt and pepper **as needed**, then gently toss the ingredients together.
4. Layer the spaghetti **Mixture** in a trifle dish or a transparent serving dish, then continue **up to** all the components are utilized.
5. Add more basil leaves as a garnish on top.
6. Serve right away with crackers, toast, or tortilla chips for dipping.

Nutrition (per serving):
Cals: 250 kcal, Protein: 9g, Fat: 12g

Carbs: 26g, Fiber: 2g

131.Chicken and Avocado Caesar Salad

Prep Time: 15 **min**s

Cook Time: 15 **min**s

Total Time: 30 **min**s

Servings: 2

Ingredients:
- 2 **cups of** cooked chicken breast, diced
- 1 ripe avocado, diced
- 1 head romaine lettuce, **chop-up**
- 1/4 **cup of finely grated** Parmesan cheese
- 1/4 **cup of** Caesar dressing
- Croutons (**non-compulsory**)

Instructions:
1. **Combine** the diced chicken, avocado, and romaine lettuce in a sizable **combining** dish.
2. Add the Caesar dressing and Parmesan cheese to the bowl. **Combine** everything and toss **up to** evenly coated.
3. For more crunch, if desired, sprinkle additional croutons on top.
4. In two Mason jars or serving bowls, divide the salad.
5. Either serve right away or store in the fridge to enjoy later.

Nutrition (per serving):
Cals: 380, Fat: 20g, **Carb**s: 14g

Protein: 35g

132.Mason Jar Sushi Salad Bowl

Prep Time: 20 **min**s

Cook Time: 0 **min**s

Total Time: 20 **min**s

Servings: 2

Ingredients:
- 1 **cup of** cooked sushi rice
- 1/2 **cup of** imitation crab meat, shredded
- 1/2 **cup of** cucumber, thinly **split**
- 1/2 avocado, diced
- 2 **tbsp** soy sauce
- 1 **tbsp** rice vinegar
- 1 **tsp** sesame oil
- Sesame seeds for garnish (**non-compulsory**)
- Nori seaweed strips for garnish (**non-compulsory**)

Instructions:
1. To prepare the dressing, **combine** the soy sauce, rice vinegar, and sesame oil in a **mini** bowl.
2. Place half of the sushi rice, shredded crab meat, cucumber slices, and **chop-up** avocado in **every** Mason jar.

3. The dressing **Must** be drizzled over the layers in **every** jar.
4. Add strips of nori seaweed and sesame seeds as a garnish, if desired.
5. Prior to serving, seal the jars and place them in the refrigerator.

Nutrition (per serving):
Cals: 320, Fat: 10g, **Carb**s: 45g

Protein: 12g

133.Layered Mediterranean Quinoa Dip

Prep Time: 20 mins

Cook Time: 15 mins

Total Time: 35 mins

Servings: 6

Ingredients:
- 1 **cup of** cooked quinoa
- 1 **cup of** hummus
- 1 **cup of** cucumber, diced
- 1 **cup of** cherry tomatoes, halved
- 1/2 **cup of** Kalamata olives, pitted and **chop-up**
- 1/2 **cup of cut up** feta cheese
- 1/4 **cup of** red onion, **lightly chop-up**
- 2 **tbsp** fresh parsley, **chop-up**

Instructions:
1. Start by putting half of the cooked quinoa in a trifle dish or other transparent glass serving dish.
2. After that, spread hummus over the quinoa.
3. On top of the hummus, keep adding layers of cucumber, cherry tomatoes, Kalamata olives, and red onion.
4. As the final layer, top with feta cheese **cut up**s and **chop-up** parsley.
5. Create individual Mason jar servings or repeat the layers for a second serving.
6. Serve with tortilla chips, vegetable sticks, or pita bread.

Nutrition (per serving):
Cals: 260, Fat: 15g, **Carb**s: 24g

Protein: 8g

134.Banana Split Parfait

Prep Time: 15 mins

Cook Time: 0 mins

Total Time: 15 mins

Servings: 2

Ingredients:
- 2 ripe bananas, **split**
- 1 **cup of** vanilla yogurt
- 1/2 **cup of** fresh strawberries, diced

- 1/2 **cup of** fresh pineapple, diced
- 1/4 **cup of** chocolate chips
- 1/4 **cup of chop-up** nuts (e.g., walnuts, almonds)
- Whipped cream for topping (**non-compulsory**)
- Maraschino cherries for garnish (**non-compulsory**)

Instructions:
1. Layer half of the **split** bananas, vanilla yogurt, strawberry and pineapple dice, chocolate chips, and **chop-up** nuts in two Mason jars.
2. To produce a lovely parfait look, repeat the layering process.
3. If preferred, garnish with whipped cream and a maraschino cherry.
4. Serve right away or chill for a cooling dessert.

Nutrition (per serving):
Cals: 380, Fat: 15g, **Carb**s: 54g

Protein: 10g

135.Mason Jar Beef and Broccoli Rice Bowl

Prep Time: 20 mins

Cook Time: 25 mins

Total Time: 45 mins

Servings: 2

Ingredients:
- 1 **cup of** cooked white or brown rice
- 8 **oz**s beef sirloin, thinly **split**
- 2 **cups of** broccoli florets
- 2 **tbsp** soy sauce
- 1 **tbsp** hoisin sauce
- 1 **tbsp** olive oil
- 1 **tsp** sesame oil
- 1 **tsp** ginger, **chop-up**
- 1 clove garlic, **chop-up**
- Sesame seeds for garnish (**non-compulsory**)
- Green onions, **chop-up**, for garnish (**non-compulsory**)

Instructions:
1. To create the marinade, **combine** the soy sauce, hoisin sauce, sesame oil, ginger, and garlic in a **mini** bowl.
2. Slices of beef **Must** be added to the marinade, and it **Must** sit for around 15 **min**s.
3. The marinated beef **Must** be stir-fried in a skillet or wok **up to** it r**every**es the appropriate **D** of doneness.
4. Broccoli florets **Must** be blanched in boiling water for two to three **min**s **up to** tender-crisp. Drain.
5. Place half of the steak, broccoli, and cooked rice in **every** Mason jar.

6. If desired, garnish with **chop-up** green onions and sesame seeds.
7. Prior to eating, seal the jars and place them in the refrigerator.

Nutrition (per serving):
Cals: 450, Fat: 15g

Carbs: 40g

Protein: 35g

136.Layered Tex-Mex Taco Dip

Prep Time: 20 **min**s

Cook Time: 0 **min**s

Total Time: 20 **min**s

Servings: 8

Ingredients:
- 1 can (16 **oz**s) refried beans
- 1 packet taco seasoning **combine**
- 1 **cup of** guacamole
- 1 **cup of** sour cream
- 1 **cup of** salsa
- 1 **cup of** shredded lettuce
- 1 **cup of** diced tomatoes
- 1 **cup of** shredded cheddar cheese
- 1/2 **cup of split** black olives
- 1/4 **cup of chop-up** fresh cilantro
- Tortilla chips, for serving

Instructions:
1. **Combine** the taco seasoning and refried beans thoroughly in a **mini** basin.
2. Layer the ingredients in a glass bowl or serving dish as follows: Refried beans and a combination of taco spice. b. Guacamole; c. Sour Cream; d. Salsa; e. Shredded Lettuce; f. Diced Tomatoes; h. **Split** Black Olives. i. Fresh cilantro, **chop-up**
3. With tortilla chips for dipping, serve right away.

Nutrition (per serving):
Cals: 250, Fat: 15g, **Carb**s: 20g

Protein: 9g, Fiber: 6g

137.Lemon Berry Chia Pudding

Prep Time: 10 **min**s

Cook Time: 0 **min**s

Total Time: 4 **hr**s 10 **min**s (includes chilling time) Servings: 4

Ingredients:
- 1 **cup of** unsweetened almond milk (or any milk of your choice)
- 1/4 **cup of** chia seeds
- 2 **tbsp** pure maple syrup (or honey)
- 1 **tsp** vanilla extract
- Zest of 1 lemon
- 1 **cup of combined** berries (blueberries, strawberries, raspberries)

Instructions:
1. **Combine** the almond milk, chia seeds, maple syrup, vanilla essence, and lemon zest in a medium bowl.
2. **Let** the chia seeds to absorb the liquid and thicken the **Mixture** by covering the bowl and placing it in the refrigerator for at least 4 **hr**s or overnight.
3. Make sure the chia pudding is thoroughly blended before serving.
4. In glasses or jars for serving, layer the chia pudding with a variety of berries.
5. Garnish with extra lemon zest and berries, if desired.

Nutrition (per serving):
Cals: 160, Fat: 6g, **Carb**s: 23g

Protein: 5g, Fiber: 9g

138.Mason Jar Shrimp and Avocado Quinoa Salad

Prep Time: 15 **min**s

Cook Time: 15 **min**s

Total Time: 30 **min**s

Servings: 2

Ingredients:
- 1/2 **cup of** quinoa, rinsed
- 1 **cup of** water or vegetable broth
- 1 **tbsp** olive oil
- 1 **tbsp** lime juice
- 1 **tsp** honey
- 1/2 **tsp** ground cumin
- 1/4 **tsp** chili powder
- Salt and pepper **as needed**
- 1 **cup of** cooked shrimp, **peel off** and deveined
- 1 avocado, diced
- 1/2 **cup of** cherry tomatoes, halved
- 1/4 **cup of chop-up** red onion
- 1/4 **cup of chop-up** fresh cilantro

Instructions:
1. Quinoa and water or vegetable broth are **combined** together in a **mini** pot. Bring to a boil, then lower the heat to a simmer, cover the pot, and cook the quinoa for about 15 **min**s, or **up to** it is tender and the liquid has been absorbed. Use a fork to fluff and **let** it to slightly cool.
2. The dressing is made by combining olive oil, lime juice, honey, ground cumin, chili powder, salt, and pepper in a separate bowl.

3. Layer the quinoa, cooked shrimp, diced avocado, cherry tomatoes, red onion, and fresh cilantro in two mason jars or serving bowls.
4. Over the layers of salad, drizzle the dressing.
5. **Up to** you're ready to serve, cover the serving bowls with plastic wrap or secure the Mason jar lids.

Nutrition (per serving):
Cals: 430, Fat: 24g
Carbs: 35g
Protein: 20g, Fiber: 9g

139.Layered Buffalo Chicken Potato Salad

Prep Time: 25 **min**s
Cook Time: 25 **min**s
Total Time: 50 **min**s
Servings: 6

Ingredients:
- 2 **lb**s red potatoes, washed and diced
- 1 **tbsp** olive oil
- Salt and pepper **as needed**
- 1 **lb** cooked chicken breast, shredded
- 1/2 **cup of** buffalo sauce
- 1 **cup of** plain Greek yogurt
- 2 **tbsp** ranch seasoning **combine**
- 1 **cup of** shredded lettuce
- 1/2 **cup of** diced celery
- 1/2 **cup of** diced carrots
- 1/4 **cup of cut up** blue cheese (**non-compulsory**)
- 2 **tbsp chop-up** green onions

Instructions:
1. Set the oven's temperature to 400°F (200°C).
2. Olive oil, salt, and pepper **Must** be **combine**d with the diced potatoes in a big dish. On a baking sheet, arrange them in a single layer.
3. The potatoes **Must** be roasted in the preheated oven for about 25 **min**s, or **up to** they are crispy and soft. **Let** them to gently cool.
4. Buffalo sauce and cooked, shredded chicken **Must** be **combine**d in a separate bowl and **combined** thoroughly.
5. **Combine** the plain Greek yogurt and ranch seasoning in a another bowl.
6. Layer the ingredients in a trifle dish or a sizable glass bowl as follows: Buffalo chicken, shredded lettuce, diced celery and carrots, ranch Greek yogurt combination, **cut up** blue cheese (**non-compulsory**), **chop-up** green onions, and roasted diced potatoes.
7. If need, repeat the layers.
8. Refrigerate with a cover **up to** ready to serve.

Nutrition (per serving):
Cals: 380, Fat: 12g, **Carb**s: 36g
Protein: 31g, Fiber: 4g

140.Berry Lemonade Delight

Prep Time: 10 **min**s
Cook Time: 0 **min**s
Total Time: 10 **min**s
Servings: 2

Ingredients:
- 1 **cup of** fresh **combined** berries (strawberries, blueberries, raspberries)
- 1/4 **cup of** freshly squeezed lemon juice
- 2 **tbsp** honey or agave syrup (adjust **as needed**)
- 1 **cup of** cold water
- Ice cubes
- Lemon slices and extra berries for garnish (**non-compulsory**)

Instructions:
1. Fresh **combined** berries, lemon juice, honey, or agave syrup, and water **Must** all be put in a blender.
2. **Up to** smooth, blend.
3. Taste the **Mixture** and, if necessary, add additional honey or agave syrup to increase the sweetness.
4. Ice cubes **Must** be placed in two glasses before the berry lemonade is poured over them.
5. If desired, add additional berries and lemon slices as a garnish.

Nutrition (per serving):
Cals: 70, Fat: 0g, **Carb**s: 18g
Protein: 0.5g, Fiber: 2g

141. Mason Jar Teriyaki Chicken and Rice

Prep Time: 15 **min**s
Cook Time: 25 **min**s
Total Time: 40 **min**s
Servings: 2

Ingredients:
- 1 **cup of** jasmine rice
- 2 **cups of** water
- 2 boneless, skinless chicken breasts, cooked and diced
- 1/4 **cup of** teriyaki sauce
- 1 **cup of** broccoli florets, steamed
- 1/2 **cup of** shredded carrots
- 2 green onions, thinly **split**
- Sesame seeds for garnish

Instructions:

1. Jasmine rice **Must** be added to boiling water in a saucepan. When the rice is ready, turn the heat down to low, cover the pot, and simmer for 15 to 18 **min**s.
2. Cooked chicken **Must** be thoroughly coated in teriyaki sauce and placed in a separate bowl.
3. The following ingredients **Must** be layered in **every** Mason jar: cooked rice, teriyaki chicken, steamed broccoli, shredded carrots, and thinly **split** green onions.
4. Sprinkle some sesame seeds on top as decoration.
5. Refrigerate after capping the jars. Shake the container lightly to **combine** the ingredients before serving, then eat.

NUTRITION INFO (per serving):
Cals: 420, Protein: 28g, **Carb**s: 56g

Fat: 8g, Fiber: 5g

142. Layered Mediterranean Hummus Quinoa Bowl

Prep Time: 20 **min**s

Cook Time: 15 **min**s

Total Time: 35 **min**s

Servings: 2

Ingredients:

- 1 **cup of** cooked quinoa
- 1 **cup of** cherry tomatoes, halved
- 1 cucumber, diced
- 1/2 **cup of** Kalamata olives, pitted and **split**
- 1/2 **cup of cut up** feta cheese
- 1 **cup of** baby spinach
- 1/4 **cup of** red onion, thinly **split**
- 1/4 **cup of** hummus
- 2 **tbsp** lemon juice
- 2 **tbsp** olive oil
- Salt and pepper **as needed**

Instructions:

1. To create the dressing, **combine** the lemon juice, olive oil, salt, and pepper in a **mini** bowl.
2. Prepared quinoa, cherry tomatoes, cucumber, Kalamata olives, feta cheese, baby spinach, and red onion **Must** be layered in that sequence in **every** Mason jar.
3. Dressing **Must** be drizzled on top.
4. Refrigerate after capping the jars. Shake the container lightly to **combine** the ingredients before serving, then eat.

NUTRITION INFO (per serving):
Cals: 450, Protein: 12g, **Carb**s: 35g

Fat: 30g, Fiber: 6g

143. Layered S'mores Parfait

Prep Time: 15 **min**s

Cook Time: 5 **min**s

Total Time: 20 **min**s

Servings: 2

Ingredients:

- 1 **cup of** graham cracker crumbs
- 1 **cup of** chocolate pudding (store-bought or homemade)
- 1 **cup of** marshm**let** cream/fluff
- 1/2 **cup of** whipped cream
- Chocolate shavings for garnish (**non-compulsory**)

Instructions:

1. Layer the following ingredients in **every** Mason jar: whipped cream, marshm**let** cream, graham cracker crumbs, and chocolate pudding.
2. Till the jars are full, keep adding layers.
3. If preferred, add some chocolate shavings as a topping.
4. Refrigerate after capping the jars. Simply tuck into the delectable s'mores parfait to serve.

NUTRITION INFO (per serving):
Cals: 550, Protein: 4g, **Carb**s: 85g

Fat: 21g, Fiber: 2g

144. Mason Jar Thai Coconut Curry Noodles

Prep Time: 15 **min**s

Cook Time: 15 **min**s

Total Time: 30 **min**s

Servings: 2

Ingredients:

- 4 **oz**s rice noodles
- 1 **tbsp** vegetable oil
- 2 **tbsp** red curry paste
- 1 can (14 **oz**s) coconut milk
- 1 **cup of combined** vegetables (bell peppers, broccoli, carrots, etc.)
- 1 **cup of** cooked and shredded chicken (**non-compulsory** for non-vegetarian version)
- 2 **tbsp** soy sauce
- 1 **tbsp** lime juice
- Fresh cilantro and lime wedges for garnish

Instructions:

1. Rice noodles **Must** be prepared per the directions on the **box/pkg**, drained, and then set aside.
2. The vegetable oil **Must** be heated in a pan over medium heat. When aromatic, add the red curry paste and stir for one to two **min**s.

3. Add the coconut milk and boil the **Mixture** while stirring.
4. When the **combined** vegetables are ready, add them and continue cooking.
5. If using chicken, stir in the cooked, shredded chicken and heat through.
6. Add the lime juice and soy sauce while seasoning **as needed**.
7. Place a layer of the cooked rice noodles and curry sauce in **every** Mason jar.
8. Lime wedges and fresh cilantro are garnishes.
9. Refrigerate after capping the jars. After giving the ingredients a gentle shake to **combine** them, serve the tasty Thai coconut curry noodles to your guests.

NUTRITION INFO (per serving, without chicken):
Cals: 450, Protein: 5g

Carbs: 70g

Fat: 17g, Fiber: 3g

145. Layered Mexican Corn Salad

Prep Time: 20 **min**s

Cook Time: 10 **min**s

Total Time: 30 **min**s

Servings: 2

Ingredients:
- 1 can (15 **oz**s) corn kernels, drained
- 1 **tbsp** olive oil
- 1 **tsp** chili powder
- 1/2 **tsp** cumin
- Salt and pepper **as needed**
- 1 **cup of** black beans, cooked and drained
- 1 **cup of** cherry tomatoes, halved
- 1 avocado, diced
- 1/2 **cup of** diced red bell pepper
- 1/4 **cup of chop-up** fresh cilantro
- 1/4 **cup of cut up** queso fresco or feta cheese

Instructions:
1. Olive oil **Must** be heated in a skillet over medium heat. Corn kernels, cumin, chili powder, salt, and pepper **Must** all be added. The corn **Must** be cooked for 5-7 **min**s, or **up to** it is slightly charred and seasoned. Take it off the stove and let it cool.
2. Layer the following ingredients in **every** Mason jar: seasoned corn, black beans, cherry tomatoes, diced red bell pepper, diced avocado, **chop-up** cilantro, and **cut up** feta or queso fresco cheese.
3. Refrigerate after capping the jars. The layered Mexican corn salad is ready to be enjoyed after a little shake of the jar to **combine** the contents.

NUTRITION INFO (per serving):
Cals: 380, Protein: 12g, **Carb**s: 44g

Fat: 20g, Fiber: 15g

146. Caramel Apple Cheesecake Parfait

Prep Time: 20 **min**s

Cook Time: 5 **min**s

Total Time: 25 **min**s

Servings: 4

Ingredients:
- 2 **cups of** graham cracker crumbs
- 1/2 **cup of** unsalted butter, **dilute**
- 16 oz cream cheese, **melted**
- 1/2 **cup of** powdered sugar
- 1 tsp vanilla extract
- 1 **cup of** caramel sauce
- 2 **cups of** diced apples (preferably Granny Smith)
- Whipped cream for garnish

Instructions:
1. Graham cracker crumbs and **dilute** butter **Must** be thoroughly **combined** in a bowl. To make the crust layer, press the **Mixture** firmly into the bottom of serving jars or glasses.
2. Cream the **melted** cream cheese, powdered sugar, and vanilla extract in a separate dish **up to** it is smooth and creamy.
3. **Every** jar's graham cracker crust **Must** be covered with a layer of the cream cheese **Mixture**.
4. Over the cream cheese layer, liberally drizzle the caramel sauce.
5. Diced apples **Must** be layered on top of the caramel.
6. The layers are repeated **up to** the jars are full, and then a dollop of whipped cream is placed on top to complete.
7. Before serving, place in the fridge for at least one **hr**.
8. You might want to top it with a scattering of **chop-up** nuts or broken graham crackers for more texture.

Nutrition (per serving):
Cals: 520 kcal, **Carb**s: 54g

Protein: 7g, Fat: 32g, Fiber: 2g

Sugar: 38g

147. Mason Jar Mediterranean Grilled Veggie Salad

Prep Time: 15 **min**s

Cook Time: 15 **min**s

Total Time: 30 **min**s

Servings: 4

Ingredients:
- 1 zucchini, **split**
- 1 yellow squash, **split**
- 1 red bell pepper, **split**
- 1 red onion, **split**
- 2 tbsp olive oil
- 1 tsp dried oregano
- Salt and pepper **as needed**
- 1 **cup of** cherry tomatoes, halved
- 1/2 **cup of** cucumber, diced
- 1/4 **cup of** Kalamata olives, pitted and halved
- 2 tbsp feta cheese, **cut up**
- 2 **cups of combined** salad greens
- Balsamic vinaigrette dressing

Instructions:
1. Heat a grill pan or the grill to medium-high temperature.
2. **Split** zucchini, yellow squash, red pepper, and red onion **Must** be **combine**d with olive oil, dried oregano, salt, and pepper in a bowl.
3. The vegetables **Must** be grilled for 3-5 **min**s on **every** side, or **up to** they have grill marks and are soft. **Take out** from fire and let them a brief moment to cool.
4. Place grilled veggies, cherry tomatoes, cucumber, Kalamata olives, feta cheese, and **combined** salad greens in a layer in **every** mason jar.
5. The layers are repeated **up to** the jars are full, and then some feta cheese is sprinkled on top to complete.
6. **Up to** you're ready to serve, seal the jars and keep them in the refrigerator.
7. Pour balsamic vinaigrette dressing over the salad and toss to blend before serving.

Nutrition (per serving):
Cals: 220 kcal, **Carb**s: 14g, Protein: 5g
Fat: 16g, Fiber: 4g, Sugar: 8g

148.Layered Caprese Quinoa Dip

Prep Time: 15 **min**s

Cook Time: 15 **min**s

Total Time: 30 **min**s

Servings: 6

Ingredients:
- 1 **cup of** quinoa, rinsed
- 2 **cups of** vegetable broth
- 1 **cup of** cherry tomatoes, halved
- 8 oz fresh mozzarella cheese, cubed
- 1/2 **cup of** fresh basil leaves, **chop-up**
- 2 tbsp balsamic glaze

- Salt and pepper **as needed**

Instructions:
1. Bring the quinoa and vegetable broth to a boil in a medium saucepan. Once the quinoa is cooked and the liquid has been absorbed, lower the heat to low, cover the pan, and simmer for about 15 **min**s.
2. Before putting the dip together, let the quinoa cool fully.
3. Layer the cooked quinoa, halved cherry tomatoes, cubed fresh mozzarella, and **chop-up** basil in a trifle dish or a sizable glass bowl.
4. Add salt and pepper **as needed** and drizzle balsamic glaze over the top layer.
5. Depending on your dish's depth, repeat the layers as necessary.
6. Serve right away or keep chilled **up to** you're ready to.
7. With pita chips, tortilla chips, or crusty toast, you can enjoy this dip.

Nutrition (per serving):
Cals: 210 kcal, **Carb**s: 19g, Protein: 11g
Fat: 10g, Fiber: 2g, Sugar: 4g

149.Mason Jar Greek Salad

Prep Time: 20 **min**s

Cook Time: 0 **min**s

Total Time: 20 **min**s

Servings: 4

Ingredients:
- 1 **cup of** cherry tomatoes, halved
- 1 **cup of** cucumber, diced
- 1/2 **cup of** red onion, thinly **split**
- 1/2 **cup of** Kalamata olives, pitted and halved
- 1/2 **cup of cut up** feta cheese
- 2 tbsp olive oil
- 2 tbsp red wine vinegar
- 1 tsp dried oregano
- Salt and pepper **as needed**
- 2 **cups of combined** salad greens

Instructions:
1. Cherry tomatoes, cucumber, red onion, Kalamata olives, and **cut up** feta cheese **Must** all be **combine**d in a bowl.
2. To create the dressing, **combine** the olive oil, red wine vinegar, dried oregano, salt, and pepper in a different bowl.
3. The vegetable combination will be covered with the dressing; stir to blend.
4. Place a layer of **combined** salad greens and the Greek salad **Mixture** in **every** mason jar.
5. Till the jars are full, keep adding layers.

6. **Up to** you're ready to serve, seal the jars and keep them in the refrigerator.
7. Shake the jar vigorously before serving to evenly distribute the dressing among the greens.

Nutrition (per serving):
Cals: 210 kcal, **Carb**s: 7g, Protein: 5g
Fat: 18g, Fiber: 2g, Sugar: 4g

150.Layered Quinoa and Chickpea Salad

Prep Time: 15 **min**s
Cook Time: 15 **min**s
Total Time: 30 **min**s
Servings: 4

Ingredients:
- 1 **cup of** quinoa, rinsed
- 2 **cups of** vegetable broth
- 1 can (15 oz) chickpeas, drained and rinsed
- 1 **cup of** diced cucumber
- 1 **cup of** halved cherry tomatoes
- 1/2 **cup of** diced red bell pepper
- 1/4 **cup of chop-up** fresh parsley
- 2 green onions, **split**
- 2 tbsp lemon juice
- 2 tbsp olive oil
- 1 tsp ground cumin
- Salt and pepper **as needed**

Instructions:
1. Bring the quinoa and vegetable broth to a boil in a medium saucepan. Once the quinoa is cooked and the liquid has been absorbed, lower the heat to low, cover the pan, and simmer for about 15 **min**s.
2. Before putting the salad together, let the quinoa to cool completely.
3. The cooked quinoa, chickpeas, cucumber, cherry tomatoes, diced red bell pepper, **chop-up** parsley, and green onions **Must** all be **combin**ed in a big bowl.
4. To prepare the dressing, **combine** the lemon juice, olive oil, ground cumin, salt, and pepper in a **mini** bowl.
5. Toss the quinoa and chickpea **Mixture** together after adding the dressing.
6. Layer the quinoa and chickpea salad in **every** mason jar **up to** it is full.
7. **Up to** you're ready to serve, seal the jars and keep them in the refrigerator.
8. This salad works well as a side dish for supper or as a light and healthy lunch.

Nutrition (per serving):
Cals: 340 kcal, **Carb**s: 49g, Protein: 12g

Fat: 12g, Fiber: 10g, Sugar: 6g

151.Zesty Southwest Black Bean Salad

Prep Time: 15 **min**s
Cook Time: 0 **min**s
Total Time: 15 **min**s
Servings: 6

Ingredients:
- 2 cans (15 oz **every**) black beans, drained and rinsed
- 1 **cup of** corn kernels (fresh, canned, or **refrigerate** and thawed)
- 1 red bell pepper, diced
- 1 **cup of** cherry tomatoes, halved
- 1/2 **cup of** diced red onion
- 1 jalapeno, seeds **take out**d and **lightly** diced (**non-compulsory**, for heat)
- 1/4 **cup of chop-up** fresh cilantro
- 2 tbsp lime juice
- 2 tbsp olive oil
- 1 tsp ground cumin
- 1/2 tsp chili powder
- Salt and pepper **as needed**
- 2 avocados, diced (**non-compulsory**, for extra creaminess)

Instructions:
1. **Combine** the black beans, corn, diced red bell pepper, halved cherry tomatoes, **split** red onion, **chop-up** cilantro, and diced jalapeño (if using) in a sizable bowl.
2. To make the dressing, **combine** the lime juice, olive oil, ground cumin, chili powder, salt, and pepper in a **mini** bowl.
3. The dressing **Must** be poured over the black bean **Mixture**, then **combined**.
4. If used, carefully incorporate the diced avocados into the salad.
5. Layer the tangy Southwest black bean salad in **every** mason jar **up to** it is full.
6. **Up to** you're ready to serve, seal the jars and keep them in the refrigerator.
7. This salad can be served as a substantial and healthy main course or as a cool side dish.

Nutrition (per serving):
Cals: 260 kcal, **Carb**s: 36g, Protein: 10g
Fat: 10g, Fiber: 12g, Sugar: 5g

152.Thai Peanut Noodle Salad:

Prep Time: 15 **min**s
Cook Time: 10 **min**s
Total Time: 25 **min**s

Servings: 4

Ingredients:

- 8 oz rice noodles
- 1 **cup of** shredded carrots
- 1 **cup of** thinly **split** cucumber
- 1 **cup of** shredded red cabbage
- 1/2 **cup of chop-up** scallions
- 1/4 **cup of chop-up** cilantro
- 1/4 **cup of chop-up** peanuts
- Lime wedges (for garnish)
- For the dressing:
- 1/4 **cup of** peanut butter
- 2 **tbsp** soy sauce
- 2 **tbsp** fresh lime juice
- 2 **tbsp** water
- 1 **tbsp** sesame oil
- 1 **tbsp** honey
- 1 **tsp finely grated** ginger
- 1 clove garlic, **chop-up**

Instructions:

1. As directed on the packaging, prepare the rice noodles. To halt the cooking process, drain and rinse under cold water. Place aside.
2. All the components for the dressing **Must** be thoroughly blended in a **mini** bowl.
3. The cooked noodles, shredded carrots, cucumber, red cabbage, onions, and cilantro **Must** all be **combine**d in a sizable **combining** dish.
4. When the salad is thoroughly covered, drizzle the dressing over it and toss to **combine**.
5. Serve with lime wedges on the side and **chop-up** peanuts as a garnish.

Nutrition (per serving):
Cals: 350, Fat: 15g, **Carb**s: 45g

Protein: 10g, Fiber: 4g

153.Caprese Salad with Balsamic Glaze:

Prep Time: 10 **min**s

Total Time: 10 **min**s

Servings: 4

Ingredients:

- 2 **Big** ripe tomatoes, **split**
- 8 oz fresh mozzarella cheese, **split**
- Fresh basil leaves
- 2 **tbsp** balsamic glaze
- 2 **tbsp** extra-virgin olive oil
- Salt and pepper **as needed**

Instructions:

1. On a serving platter, arrange the tomato and mozzarella slices in an overlapping, alternating pattern.
2. Place some fresh basil between the mozzarella and tomato pieces.
3. Olive oil and balsamic glaze **Must** be drizzled over the salad.
4. **As needed**, add salt and pepper to the food.
5. Serve right away as a cool starter or side dish.

Nutrition (per serving):
Cals: 250, Fat: 18g

Carbs: 8g, Protein: 12g

Fiber: 1g

154.Mason Jar Cobb Salad:

Prep Time: 20 **min**s

Total Time: 20 **min**s

Servings: 2

Ingredients:

- 4 **cups of chop-up** lettuce (romaine or **combined** greens)
- 1 **cup of** cooked and diced chicken breast
- 1 avocado, diced
- 1/2 **cup of** cherry tomatoes, halved
- 1/4 **cup of cut up** blue cheese
- 2 boiled eggs, **chop-up**
- 4 slices cooked bacon, **cut up**
- Ranch dressing (or dressing of your choice)

Instructions:

1. Layer the **chop-up** lettuce, diced chicken, cherry tomatoes, avocado, blue cheese, **chop-up** boiled eggs, and **cut up** bacon in two mason jars.
2. Prior to serving, seal the jars and place them in the refrigerator.
3. When you're ready to dine, add the proper quantity of dressing to the salad in the jar, secure the lid, and shake vigorously to evenly distribute the dressing over the contents.
4. You may either serve the salad from the jar or pour it onto a platter.

Nutrition (per serving):
Cals: 450, Fat: 30g

Carbs: 12g

Protein: 30g, Fiber: 6g

155.Rainbow Veggie and Hummus Snack:

Prep Time: 15 **min**s

Total Time: 15 mins

Servings: 4

Ingredients:

- 1 **Big** red bell pepper, **split**
- 1 **Big** yellow bell pepper, **split**
- 1 **Big** orange bell pepper, **split**
- 2 medium carrots, **slice** into sticks
- 1 **cup of** cherry tomatoes, halved
- 1 **cup of** sugar snap peas
- 1 **cup of** broccoli florets
- 1 **cup of** cauliflower florets
- 1 **cup of** hummus (store-bought or homemade)

Instructions:

1. On a sizable serving tray, arrange the **split** bell peppers, carrot sticks, cherry tomatoes, sugar snap peas, broccoli florets, and cauliflower florets.
2. In the middle of the platter, place a bowl of hummus for dipping.
3. Serve as a quick appetizer or a bright and wholesome party snack.

Nutrition (per serving):

Cals: 150, Fat: 8g, **Carb**s: 20g

Protein: 6g, Fiber: 8g

156.Classic Caesar Salad with Croutons:

Prep Time: 15 mins

Cook Time: 10 mins

Total Time: 25 mins

Servings: 4

Ingredients:

- 1 **Big** head of romaine lettuce, **chop-up**
- 1/2 **cup of** Caesar dressing (store-bought or homemade)
- 1/2 **cup of finely grated** Parmesan cheese
- 1 **cup of** croutons
- 1/4 **cup of chop-up** fresh parsley (**non-compulsory**)
- Salt and pepper **as needed**
- For the dressing:
- 1/4 **cup of** mayonnaise
- 2 **tbsp** lemon juice
- 2 **tbsp finely grated** Parmesan cheese
- 1 **tbsp** Dijon mustard
- 1 clove garlic, **chop-up**
- 1 anchovy fillet (**non-compulsory**)
- Salt and pepper **as needed**

Instructions:

1. **Combine** the **chop-up** romaine lettuce, Caesar dressing, and **finely grated** Parmesan cheese in a

big salad bowl. Toss the lettuce with the dressing **up to** it is well distributed.

2. Throw in the croutons one more.
3. For more taste and color, you can top the salad with **chop-up** fresh parsley.
4. **As needed**, add salt and pepper to the food.
5. As a wonderful and traditional Caesar salad, serve right away.

Nutrition (per serving):

Cals: 300, Fat: 22g

Carbs: 12g

Protein: 10g, Fiber: 4g

157.Mediterranean Couscous Salad

Prep Time: 15 mins

Cook Time: 10 mins

Total Time: 25 mins

Servings: 4

Ingredients:

- 1 **cup of** couscous
- 1 1/4 **cups of** vegetable broth
- 1 **cup of** cherry tomatoes, halved
- 1 cucumber, diced
- 1/2 red onion, **lightly chop-up**
- 1/2 **cup of** Kalamata olives, pitted and **split**
- 1/3 **cup of cut up** feta cheese
- 1/4 **cup of** fresh parsley, **chop-up**
- 3 **tbsp** olive oil
- 2 **tbsp** lemon juice
- 1 garlic clove, **chop-up**
- Salt and pepper **as needed**

Instructions:

1. Bring the vegetable broth to a boil in a medium saucepan. Add the couscous, cover, and turn the heat off. After letting it stand for five **mins**, fluff it with a fork.
2. Cooked couscous, Kalamata olives, cucumber, red onion, feta cheese, and parsley **Must** all be **combine**d in a big bowl.
3. To create the dressing, **combine** the olive oil, lemon juice, garlic that has been **chop-up**, salt, and pepper in a **mini** bowl.
4. Toss the couscous salad thoroughly after adding the dressing.
5. Serve right away or store in the fridge for later. You can drink it warm or cold.

NUTRITION INFO (per serving):

Cals: 320 kcal, Fat: 14g, **Carb**s: 40g

Fiber: 4g, Protein: 8g

158.Mason Jar Taco Salad

Prep Time: 20 **min**s

Cook Time: 10 **min**s

Total Time: 30 **min**s

Servings: 2

Ingredients:

- 1 **cup of** cooked ground beef or turkey (seasoned with taco seasoning)
- 1 **cup of** black beans, drained and rinsed
- 1 **cup of** cherry tomatoes, halved
- 1 **cup of** corn kernels (fresh, **refrigerate**, or canned)
- 1 **cup of** shredded lettuce
- 1/2 **cup of** shredded cheddar cheese
- 1/4 **cup of** diced red onion
- 1/4 **cup of** diced bell peppers (any color)
- 1/4 **cup of** salsa
- 1/4 **cup of** sour cream
- 1 **tbsp chop-up** fresh cilantro (**non-compulsory**)
- 1 lime, **slice** into wedges

Instructions:

1. Cook the ground beef or turkey in a **Big** skillet over medium heat. Incorporate the taco seasoning as directed on the packet. Set apart for cooling.
2. Layer the following ingredients in two mason jars: bell peppers, **chop-up** red onion, diced red onion, black beans, cherry tomatoes, corn, lettuce, cooked and cooled meat, shredded cheddar cheese, and shredded lettuce.
3. Add salsa, sour cream, and **chop-up** cilantro (if using) to the top of **every** jar.
4. Prior to eating, seal the jars and place them in the refrigerator. When serving, thoroughly **combine** the salad and squeeze a lime wedge over it.

NUTRITION INFO (per serving):

Cals: 550 kcal, Fat: 30g, **Carb**s: 45g

Fiber: 10g, Protein: 30g

159. Buffalo Chicken Mason Jar Salad

Prep Time: 15 **min**s

Cook Time: 20 **min**s

Total Time: 35 **min**s

Servings: 2

Ingredients:

- 1 **cup of** cooked chicken breast, shredded or diced
- 1/4 **cup of** buffalo sauce
- 1 **cup of** cherry tomatoes, halved
- 1/2 **cup of** diced celery
- 1/2 **cup of** shredded carrots
- 1/4 **cup of cut up** blue cheese
- 1/4 **cup of** ranch dressing
- 1 **tbsp chop-up** green onions (**non-compulsory**)
- 1 **tbsp chop-up** fresh cilantro (**non-compulsory**)

Instructions:

1. Buffalo sauce **Must** be well **combine**d with the cooked chicken in a bowl.
2. Layer the ingredients in two mason jars as follows: buffalo chicken, cherry tomatoes, **split** celery, shredded carrots, and blue cheese **cut up**s.
3. Ranch dressing **Must** be added to **every** jar, and green onions and cilantro (if using) **Must** be garnished.
4. Prior to eating, seal the jars and place them in the refrigerator. Shake the container to **combine** the contents before serving, then eat.

NUTRITION INFO (per serving):

Fat: 25g, **Carb**s: 12g, Fiber: 3g

Protein: 30g

160. Mason Jar Ramen Soup

Prep Time: 10 **min**s

Cook Time: 15 **min**s

Total Time: 25 **min**s

Servings: 2

Ingredients:

- 2 packs of instant ramen noodles (discard the seasoning packets)
- 4 **cups of** chicken or vegetable broth
- 1 **cup of split** mushrooms
- 1 **cup of** baby spinach or bok choy
- 1/2 **cup of split** carrots
- 1/4 **cup of split** green onions
- 2 boiled eggs, halved
- 2 **tsp** soy sauce
- 1 **tsp** sesame oil
- 1/2 **tsp** sriracha sauce (**non-compulsory**)

Instructions:

1. The instant ramen noodles **Must** be prepared as directed on the packaging. Drain, then set apart.
2. Bring the chicken or vegetable broth to a simmer in a saucepan. **Split** carrots, baby spinach or bok choy, **split** mushrooms, and half of the green onions **Must** all be added. **Up to** the vegetables are cooked, simmer for about 5-7 **min**s.
3. Layer half of the cooked ramen noodles in **every** mason jar and then pour half of the hot veggie broth over them.
4. 1 **tsp** soy sauce and 1/2 **tsp** sesame oil **Must** be added to **every** container. Sriracha sauce **Must** be used as well if you prefer it spicy.

5. Add a boiled egg **slice** in half and the remaining green onions, **split**, to the top of **every** jar.
6. Prior to eating, seal the jars and place them in the refrigerator. When serving, take off the lid, give the ramen soup in the mason jar a good swirl, and then devour!

NUTRITION INFO (per serving):
Cals: 350 kcal, Fat: 15g, **Carb**s: 35g
Fiber: 3g, Protein: 18g

161.Creamy Tomato Basil Soup

Prep Time: 10 **min**s
Cook Time: 25 **min**s
Total Time: 35 **min**s
Servings: 4

Ingredients:
- 2 **tbsp** olive oil
- 1 onion, **chop-up**
- 2 cloves garlic, **chop-up**
- 2 cans (28 oz **every**) whole **peel off** tomatoes
- 1 **cup of** vegetable broth
- 1/2 **cup of** heavy cream
- 1/4 **cup of** fresh basil leaves, **chop-up**
- Salt and pepper **as needed**
- Croutons and additional fresh basil for garnish (**non-compulsory**)

Instructions:
1. Olive oil **Must** be heated in a sizable pot over medium heat. About 5 **min**s after adding the onion, it **Must** be tender. Cook for another **min** after adding the **chop-up** garlic.
2. Add the veggie broth together with the canned tomatoes and their juice. **Let** the **Mixture** to simmer for about 15 **min**s so that the flavors may blend.
3. Puree the soup using a conventional or immersion blender **up to** it is smooth.
4. If using a conventional blender, pour the soup back into the pot and add the heavy cream and basil. **As needed**, add salt and pepper to the food.
5. The soup **Must** be heated through and given an additional five **min**s of simmering to **let** the flavors to meld.
6. Pour the smooth tomato basil soup into mason jars and, if preferred, top with croutons and fresh basil.

NUTRITION INFO (per serving):
Cals: 250 kcal, Fat: 18g, **Carb**s: 20g
Fiber: 4g, Protein: 4g

162.Butternut Squash and Apple Soup

Prep Time: 15 **min**s
Cook Time: 35 **min**s
Total Time: 50 **min**s
Servings: 4

Ingredients:
- 1 medium butternut squash, **peel off**, seeded, and **chop-up**
- 2 apples, **peel off**, cored, and **chop-up**
- 1 onion, **chop-up**
- 2 cloves garlic, **chop-up**
- 1 **tbsp** olive oil
- 4 **cups of** vegetable broth
- 1 **tsp** ground cinnamon
- 1/2 **tsp** ground nutmeg
- Salt and pepper **as needed**
- 1/2 **cup of** heavy cream (**non-compulsory**, for a creamier version)

Instructions:
1. Olive oil is heated over medium heat in a big pot. Add **chop-up** garlic and onion, **chop-up**. Sauté onions **up to** they are transparent.
2. Apples and butternut squash diced, add to the saucepan. For a few **min**s, cook while stirring.
3. Add nutmeg and cinnamon powder along with the veggie broth. Add salt and pepper **as needed**.
4. Heat **Must** be turned down once the **Mixture** comes to a boil. For about 25 to 30 **min**s, or **up to** the squash is soft, simmer the **Mixture** with the cover on.
5. To purée the soup **up to** it is smooth, either use an immersion blender or transfer it to a blender.
6. If you want the soup to be creamier, whisk in the heavy cream.
7. If preferred, top with a dusting of ground cinnamon and serve hot.

NUTRITION INFO (per serving):
Cals: 200 kcal, Protein: 3g, Fat: 10g
Carbs: 28g, Fiber: 6g, Vitamin A: 300% DV
Vitamin C: 30% DV

163. Hearty Minestrone Soup

Prep Time: 20 **min**s
Cook Time: 40 **min**s
Total Time: 1 **hr**
Servings: 6

Ingredients:
- 2 **tbsp** olive oil
- 1 onion, **chop-up**

- 2 carrots, diced
- 2 celery stalks, diced
- 3 cloves garlic, **chop-up**
- 1 zucchini, diced
- 1 yellow squash, diced
- 1 can (14 oz) diced tomatoes
- 4 **cups of** vegetable broth
- 2 **cups of** water
- 1 can (15 oz) kidney beans, drained and rinsed
- 1 can (15 oz) cannellini beans, drained and rinsed
- 1 **cup of mini** pasta (e.g., macaroni, ditalini)
- 2 **tsp** dried oregano
- 1 **tsp** dried basil
- Salt and pepper **as needed**
- **Finely grated** Parmesan cheese for serving (**non-compulsory**)

Instructions:

1. Olive oil is heated over medium heat in a big pot. Add diced celery, carrots, and onion, all **chop-up**. Sauté the vegetables **up to** they begin to soften.
2. Zucchini, yellow squash, and **chop-up** garlic **Must** all be added to the pot. Add a couple more **min**s of cooking.
3. Add the water, vegetable broth, and diced tomatoes. The **Mixture Must** boil.
4. Add the kidney and cannellini beans to the saucepan once they have been rinsed and drained. Add the dried basil and oregano. Add salt and pepper **as needed**.
5. For around 20 **min**s, simmer the soup on low heat with the lid on.
6. Cook the little pasta separately in the meantime according the directions on the **box/pkg**.
7. Just before serving, stir the cooked pasta into the soup.
8. Garnish with freshly **finely grated** Parmesan cheese before serving hot.

NUTRITION INFO (per serving):
Cals: 300 kcal, Protein: 10g, Fat: 6g

Carbs: 50g, Fiber: 10g, Vitamin A: 100% DV

Vitamin C: 25% DV

164. Mason Jar Tortilla Soup

Prep Time: 15 **min**s

Cook Time: 25 **min**s

Total Time: 40 **min**s

Servings: 4

Ingredients:

- 1 **tbsp** olive oil
- 1 **mini** onion, **chop-up**
- 1 bell pepper, diced (any color you prefer)

- 2 cloves garlic, **chop-up**
- 1 can (14 oz) diced tomatoes
- 1 can (14 oz) black beans, drained and rinsed
- 1 **cup of** corn kernels (fresh, **refrigerate**, or canned)
- 4 **cups of** vegetable broth
- 1 **tsp** chili powder
- 1/2 **tsp** ground cumin
- Salt and pepper **as needed**
- Tortilla chips, avocado slices, fresh cilantro, lime wedges for serving

Instructions:

1. Olive oil is heated over medium heat in a big pot. Add diced bell pepper and **chop-up** onion. Sauté onions **up to** they are transparent.
2. Cook the **chop-up** garlic in the pot for a further **min**.
3. Add the corn kernels, black beans, and diced tomatoes. Add the ground cumin and chili powder after that. Add salt and pepper **as needed**.
4. Bring the **Mixture** to a boil after adding the veggie broth to the pan.
5. Turn down the heat to low, cover the pot, and simmer the soup for 15 to 20 **min**s.
6. Serve the tortilla soup hot, topped with avocado slices, fresh cilantro, **cut up** tortilla chips, and a squeeze of lime juice.

NUTRITION INFO (per serving):
Cals: 250 kcal, Protein: 8g, Fat: 6g, **Carb**s: 42g, Fiber: 10g, Vitamin A: 15% DV, Vitamin C: 60% DV

165.Lentil and Vegetable Soup

Prep Time: 15 **min**s

Cook Time: 40 **min**s

Total Time: 55 **min**s

Servings: 6

Ingredients:

- 1 **cup of** dried green or brown lentils, rinsed
- 2 **tbsp** olive oil
- 1 onion, **chop-up**
- 2 carrots, diced
- 2 celery stalks, diced
- 2 cloves garlic, **chop-up**
- 1 can (14 oz) diced tomatoes
- 6 **cups of** vegetable broth
- 2 bay leaves
- 1 **tsp** dried thyme
- Salt and pepper **as needed**
- Fresh parsley for garnish

Instructions:

1. Olive oil is heated over medium heat in a big pot. Add diced celery, carrots, and onion, all **chop-up**. Sauté the vegetables **up to** they begin to soften.
2. Cook the **chop-up** garlic in the pot for a further **min**.
3. Add the vegetable broth, **chop-up** tomatoes, bay leaves, and dried thyme along with the rinsed lentils. Add salt and pepper **as needed**.
4. The soup **Must** simmer for about 30-35 **min**s, or **up to** the lentils are cooked, after the **Mixture** comes to a boil.
5. Before serving, take off the bay leaves.
6. Add some fresh parsley to the lentil and vegetable soup as a garnish.

NUTRITION INFO (per serving):
Cals: 220 kcal, Protein: 10g, Fat: 5g

Carbs: 35g, Fiber: 10g, Vitamin A: 80% DV

Vitamin C: 20% DV

166. Creamy Broccoli Cheddar Soup

Prep Time: 10 **min**s

Cook Time: 25 **min**s

Total Time: 35 **min**s

Servings: 4

Ingredients:

- 1 **tbsp** butter
- 1 onion, **chop-up**
- 2 cloves garlic, **chop-up**
- 3 **cups of chop-up** broccoli florets
- 2 **cups of** vegetable broth
- 2 **cups of** milk (whole or 2%)
- 2 **tbsp** all-purpose flour
- 2 **cups of** shredded cheddar cheese
- Salt and pepper **as needed**
- Croutons for serving (**non-compulsory**)

Instructions:

1. Melt the butter in a **Big** pot over medium heat. Sauté the **chop-up** onion after adding it **up to** it turns translucent.
2. Cook the **chop-up** garlic in the pot for a further **min**.
3. Add vegetable broth and **chop-up** broccoli florets. After bringing the **Mixture** to a boil, turn the heat down to low, cover the saucepan, and cook the broccoli for 8 to 10 **min**s, or **up to** it is soft.
4. Make sure there are no lumps when you **combine** the milk and all-purpose flour in a different bowl.
5. Fill the pot with the cooked broccoli and add the milk **Mixture** to it. Stir thoroughly, then let the

soup simmer for an additional few **min**s to slightly thicken.
6. The cheddar cheese has been added; stir **up to** it has **dilute** completely and been inte**finely grated** into the soup.
7. **As needed**, add salt and pepper to the food.
8. Serve the hot, creamy broccoli cheddar soup with or without croutons.

NUTRITION INFO (per serving):
Cals: 400 kcal, Protein: 20g, Fat: 25g

Carbs: 25g, Fiber: 3g, Vitamin A: 60% DV

Vitamin C: 80% DV

167.Mason Jar Gazpacho

Prep Time: 15 **min**s

Total Time: 15 **min**s

Servings: 2

Ingredients:

- 2 **Big** tomatoes, **chop-up**
- 1 cucumber, **peel off** and **chop-up**
- 1 red bell pepper, **chop-up**
- 1 **mini** red onion, **chop-up**
- 2 cloves garlic, **chop-up**
- 2 **cups of** tomato juice
- 2 **tbsp** red wine vinegar
- 2 **tbsp** olive oil
- 1 **tsp** salt
- 1/2 **tsp** black pepper
- 1/2 **tsp** cumin
- Fresh basil leaves, for garnish

Instructions:

1. The diced tomatoes, cucumber, red bell pepper, red onion, and **chop-up** garlic **Must** all be **combine**d in a bowl.
2. Add the salt, black pepper, cumin, tomato juice, red wine vinegar, and olive oil. Stir to **combine**.
3. Ladle the gazpacho carefully into two mason jars.
4. Fresh basil leaves are a nice garnish.
5. Before serving, chill the jars for at least one **hr** after sealing.

NUTRITION INFO (per serving):
Cals: 120 kcal, **Carb**s: 15g, Protein: 3g

Fat: 6g, Fiber: 3g

168.Chicken and Wild Rice Soup

Prep Time: 10 **min**s

Cook Time: 30 **min**s

Total Time: 40 **min**s

Servings: 4

Ingredients:

- 1 **tbsp** olive oil
- 1 onion, diced
- 2 carrots, diced
- 2 celery stalks, diced
- 2 cloves garlic, **chop-up**
- 4 **cups of** chicken broth
- 1 **cup of** cooked wild rice
- 2 **cups of** cooked chicken, shredded
- 1 **tsp** dried thyme
- Salt and pepper **as needed**
- Fresh parsley, **chop-up**, for garnish

Instructions:

1. Olive oil **Must** be heated in a sizable pot over medium heat. Add the celery, carrots, and onion, all **chop-up**. Cook for about 5 **min**s, or **up to melted**.
2. Add the **chop-up** garlic, stir, and cook for one more **min**.
3. Bring to a boil after adding the chicken broth. Simmer the heat down.
4. Add the chicken that has been shredded, the cooked wild rice, salt, and pepper. For 15 to 20 **min**s, simmer.
5. Pour the soup into mason jars, top with fresh parsley that has been **chop-up**, and serve.

NUTRITION INFO (per serving):
Cals: 250 kcal, **Carb**s: 18g, Protein: 20g

Fat: 10g, Fiber: 3g

169.Mason Jar Spinach and Artichoke Dip

Prep Time: 15 **min**s

Cook Time: 25 **min**s

Total Time: 40 **min**s

Servings: 6

Ingredients:

- 1 **cup of refrigerate chop-up** spinach, thawed and drained
- 1 **cup of** canned artichoke hearts, **chop-up**
- 1/2 **cup of** mayonnaise
- 1/2 **cup of** sour cream
- 1 **cup of** shredded mozzarella cheese
- 1/4 **cup of finely grated** parmesan cheese
- 1 **tsp** garlic powder
- 1/2 **tsp** onion powder
- Salt and pepper **as needed**
- Tortilla chips or pita chips, for serving

Instructions:

1. Turn on the oven to 350 °F (175 °C).
2. Chop the spinach and artichoke hearts. **Combine** the mayonnaise, sour cream, mozzarella cheese,

finely grated parmesan cheese, garlic powder, onion powder, salt, and pepper in a **combining** bowl.
3. All materials **Must** be thoroughly blended after **combining**.
4. Fill the mason jars with the **Mixture**, **let**ing space at the top for expansion.
5. Bake the jars in the preheated oven for about 25 **min**s, or **up to** the dip is bubbling and the tops are just beginning to brown.
6. Before serving with tortilla or pita chips, take it out of the oven and let it a brief moment to cool.

NUTRITION INFO (per serving):
Cals: 220 kcal, **Carb**s: 5g, Protein: 7g

Fat: 19g, Fiber: 2g

170.Layered Mexican Bean Dip

Prep Time: 20 **min**s

Total Time: 20 **min**s

Servings: 8

Ingredients:

- 1 can (16 oz) refried beans
- 1 **cup of** guacamole
- 1 **cup of** sour cream
- 1 **cup of** salsa
- 1 **cup of** shredded cheddar cheese
- 1/2 **cup of chop-up** tomatoes
- 1/2 **cup of chop-up** green onions
- 1/4 **cup of split** black olives
- 1/4 **cup of chop-up** fresh cilantro

Instructions:

1. An even layer of refried beans **Must** be put at the bottom of a trifle dish or clear glass mason jar.
2. On top of the beans, add the guacamole, then the sour cream, then the salsa.
3. Cheddar cheese **cut up**s **Must** be scattered over the salsa layer.
4. For a vivid presentation, garnish with **split** tomatoes, green onions, black olives, and fresh cilantro.
5. Serve with tortilla chips right away.

NUTRITION INFO (per serving):
Cals: 220 kcal, **Carb**s: 10g, Protein: 8g

Fat: 16g, Fiber: 3g

171.Avocado and Mango Salsa

Prep Time: 15 **min**s

Total Time: 15 **min**s

Servings: 4

Ingredients:

- 2 ripe avocados, diced

- 1 ripe mango, diced
- 1/2 red onion, **lightly chop-up**
- 1 jalapeño, seeds **take out**d and **lightly chop-up**
- 1/4 **cup of** fresh cilantro, **chop-up**
- Juice of 1 lime
- Salt and pepper **as needed**
- Tortilla chips, for serving

Instructions:
1. The diced avocados, diced mango, red onion, jalapenos, and fresh cilantro **Must** all be **combine**d in a bowl.
2. Lime juice **Must** be squeezed over the **Mixture** and gently **combined** in.
3. **As needed**, add salt and pepper to the food.
4. Spoon the salsa made from mango and avocado into mason jars with care.
5. Serve with tortilla chips right away.

NUTRITION INFO (per serving):
Cals: 160 kcal, **Carb**s: 16g

Protein: 2g, Fat: 11g

Fiber: 6g

172.Mason Jar Buffalo Chicken Dip

Prep Time: 15 **min**s

Cook Time: 20 **min**s

Total Time: 35 **min**s

Servings: 6

Ingredients:
- 2 **cups of** cooked chicken, shredded
- 1/2 **cup of** buffalo sauce
- 1 **cup of** cream cheese, **melted**
- 1 **cup of** sour cream
- 1 **cup of** shredded cheddar cheese
- 1/4 **cup of chop-up** green onions
- 1/4 **cup of cut up** blue cheese (**non-compulsory**)
- Salt and pepper **as needed**
- Celery sticks and tortilla chips for serving

Instructions:
1. Shredded chicken and buffalo sauce **Must** be **combine**d in a medium bowl so that the chicken is thoroughly coated.
2. **Combine** the cream cheese, sour cream, cheddar cheese, green onions, and blue cheese (if using) in a different bowl.
3. **Combine** thoroughly after taste-adjusting the salt and pepper.
4. Layer the buffalo chicken **Mixture** and the cream cheese **Mixture** alternately in **mini** or **Big** mason jars.
5. Before serving, cover the mason jar(s) and place them in the refrigerator.

6. Serve the Buffalo Chicken Dip with tortilla chips for dipping and celery sticks.

Nutrition (per serving):
Cals: 350, Fat: 25g, **Carb**s: 10g

Protein: 22g, Fiber: 1g

173. Spinach and Feta Dip with Pita Chips

Prep Time: 10 **min**s

Cook Time: 15 **min**s

Total Time: 25 **min**s

Servings: 4

Ingredients:
- 1 **cup of refrigerate chop-up** spinach, thawed and drained
- 1 **cup of cut up** feta cheese
- 1/2 **cup of** plain Greek yogurt
- 1/4 **cup of** mayonnaise
- 2 cloves garlic, **chop-up**
- 1 **tbsp** lemon juice
- Salt and pepper **as needed**
- Pita chips for serving

Instructions:
1. The **chop-up** spinach, feta cheese, Greek yogurt, mayonnaise, garlic, and lemon juice **Must** all be **combine**d in a medium bowl.
2. All of the ingredients **Must** be thoroughly **combine**d after **combining**.
3. **As needed**, add salt and pepper to the food.
4. When ready to serve, pour the dip into a serving bowl and place in the refrigerator.
5. Serve the Spinach and Feta Dip with pita chips for dipping.

Nutrition (per serving):
Cals: 220, Fat: 16g, **Carb**s: 7g

Protein: 10g, Fiber: 1g

174. Greek Yogurt Ranch Dip

Prep Time: 5 **min**s

Cook Time: 0 **min**s

Total Time: 5 **min**s

Servings: 4

Ingredients:
- 1 **cup of** plain Greek yogurt
- 1 **tbsp** dried dill
- 1 **tbsp** dried parsley
- 1 **tsp** garlic powder
- 1 **tsp** onion powder
- 1/2 **tsp** dried chives
- 1/2 **tsp** salt

- 1/4 **tsp** black pepper

Instructions:
1. Greek yogurt, dried dill, dried parsley, dried chives, garlic powder, onion powder, salt, and black pepper **Must** all be **combine**d in a bowl.
2. Greek yogurt and all the herbs and spices **Must** be thoroughly **combined**.
3. Keep the dip cold **up to** you're ready to serve it.
4. Serve your favorite chips or fresh vegetables with the Greek yogurt ranch dip.

Nutrition (per serving):
Cals: 60, Fat: 0g, **Carb**s: 4g

Protein: 11g, Fiber: 0g

175. Mason Jar Tzatziki Sauce

Prep Time: 10 **min**s

Cook Time: 0 **min**s

Total Time: 10 **min**s

Servings: 6

Ingredients:
- 1 **cup of** cucumber, **finely grated** and drained
- 1 1/2 **cups of** Greek yogurt
- 2 cloves garlic, **chop-up**
- 1 **tbsp** fresh dill, **chop-up**
- 1 **tbsp** fresh mint, **chop-up**
- 1 **tbsp** lemon juice
- Salt and pepper **as needed**

Instructions:
1. To **take out** extra water, grate the cucumber and lay it in a cheesecloth or fine-mesh sieve.
2. **Finely grated** cucumber, Greek yogurt, **chop-up** garlic, **chop-up** dill, **chop-up** mint, and lemon juice **Must** all be **combine**d in a bowl.
3. **Combine** thoroughly **up to** all components are distributed equally.
4. **As needed**, add salt and pepper to the food.
5. When you're ready to serve, pour the tzatziki sauce into mason jars and put them in the fridge.
6. Serve pita bread, grilled meats, or fresh veggies as a dip with the tzatziki sauce.

Nutrition (per serving):
Cals: 70, Fat: 2g, **Carb**s: 6g

Protein: 7g, Fiber: 1g

176. Fresh Guacamole with Tortilla Chips

Prep Time: 15 **min**s

Cook Time: 0 **min**s

Total Time: 15 **min**s

Servings: 4

Ingredients:
- 3 ripe avocados, pitted and **peel off**
- 1/4 **cup of** red onion, **lightly** diced
- 1/4 **cup of** fresh cilantro, **chop-up**
- 1 jalapeño, seeded and **lightly** diced
- 1 **Big** tomato, diced
- 1 clove garlic, **chop-up**
- 1 lime, juiced
- Salt and pepper **as needed**
- Tortilla chips for serving

Instructions:
1. Use a fork or potato masher to mash the ripe avocados in a bowl **up to** the appropriate consistency is achieved.
2. The mashed avocados **Must** be **combined** with the **lightly split** red onion, **chop-up** cilantro, **lightly** diced jalapeo, diced tomato, **chop-up** garlic, and lime juice.
3. All the components **Must** be thoroughly **combined**.
4. **As needed**, add salt and pepper to the food.
5. Serve tortilla chips with the fresh guacamole for dipping.

Nutrition (per serving):
Cals: 190, Fat: 15g, **Carb**s: 14g

Protein: 3g, Fiber: 9g

177. Mason Jar Pesto Pasta Salad

Prep Time: 15 **min**s

Cook Time: 10 **min**s

Total Time: 25 **min**s

Servings: 2

Ingredients:
- 1 **cup of** cooked pasta (such as fusilli or penne)
- 1/4 **cup of** cherry tomatoes, halved
- 1/4 **cup of** fresh mozzarella balls, halved
- 1/4 **cup of** black olives, pitted and **split**
- 2 **tbsp** pesto sauce
- 1 **tbsp** pine nuts
- Fresh basil leaves for garnish
- Salt and pepper **as needed**

Instructions:
1. Place the cooked spaghetti, cherry tomatoes, mozzarella balls, and black olives in a mason jar.
2. Pine nuts **Must** be added together with the pesto sauce.
3. **As needed**, add salt and pepper to the food.
4. Fresh basil leaves are a nice garnish.
5. Before serving, seal the Mason jar and place it in the refrigerator.

6. When you're ready to eat, give the jar a gentle shake to **combine** the ingredients.

Nutrition (per serving):
Cals: 400 kcal, **Carb**s: 32g

Protein: 12g, Fat: 25g, Fiber: 4g

178. Layered Antipasto Pasta Salad

Prep Time: 20 **min**s

Cook Time: 10 **min**s

Total Time: 30 **min**s

Servings: 4

Ingredients:
- 2 **cups of** cooked rotini pasta
- 1/2 **cup of** cherry tomatoes, halved
- 1/2 **cup of** fresh mozzarella balls
- 1/2 **cup of** marinated artichoke hearts, drained and **chop-up**
- 1/4 **cup of split** pepperoni
- 1/4 **cup of split** black olives
- 1/4 **cup of split** red onion
- 1/4 **cup of chop-up** roasted red peppers
- 1/4 **cup of** Italian salad dressing
- Fresh basil leaves for garnish
- Salt and pepper **as needed**

Instructions:
1. Prepared spaghetti, cherry tomatoes, mozzarella balls, artichoke hearts, pepperoni, black olives, red onion, and roasted red peppers **Must** all be **combine**d in a big bowl.
2. The items **Must** be evenly covered with the Italian salad dressing after being poured over them.
3. **As needed**, add salt and pepper to the food.
4. Layer the spaghetti **Mixture** in a serving dish, carefully pressing down between **every** layer to compact it.
5. Fresh basil leaves are a nice garnish.
6. Refrigerate with a cover **up to** ready to serve.

Nutrition (per serving):
Cals: 380 kcal, **Carb**s: 24g, Protein: 14g

Fat: 26g, Fiber: 3g

179. Mason Jar Macaroni and Cheese

Prep Time: 10 **min**s

Cook Time: 20 **min**s

Total Time: 30 **min**s

Servings: 2

Ingredients:
- 1 **cup of** uncooked elbow macaroni
- 1 1/2 **cups of** milk
- 1 **cup of** shredded cheddar cheese
- 2 **tbsp** unsalted butter
- 2 **tbsp** all-purpose flour
- 1/4 **tsp** garlic powder
- 1/4 **tsp** onion powder
- Salt and pepper **as needed**

Instructions:
1. The macaroni **Must** be prepared as directed on the **box/pkg**, drained, and set aside.
2. Melt the butter in a saucepan over medium heat. The flour **Must** be stirred in and cooked for 1-2 **min**s, or **up to** a roux develops.
3. Adding the milk to the roux gradually while continually stirring to prevent lumps. Cook the sauce **up to** it thickens.
4. Add the shredded cheddar cheese, garlic powder, onion powder, salt, and pepper after lowering the heat. The sauce **Must** be smooth and the cheese **Must** be **dilute**.
5. Layer the cheese sauce and cooked macaroni in mason jars **up to** all the ingredients have been utilized.
6. Before serving, seal the Mason jars and place them in the refrigerator.
7. When ready to serve, microwave the jars of macaroni and cheese **up to** they are hot and creamy.

Nutrition (per serving):
Cals: 550 kcal, **Carb**s: 39g, Protein: 23g

Fat: 33g, Fiber: 2g

180. Classic Spaghetti and Meatballs

Prep Time: 30 **min**s

Cook Time: 30 **min**s

Total Time: 1 **hr**

Servings: 4

Ingredients:
- 8 **oz**s spaghetti
- 1 **lb** ground beef
- 1/2 **cup of** breadcrumbs
- 1/4 **cup of finely grated** Parmesan cheese
- 1/4 **cup of chop-up** fresh parsley
- 1 egg, beaten
- 2 **cups of** marinara sauce
- 1 **tbsp** olive oil
- 2 garlic cloves, **chop-up**
- Salt and pepper **as needed**

Instructions:

1. Spaghetti **Must** be prepared as directed on the **box/pkg**, drained, and then set aside.
2. Ground beef, breadcrumbs, **finely grated** Parmesan cheese, **chop-up** parsley, beaten egg, **chop-up** garlic, salt, and pepper **Must** all be **combine**d in a **combining** bowl. **Combine** thoroughly after **combining**.
3. Make meatballs out of the **Mixture** that are about an inch in diameter.
4. Over medium heat, warm the olive oil in a skillet. Add the meatballs, and simmer for 8 to 10 **min**s, or **up to** thoroughly cooked on all sides.
5. The marinara sauce **Must** be warmed through on a medium-low heat in a different pan.
6. Serve the cooked spaghetti with meatballs and marinara sauce on top. If preferred, add more Parmesan cheese and parsley as a garnish.

Nutrition (per serving):
Cals: 650 kcal, **Carb**s: 53g, Protein: 34g

Fat: 32g, Fiber: 4g

181. Creamy Chicken Alfredo

Prep Time: 15 **min**s

Cook Time: 20 **min**s

Total Time: 35 **min**s

Servings: 4

Ingredients:
- 8 **oz**s fettuccine
- 2 boneless, skinless chicken breasts, cooked and **split**
- 2 **cups of** heavy cream
- 1/2 **cup of finely grated** Parmesan cheese
- 1/4 **cup of** unsalted butter
- 3 garlic cloves, **chop-up**
- 1 **tbsp** olive oil
- 1 **tsp** dried parsley
- Salt and pepper **as needed**

Instructions:
1. The fettuccine **Must** be prepared per the directions on the **box/pkg**, drained, and then set aside.
2. The olive oil **Must** be heated in a saucepan over medium heat. Sauté the **chop-up** garlic **up to** fragrant after adding it.
3. Add the heavy cream, Parmesan cheese, and unsalted butter after lowering the heat. Stir the sauce **up to** it becomes creamy and smooth.
4. Add salt, pepper, and dry parsley **as needed** to the sauce.

5. The chicken **Must** be heated through after being added to the sauce after being cooked and **slice** into slices.
6. Over the cooked fettuccine, dish out the creamy chicken Alfredo.

Nutrition (per serving):
Cals: 800 kcal, **Carb**s: 54g, Protein: 32g

Fat: 52g, Fiber: 2g

182. Overnight Chia Seed Pudding

Prep Time: 10 **min**s

Total Time: 8 **hrs** 10 **min**s

Servings: 2

Ingredients:
- 1/4 **cup of** chia seeds
- 1 **cup of** almond milk (or any milk of your choice)
- 1 **tbsp** maple syrup or honey
- 1/2 **tsp** vanilla extract
- Fresh fruits (such as berries or **split** bananas) for topping

Instructions:
1. **Combine** the chia seeds, almond milk, maple syrup (or honey), and vanilla essence in a mason jar or other airtight container.
2. Make sure to completely **combine** all the components by stirring.
3. Place the jar in the refrigerator, covered, for at least 8 **hr**s or overnight.
4. Give the **Mixture** a brisk swirl just before serving to spread the chia seeds evenly.
5. Enjoy your wonderful overnight chia seed pudding with a sprinkle of your favorite fresh fruits!

Nutrition (per serving):
Cals: 210 kcal, Fat: 10g, **Carb**s: 24g

Fiber: 12g, Protein: 6g

183. Mason Jar Breakfast Burrito

Prep Time: 15 **min**s

Cook Time: 10 **min**s

Total Time: 25 **min**s

Servings: 1

Ingredients:
- 2 **Big** eggs
- 2 **tbsp** milk
- Salt and pepper **as needed**
- 1/4 **cup of** shredded cheddar cheese

- 1/4 **cup of** cooked **cut up** sausage or bacon
- 1/4 **cup of** diced bell peppers
- 1/4 **cup of** diced onions
- 1/4 **cup of** diced tomatoes
- 1 **mini** flour tortilla

Instructions:

1. **Combine** the eggs, milk, salt, and pepper in a bowl.
2. The eggs **Must** be scrambled in a nonstick pan over medium heat **up to** they are barely set.
3. On a spotless surface, spread the flour tortilla out flat.
4. Scrambled eggs, shredded cheddar cheese, cooked sausage or bacon, diced bell peppers, diced onions, and diced tomatoes **Must** be layered in the mason jar starting with the last ingredient.
5. Make sure the ingredients are tightly packed before placing the loaded tortilla in the mason jar.
6. Refrigerate the mason jar with the lid **up to** you're ready to eat.
7. **Take out** the cover, then either eat the burrito from the jar or move it to a platter before serving.

Nutrition (per serving):

Cals: 480 kcal, Fat: 31g, **Carb**s: 24g, Fiber: 3g

Protein: 26g

184.Mason Jar Pancakes with Maple Syrup

Prep Time: 10 **min**s

Cook Time: 10 **min**s

Total Time: 20 **min**s

Servings: 1

Ingredients:

- 1/2 **cup of** pancake **combine**
- 1/3 **cup of** milk
- 1 **tbsp** vegetable oil
- 1 **tbsp** maple syrup

Instructions:

1. The pancake **combine**, milk, vegetable oil, and maple syrup **Must** all be **combine**d into a smooth batter in a bowl.
2. Heat a nonstick pan to medium-high temperature.
3. Fill the greased Mason jar only halfway with the pancake batter to **let** for expansion.
4. For about 2-3 **min**s, or **up to** bubbles appear on the surface, cook the pancake in the mason jar.
5. Using oven mitts, carefully turn the mason jar over to cook the other side of the pancake **up to** it is golden brown.

6. Before enjoying your Mason jar pancakes with maple syrup, **take out** the mason jar from the pan and let it cool somewhat.

Nutrition (per serving):

Cals: 520 kcal, Fat: 20g, **Carb**s: 75g

Fiber: 2g, Protein: 10g

185.Layered Fruit Salad with Honey-Lime Dressing

Prep Time: 20 **min**s

Total Time: 20 **min**s

Servings: 2

Ingredients:

- 1 **cup of combined** fresh fruits (such as strawberries, blueberries, kiwi, and grapes), diced or **split**
- 1 **tbsp** honey
- 1 **tbsp** lime juice
- 1/2 **tsp** lime zest
- Fresh mint leaves for garnish (**non-compulsory**)

Instructions:

1. To prepare the dressing, **combine** the honey, lime juice, and zest in a **mini** bowl.
2. The assorted fresh fruits **Must** be layered in Mason jars or serving glasses.
3. Over the fruits, drizzle the honey-lime dressing.
4. If desired, garnish with fresh mint leaves.
5. Serve right now or keep chilled **up to** you're ready to dine.

Nutrition (per serving):

Cals: 80 kcal, Fat: 0.5g, **Carb**s: 21g

Fiber: 3g, Protein: 1g

186.Mason Jar Raspberry Oatmeal

Prep Time: 10 **min**s

Cook Time: 5 **min**s

Total Time: 15 **min**s

Servings: 1

Ingredients:

- 1/2 **cup of** rolled oats
- 1 **cup of** milk (dairy or plant-based)
- 1/4 **cup of** fresh raspberries
- 1 **tbsp** honey or maple syrup
- 1/4 **tsp** vanilla extract
- Pinch of salt

Instructions:

1. The milk, raspberries, honey (or maple syrup), vanilla extract, salt, and rolled oats **Must** all be **combine**d in a pot.
2. Cook the oats for about 5 **min**s, or **up to** it **revery**es the desired consistency, over medium heat, stirring regularly.
3. Lavishly let the oatmeal to cool.
4. When ready to eat, pour the cooked oats into a mason jar, seal it, and place it in the refrigerator.
5. For added taste and presentation, garnish the dish with more fresh raspberries before serving.

Nutrition (per serving):

Cals: 320 kcal, Fat: 6g, **Carb**s: 55g

Fiber: 9g, Protein: 10g

187.Mason Jar Chili Mac

Prep Time: 15 **min**s

Cook Time: 25 **min**s

Total Time: 40 **min**s

Servings: 4

Ingredients:

- 1 **cup of** elbow macaroni
- 1 lb ground beef
- 1 can (14.5 oz) diced tomatoes
- 1 can (8 oz) tomato sauce
- 1/2 **cup of** diced onions
- 1/2 **cup of** diced bell peppers
- 1/2 **cup of** kidney beans (drained and rinsed)
- 1/2 **cup of** corn kernels
- 1 **tbsp** chili powder
- 1 **tsp** ground cumin
- Salt and pepper **as needed**
- 1 **cup of** shredded cheddar cheese
- **Chop-up** green onions for garnish

Instructions:

1. Follow the directions on the **box/pkg** to prepare the elbow macaroni. Drain, then set apart.
2. Cook the ground beef in a **Big** skillet over medium heat. **Take out** any extra fat.
3. Cook the bell peppers and **chop-up** onions in the skillet **up to** they are tender.
4. Add the **chop-up** tomatoes, tomato sauce, kidney beans, corn, cumin, chili powder, salt, and pepper after stirring. Cook for ten **min**s.
5. Cooked macaroni, chili **Mixture**, and shredded cheddar cheese **Must** be arranged in the Mason jars in that order. Till the jars are full, keep adding layers.
6. Add **chop-up** green onions as a garnish.

7. Place the Mason jars in the refrigerator after sealing. Reheat in the microwave before serving, or consume cold.

NUTRITION INFO (per serving):

Cals: 450 kcal, Protein: 27g, Fat: 18g

Carbs: 43g, Fiber: 6g

188.Mason Jar Lasagna

Prep Time: 20 **min**s

Cook Time: 30 **min**s

Total Time: 50 **min**s

Servings: 4

Ingredients:

- 8 lasagna noodles, cooked and drained
- 1 **cup of** ricotta cheese
- 1 **cup of** shredded mozzarella cheese
- 1 **cup of finely grated** Parmesan cheese
- 1 **cup of** marinara sauce
- 1/2 **cup of** cooked and **cut up** Italian sausage (**non-compulsory**)
- 1/2 **cup of chop-up** spinach
- 1 **tsp** dried oregano
- Salt and pepper **as needed**
- Fresh basil leaves for garnish

Instructions:

1. Set the oven's temperature to 375°F (190°C).
2. **Combine** the ricotta cheese, half of the shredded mozzarella, and half of the Parmesan cheese in a bowl. Add salt, pepper, and dried oregano as seasonings.
3. A dollop of marinara sauce, a layer of cooked lasagna noodles (break them to fit), a layer of the cheese **Mixture**, some **chop-up** spinach, and some **cut up** Italian sausage (if used) **Must** be arranged in **every** Mason jar.
4. The layers are repeated **up to** the jars are full, and then a layer of marinara sauce is placed on top.
5. The remaining mozzarella and Parmesan cheese **Must** be added on top.
6. The filled Mason jars **Must** be placed on a baking sheet and baked for 15 to 20 **min**s in a preheated oven, or **up to** the cheese is **dilute** and bubbling.
7. Before serving, garnish with fresh basil leaves.

NUTRITION INFO (per serving):

Cals: 520 kcal, Protein: 28g, Fat: 28g, **Carb**s: 39g, Fiber: 3g

189.Mason Jar Huevos Rancheros

Prep Time: 10 **min**s

Cook Time: 15 **min**s

Total Time: 25 **min**s

Servings: 2

Ingredients:

- 4 **Big** eggs
- 1 **cup of** black beans (canned or cooked)
- 1 **cup of** diced tomatoes (canned or fresh)
- 1/2 **cup of** diced bell peppers
- 1/2 **cup of** diced onions
- 1/2 **cup of** shredded cheddar cheese
- 1/4 **cup of chop-up** cilantro
- 1 **tbsp** olive oil
- 1 **tsp** chili powder
- Salt and pepper **as needed**
- Hot sauce or salsa (**non-compulsory**)

Instructions:

1. Olive oil **Must** be heated in a skillet over medium heat. Add the bell peppers and onion dice, and cook **up to** they are tender.
2. Add the chili powder and diced tomatoes after **combining**. Cook for a further 2 to 3 **min**s, or **up to** the **Mixture** slightly thickens.
3. Fry the eggs to your preferred doneness or sunny side up in a separate pan.
4. Layer black beans, a tomato and pepper **Mixture**, shredded cheddar cheese, and a fried egg on top in **every** Mason jar.
5. **As needed**, add salt and pepper to the food.
6. If preferred, serve with salsa or spicy sauce and garnish with **chop-up** cilantro.

NUTRITION INFO (per serving):

Cals: 390 kcal, Protein: 21g, Fat: 24g

Carbs: 24g, Fiber: 7g

190.Layered Breakfast Parfait

Prep Time: 10 **min**s

Cook Time: 0 **min**s

Total Time: 10 **min**s

Servings: 2

Ingredients:

- 1 **cup of** Greek yogurt
- 1 **cup of** granola
- 1 **cup of combined** fresh berries (strawberries, blueberries, raspberries)
- 2 **tbsp** honey
- 1/4 **cup of chop-up** nuts (almonds, walnuts, or your choice)

Instructions:

1. Greek yogurt, a drizzle of honey, granola, **combined** berries, and **chop-up** nuts **Must** all be layered in a Mason jar.
2. The layers **Must** be repeated **up to** the jars are completely full.

3. For a little extra flavor, you might top it with some cinnamon or more honey.
4. To let the flavors mingle, either serve right away or chill for a few **hr**s.

NUTRITION INFO (per serving):

Cals: 400 kcal, Protein: 15g, Fat: 18g, **Carb**s: 45g, Fiber: 6g

191.Mason Jar Greek Yogurt with Berries

Prep Time: 5 **min**s

Cook Time: 0 **min**s

Total Time: 5 **min**s

Servings: 1

Ingredients:

- 1 **cup of** Greek yogurt
- 1/2 **cup of combined** fresh berries (blueberries, strawberries, raspberries)
- 2 **tbsp** honey
- 1/4 **cup of** granola
- Fresh mint leaves for garnish (**non-compulsory**)

Instructions:

1. Place the Greek yogurt at the bottom of a Mason jar.
2. Honey **Must** be drizzled over the yogurt.
3. Granola **Must** be scattered on top of the honey.
4. The following layer **Must** be the **combined** berries.
5. Up till the jar is full, keep adding layers.
6. If desired, garnish with fresh mint leaves.

NUTRITION INFO (per serving):

Cals: 400 kcal, Protein: 20g, Fat: 10g, **Carb**s: 60g, Fiber: 5g

192.Mason Jar Banana Bread

Prep Time: 15 **min**s

Cook Time: 1 **hr**

Total Time: 1 **hr** 15 **min**s

Servings: 8

Ingredients:

- 1 1/2 **cups of** all-purpose flour
- 1 **tsp** baking soda
- 1/2 **tsp** salt
- 1/2 **cup of** unsalted butter, **dilute**
- 3/4 **cup of** brown sugar, packed
- 2 **Big** eggs
- 1 **tsp** vanilla extract
- 3 ripe bananas, mashed

- 1/4 **cup of** milk
- 1/2 **cup of chop-up** walnuts (**non-compulsory**)

Instructions:
1. Turn on the oven to 350 °F (175 °C). 8 half-pint Mason jars **Must** be floured and greased.
2. **Combine** the salt, baking soda, and flour in a **Big** bowl.
3. The **dilute** butter and brown sugar **Must** be thoroughly **combined** in a different basin. Blend in the eggs and vanilla extract after adding them.
4. Once the milk and mashed bananas have been added, stir everything together thoroughly.
5. The dry components **Must** be added to the wet ingredients gradually while being stirred just **up to combine**d. Add the **chop-up** walnuts if desired.
6. Fill **every** mason jar to about two-thirds full and distribute the batter among them evenly.
7. On a baking sheet, arrange the filled jars and bake for approximately an **hr**, or **up to** a toothpick inserted in the center comes out clean.
8. Before moving the banana bread to a wire rack to finish cooling, give it a few **mins** to cool in the jars.

Nutrition (per serving):
Cals: 295 kcal, **Carb**s: 41g, Protein: 4g
Fat: 14g, Fiber: 2g

193.Mason Jar Lemon Blueberry Muffins

Prep Time: 20 **min**s

Cook Time: 25 **min**s

Total Time: 45 **min**s

Servings: 12

Ingredients:
- 2 **cups of** all-purpose flour
- 1/2 **cup of** granulated sugar
- 1 **tbsp** baking powder
- 1/2 **tsp** baking soda
- 1/4 **tsp** salt
- 1 **cup of** plain yogurt
- 1/4 **cup of** unsalted butter, **dilute**
- 2 **Big** eggs
- 1 **tsp** vanilla extract
- 1 **tbsp** lemon zest
- 1 **cup of** fresh blueberries

Instructions:
1. Set your oven's temperature to 375°F (190°C). 12 half-pint Mason jars **Must** be greased or lined with paper liners.
2. **Combine** the flour, sugar, baking soda, baking powder, and salt in a big bowl.

3. **Combine** the yogurt, **dilute** butter, eggs, vanilla extract, and lemon zest thoroughly in a different bowl.
4. Stirring constantly, add the wet components little by little to the dry ingredients. Fold in the fresh blueberries gently.
5. Fill **every** mason jar to about two-thirds full and distribute the batter among them evenly.
6. Bake the filled jars for about 25 **min**s, or **up to** a toothpick inserted into the center of a muffin comes out clean, on a baking sheet in the preheated oven.
7. The muffins **Must** cool in the jars for a little while before being transferred to a wire rack to finish cooling.

Nutrition (per serving):
Cals: 198 kcal, **Carb**s: 30g, Protein: 4g
Fat: 7g, Fiber: 1g

194.Mason Jar Chicken Pot Pie

Prep Time: 30 **min**s

Cook Time: 40 **min**s

Total Time: 1 **hr** 10 **min**s

Servings: 4

Ingredients:
- 1 sheet of puff pastry, thawed
- 2 **tbsp** unsalted butter
- 1/4 **cup of** all-purpose flour
- 1 3/4 **cups of** chicken broth
- 1/2 **cup of** milk
- 1/2 **tsp** salt
- 1/4 **tsp** black pepper
- 2 **cups of** cooked chicken, diced
- 1 **cup of refrigerate combined** vegetables (carrots, peas, corn, green beans)
- 1/4 **cup of chop-up** onions
- 2 **tbsp chop-up** fresh parsley

Instructions:
1. Set your oven's temperature to 375°F (190°C).
2. The puff pastry sheet **Must** be rolled out and **slice** into four circles that are about the same size as the mason jar openings. Place aside.
3. Melt the butter in a **Big** pot over medium heat. Once they are transparent, add the **split** onions.
4. Add the flour and heat while constantly stirring for one or two **min**s.
5. As the sauce thickens, gradually include the milk and chicken broth.
6. Add the cooked chicken, black pepper, **refrigerate combined** veggies, and parsley that has been **chop-up**. Stir **every** component together thoroughly.

7. Turn off the heat and **take out** the pot. Put roughly three-quarters of the chicken pot pie filling into **every** mason jar as you spoon it in.
8. **Every** jar **Must** have a puff pastry circle on top. Gently press the sides together to form a crust.
9. **Every** pastry **Must** have a **mini** slit in the center **slice** out to let steam to escape while baking.
10. Bake the filled jars for about 40 **min**s, or **up to** the dough is golden brown and the filling is bubbly, on a baking sheet in the preheated oven.

Nutrition (per serving):
Cals: 489 kcal, **Carb**s: 32g, Protein: 23g
Fat: 31g, Fiber: 4g

195. Layered Shepherd's Pie

Prep Time: 30 **min**s
Cook Time: 30 **min**s
Total Time: 1 **hr**
Servings: 6

Ingredients:
- 1 **lb** ground beef
- 1 onion, **chop-up**
- 2 cloves garlic, **chop-up**
- 2 **cups of refrigerate combined** vegetables (carrots, peas, corn, green beans)
- 2 **tbsp** tomato paste
- 1 **cup of** beef broth
- 1 **tbsp** Worcestershire sauce
- 1 **tsp** dried thyme
- Salt and pepper **as needed**
- 4 **cups of** mashed potatoes (prepared from 2 **lb**s potatoes)
- 1 **cup of** shredded cheddar cheese

Instructions:
1. Set your oven's temperature to 375°F (190°C).
2. Cook the ground beef to desired doneness in a **Big** skillet over medium-high heat. Delete extra fat if necessary.
3. To the skillet containing the ground meat, add the **chop-up** garlic and onion. Cook the onion **up to** it turns translucent.
4. Add the tomato paste, beef broth, Worcestershire sauce, dried thyme, salt, and pepper along with the **refrigerate combined** vegetables. **Up to** the vegetables are thoroughly heated and the sauce starts to thicken, simmer the **Mixture** for a few **min**s.
5. Layer the beef and vegetable combination, then the mashed potatoes, in 6 half-pint Mason jars. Continue the layering, and then add a final layer of mashed potatoes on top.

6. **Every** Mason jar **Must** have cheddar cheese sprinkled on top of it.
7. Bake the filled jars for about 30 **min**s, or **up to** the cheese is **dilute** and bubbling, on a baking sheet in a preheated oven.

Nutrition (per serving):
Cals: 446 kcal, **Carb**s: 39g, Protein: 21g
Fat: 22g, Fiber: 5g

196. Mason Jar Beef and Broccoli Stir-Fry

Prep Time: 15 **min**s
Cook Time: 15 **min**s
Total Time: 30 **min**s
Servings: 4

Ingredients:
- 1 **lb** flank steak, thinly **split**
- 1/4 **cup of** soy sauce
- 2 **tbsp** oyster sauce
- 1 **tbsp** hoisin sauce
- 1 **tbsp** cornstarch
- 2 **tbsp** vegetable oil, **slice up**
- 3 **cups of** broccoli florets
- 1 red bell pepper, **split**
- 2 cloves garlic, **chop-up**
- 1 **tbsp finely grated** fresh ginger
- Cooked white rice, for serving

Instructions:
1. **Combine** the cornstarch, hoisin sauce, oyster sauce, and soy sauce in a bowl. Flank steak that has been thinly **slice Must** be added to the bowl and **combined** with the marinade. Give it at least 10 **min**s to marinate.
2. 1 **tbsp** of vegetable oil **Must** be heated over high heat in a sizable skillet or wok. Stir-fry the beef with the marinade for two to three **min**s, or **up to** it is browned and thoroughly cooked. From the skillet, take out the beef, and set it aside.
3. Add the final **tbsp** of vegetable oil to the same skillet. Garlic and ginger **Must** be stir-fried for about a **min** to release their fragrance.
4. Broccoli florets and red bell pepper slices **Must** be added to the skillet. Vegetables **Must** be stir-fried for 3–4 **min**s to achieve tender-crispness.
5. Add the cooked beef back to the skillet and stir everything together thoroughly.

Nutrition (per serving):
Cals: 328 kcal, **Carb**s: 14g, Protein: 26g

Fat: 19g, Fiber: 3g

197. Mason Jar Teriyaki Salmon with Sesame Seeds

Prep Time: 15 mins

Cook Time: 20 mins

Total Time: 35 mins

Servings: 2

Ingredients:
- 2 salmon fillets
- 1/4 **cup of** teriyaki sauce
- 1 **tbsp** sesame oil
- 1 **tbsp** soy sauce
- 1 **tbsp** honey
- 1 **tsp chop-up** garlic
- 1 **tsp finely grated** ginger
- 1 **tbsp** sesame seeds
- 1 **cup of** cooked white rice
- 1 **cup of** broccoli florets
- 1/2 **cup of** shredded carrots
- 1/4 **cup of split** green onions

Instructions:
1. **Combine** the teriyaki sauce, sesame oil, soy sauce, honey, **chop-up** garlic, and **finely grated** ginger in a **mini** bowl.
2. For around 10 **mins**, marinate the salmon fillets in half the sauce.
3. Set the oven's temperature to 375°F (190°C). Sesame seeds **Must** be added to the salmon fillets before placing them on a baking pan.
4. Salmon **Must** be baked for 15 to 20 **mins**, or **up to** fully done.
5. Layer the cooked white rice, broccoli, shredded carrots, **split** green onions, and the rest of the teriyaki sauce in two Mason jars.
6. **Every** jar **Must** have a grilled salmon fillet on top.
7. Prior to serving, seal the jars and place them in the refrigerator.

Nutrition (per serving):
Cals: 400 kcal, Fat: 15g

Carbs: 40g

Protein: 30g, Fiber: 4g

198. Layered Ratatouille

Prep Time: 20 mins

Cook Time: 40 mins

Total Time: 1 hr

Servings: 4

Ingredients:
- 1 **Big** eggplant, **split**

- 2 medium zucchinis, **split**
- 2 **Big** tomatoes, **split**
- 1 red bell pepper, **split**
- 1 yellow bell pepper, **split**
- 1/4 **cup of** olive oil
- 2 cloves garlic, **chop-up**
- 1 **tbsp** fresh thyme leaves
- Salt and pepper **as needed**
- 1 **cup of** tomato sauce
- 1/2 **cup of** shredded mozzarella cheese

Instructions:
1. Set the oven's temperature to 375°F (190°C).
2. Olive oil **Must** be heated in a sizable skillet over medium heat. When aromatic, add the **chop-up** garlic and stir for one to two **mins**.
3. **Split** tomatoes, red and yellow bell peppers, eggplant, zucchini, and other vegetables, and add to the skillet. Add fresh thyme leaves, pepper, and salt **as needed**. Cook the vegetables for about 5 **mins**, or **up to** they start to soften.
4. Layer the cooked vegetables in a baking dish, rotating between several vegetable varieties.
5. Make sure the tomato sauce is distributed evenly when you pour it over the layers of vegetables.
6. Add some mozzarella cheese shredded on top.
7. Bake for 30-35 **mins** in a preheated oven, or **up to** the cheese is bubbling and golden.

Nutrition (per serving):
Cals: 220 kcal, Fat: 15g

Carbs: 18g

Protein: 6g, Fiber: 6g

199. Mason Jar Egg Fried Rice

Prep Time: 10 mins

Cook Time: 15 mins

Total Time: 25 mins

Servings: 2

Ingredients:
- 2 **cups of** cooked white rice
- 2 **tbsp** vegetable oil
- 2 **Big** eggs, beaten
- 1 **cup of refrigerate combined** vegetables (peas, carrots, corn)
- 2 **tbsp** soy sauce
- 1 **tbsp** oyster sauce (**non-compulsory**)
- 1/2 **tsp** garlic powder
- 1/2 **tsp** onion powder
- 1/4 **cup of chop-up** green onions

Instructions:
1. In a sizable skillet or wok, heat one **tbsp** of vegetable oil over medium heat.

2. Add the scrambled eggs and heat them through **up to** done. The eggs **Must** be taken out of the skillet and put aside.
3. Stir-fry the **refrigerate combined** vegetables in the same skillet with an additional **tbsp** of vegetable oil **up to** heated through.
4. When adding the cooked white rice to the skillet, use a spatula to separate any clumps.
5. Rice **Must** be covered with soy sauce and oyster sauce, if using.
6. Stir the rice as you sprinkle on the garlic and onion powders to incorporate the flavors.
7. After turning off the heat, let the fried rice cool in the skillet.
8. Construction in Mason jars:
9. Layer the cooked egg fried rice in two Mason jars.
10. Add **chop-up** green onions to the top of **every** jar.
11. Prior to serving, seal the jars and place them in the refrigerator.

Nutrition (per serving):
Cals: 380 kcal, Fat: 15g, **Carbs**: 48g
Protein: 12g, Fiber: 4g

200. Mason Jar Shrimp and Quinoa Bowl

Prep Time: 15 **min**s
Cook Time: 20 **min**s
Total Time: 35 **min**s
Servings: 2

Ingredients:
- 1 **cup of** quinoa, rinsed
- 1 3/4 **cups of** water or vegetable broth
- 1 **tbsp** olive oil
- 1/2 **lb** medium shrimp, **peel off** and deveined
- 1 **tsp** paprika
- 1/2 **tsp** garlic powder
- Salt and pepper **as needed**
- 1 **cup of** cherry tomatoes, halved
- 1 **cup of** cucumber, diced
- 1/4 **cup of** feta cheese, **cut up**
- 2 **tbsp chop-up** fresh parsley

Instructions:
1. Bring the water or vegetable broth to a boil in a medium saucepan. Add a dash of salt and the rinsed quinoa. Once the quinoa is cooked and the liquid has been absorbed, lower the heat to low, cover the pan, and simmer for 15 to 20 **min**s.
2. Olive oil **Must** be heated in a different skillet over a medium-high heat. Add the shrimp and season with salt, pepper, paprika, and garlic powder. The shrimp **Must** be cooked for two to three **min**s on **every** side, or **up to** pink and opaque.

3. Layer the cooked quinoa, cooked shrimp, cherry tomatoes, cucumber, feta cheese, and fresh parsley in two Mason jars.
4. Prior to serving, seal the jars and place them in the refrigerator.

Nutrition (per serving):
Cals: 420 kcal, Fat: 15g
Carbs: 50g, Protein: 25g, Fiber: 7g

201. Layered BBQ Pulled Pork with Coleslaw

Prep Time: 20 **min**s
Cook Time: 4 **hr**s
Total Time: 4 **hr**s 20 **min**s
Servings: 4

Ingredients:
- 1 1/2 **lb**s pork **Must**er or pork butt
- 1 **cup of** BBQ sauce
- 1/2 **cup of** chicken broth or water
- 4 hamburger buns or slider buns
- 1 **cup of** coleslaw

Instructions:
1. Salt and pepper **Must** be used to season the pork **Must**er or pig butt.
2. Put the seasoned pork in a slow cooker and cover it with water or chicken stock.
3. Pork **Must** be soft and easy to tear apart after 8 **hr**s of cooking on low heat or 4 **hr**s on high heat.
4. Using two forks, **take out** the pork from the slow cooker and shred it.
5. The BBQ sauce **Must** be warmed up in a skillet over low heat. When the pork is properly coated, add it to the sauce and toss.
6. Layer the coleslaw with BBQ pulled pork in four serving bowls or Mason jars.
7. Serve the pulled pork on slider or hamburger buns.

Nutrition (per serving):
Cals: 600 kcal, Fat: 25g, **Carbs**: 50g
Protein: 45g, Fiber: 3g

202. Layered Caprese Chicken

Prep Time: 15 **min**s
Cook Time: 25 **min**s
Total Time: 40 **min**s
Servings: 4

Ingredients:
- 4 boneless, skinless chicken breasts

- 2 **Big** tomatoes, **split**
- 8 oz fresh mozzarella cheese, **split**
- Fresh basil leaves
- Balsamic glaze
- Salt and pepper **as needed**

Instructions:

1. Set the oven's temperature to 375°F (190°C).
2. Chicken breasts **Must** be salted and peppered.
3. Place **every** chicken breast in a baking dish and top with **split** tomatoes, fresh mozzarella, and basil leaves.
4. Balsamic glaze **Must** be drizzled on top.
5. Bake for 25 **min**s in a preheated oven, or **up to** the cheese is **dilute** and bubbling and the chicken is thoroughly cooked.
6. Serving hot, please.

Nutrition (per serving):

Cals: 350 kcal, Fat: 15g

Carbs: 8g, Protein: 40g

203.Mason Jar Honey Mustard Chicken

Prep Time: 10 **min**s

Cook Time: 20 **min**s

Total Time: 30 **min**s

Servings: 2

Ingredients:

- 2 boneless, skinless chicken breasts, **slice** into bite-sized pieces
- 2 **tbsp** Dijon mustard
- 1 **tbsp** honey
- 1 **tbsp** olive oil
- 1 clove garlic, **chop-up**
- Salt and pepper **as needed**
- Fresh parsley for garnish (**non-compulsory**)

Instructions:

1. **Combine** the Dijon mustard, honey, olive oil, garlic powder, salt, and pepper in a bowl.
2. When the chicken pieces are thoroughly coated, add them to the **Mixture** and toss again.
3. The chicken has been marinated, so heat a skillet over medium heat.
4. Cook the chicken for 15 to 20 **min**s, or **up to** it is thoroughly cooked and beginning to caramelize.
5. If desired, garnish with fresh parsley.
6. For a colorful presentation, serve the honey mustard chicken in Mason jars.

Nutrition (per serving):

Cals: 320 kcal, Fat: 12g, **Carb**s: 15g

Protein: 38g

204.Mason Jar BBQ Chicken with Cornbread

Prep Time: 15 **min**s

Cook Time: 25 **min**s

Total Time: 40 **min**s

Servings: 2

Ingredients:

- 2 boneless, skinless chicken breasts, diced
- 1/2 **cup of** BBQ sauce
- 1 **cup of** cornbread **combine**
- 1/3 **cup of** milk
- 1 egg
- 1/2 **cup of** corn kernels (fresh, canned, or **refrigerate**)
- Salt and pepper **as needed**
- Fresh cilantro for garnish (**non-compulsory**)

Instructions:

1. Set the oven's temperature to 375°F (190°C).
2. Cornbread **combine**, milk, egg, corn kernels, salt, and pepper **Must** all be thoroughly blended in a bowl.
3. Chicken dice **Must** be covered uniformly in BBQ sauce in a separate bowl.
4. The BBQ chicken **Mixture Must** be placed halfway up **every** Mason jar.
5. Fill the jar roughly three-quarters full with the cornmeal batter before pouring it over the chicken.
6. The Mason jars **Must** be baked for 20 to 25 **min**s, or **up to** the cornbread is golden and the chicken is thoroughly cooked.
7. If desired, garnish with fresh cilantro.

Nutrition (per serving):

Cals: 450 kcal, Fat: 10g

Carbs: 55g

Protein: 35g

205.Mason Jar Garlic Butter Shrimp

Prep Time: 10 **min**s

Cook Time: 10 **min**s

Total Time: 20 **min**s

Servings: 2

Ingredients:

- 1 lb **Big** shrimp, **peel off** and deveined
- 4 **tbsp** unsalted butter, **dilute**
- 4 cloves garlic, **chop-up**
- 1 **tbsp** lemon juice
- 1 **tbsp chop-up** parsley
- Salt and pepper **as needed**
- Cooked rice or pasta for serving

Instructions:

1. Set the oven's temperature to 375°F (190°C).

2. **Dilute** butter, **chop-up** garlic, lemon juice, parsley that has been **slice**, salt, and pepper **Must** all be **combine**d in a bowl.
3. The shrimp **Must** be thoroughly coated before being added to the garlic butter **Mixture**.
4. Between two Mason jars, distribute the shrimp and garlic butter **Mixture** equally.
5. Bake the Mason jars for 8 to 10 **min**s, or **up to** the shrimp are pink and cooked all the way through.
6. Serve the shrimp with garlic and butter over cooked pasta or rice.

Nutrition (per serving):
Cals: 350 kcal, Fat: 20g

Carbs: 3g

Protein: 35g

206.Layered Lemon Dill Salmon

Prep Time: 15 **min**s

Cook Time: 15 **min**s

Total Time: 30 **min**s

Servings: 4

Ingredients:
- 4 salmon fillets
- 1 lemon, thinly **split**
- 2 **tbsp** olive oil
- 2 **tbsp** fresh dill, **chop-up**
- Salt and pepper **as needed**

Instructions:
1. Set the oven's temperature to 375°F (190°C).
2. Add salt and pepper to the salmon fillets.
3. Slices of lemon **Must** be layered in a baking dish, and then some **chop-up** dill **Must** be added.
4. On top of the lemon and dill layer, arrange the salmon fillets with seasoning.
5. Add extra lemon slices and dill on top of the salmon after drizzling it with olive oil.
6. Bake for about 15 **min**s, or **up to** the salmon is cooked through and flakes readily with a fork, in the preheated oven.
7. If desired, add more fresh dill to the serving dish as a garnish.

Nutrition (per serving):
Cals: 300 kcal, Fat: 18g, **Carb**s: 2g

Protein: 32g

207.Mason Jar Chicken Caesar Wraps

Prep Time: 15 **min**s

Cook Time: 0 **min**s

Total Time: 15 **min**s

Servings: 2

Ingredients:
- 1 **cup of** cooked chicken, shredded or diced
- 1/2 **cup of** cherry tomatoes, halved
- 1/4 **cup of finely grated** Parmesan cheese
- 1/4 **cup of** Caesar dressing
- 1 **cup of** romaine lettuce, **chop-up**
- 1/4 **cup of** croutons
- 2 **Big** whole wheat tortillas

Instructions:
1. **Combine** the cooked chicken, cherry tomatoes, and Caesar dressing in a **combining** dish. Toss to thoroughly coat.
2. Divide the chicken **Mixture** equally between two mason jars.
3. Over the chicken **Mixture** in **every** jar, arrange the **chop-up** romaine lettuce.
4. Croutons and freshly **finely grated** Parmesan cheese **Must** be added to the greens.
5. The whole wheat tortillas **Must** be tightly rolled before being **slice** into bite-sized pieces. **Every** mason jar **Must** have the tortilla pieces added to the top.
6. Prior to serving, seal the Mason jars and place in the refrigerator.
7. Shake the jar's contents to **combine** everything before you start eating the wraps. After that, either serve the **Mixture** directly from the jar or onto a platter.

NUTRITION INFO (per serving):
Cals: 380 kcal **Carb**s: 22g Protein: 26g Fat: 20g Saturated Fat: 5g Cholesterol: 75mg Sodium: 850mg Fiber: 3g Sugar: 3g

208.Mason Jar Buffalo Chicken Wrap

Prep Time: 15 **min**s

Cook Time: 0 **min**s

Total Time: 15 **min**s

Servings: 2

Ingredients:
- 1 **cup of** cooked chicken, shredded
- 1/4 **cup of** buffalo sauce
- 1/2 **cup of** shredded carrots
- 1/2 **cup of** celery, thinly **split**
- 1/4 **cup of** blue cheese dressing
- 1 **cup of** lettuce, shredded
- 2 **Big** whole wheat tortillas

Instructions:
1. Buffalo sauce **Must** be well **combine**d with the cooked chicken in a bowl.
2. Divide the buffalo chicken evenly between two mason jars.

3. Over the chicken in **every** jar, arrange the celery slices and carrot shreds.
4. Over the vegetables, drizzle the blue cheese dressing.
5. **Every** jar of dressing **Must** have the lettuce shreds added on top.
6. The whole wheat tortillas **Must** be tightly rolled before being **slice** into bite-sized pieces. **Every** mason jar **Must** have the tortilla pieces added to the top.
7. Prior to serving, seal the Mason jars and place in the refrigerator.
8. Shake the jar's contents to **combine** everything before you start eating the wrap. After that, either serve the **Mixture** directly from the jar or onto a platter.

NUTRITION INFO (per serving):
Cals: 420 kcal **Carb**s: 27g Protein: 24g Fat: 25g Saturated Fat: 8g Cholesterol: 80mg Sodium: 1550mg Fiber: 4g Sugar: 5g

209.Layered Veggie Burrito Bowl

Prep Time: 20 **min**s

Cook Time: 10 **min**s

Total Time: 30 **min**s

Servings: 2

Ingredients:

- 1 **cup of** cooked brown rice
- 1 **cup of** black beans, canned or cooked
- 1 **cup of** corn kernels, cooked
- 1 **cup of** cherry tomatoes, halved
- 1 avocado, diced
- 1/4 **cup of** red onion, **lightly chop-up**
- 1/4 **cup of** fresh cilantro, **chop-up**
- 1/4 **cup of** lime juice
- Salt and pepper **as needed**
- 1/4 **cup of** Greek yogurt (**non-compulsory**, for topping)

Instructions:

1. The avocado salsa is made by combining diced avocado, red onion, fresh cilantro, lime juice, salt, and pepper in a **mini** bowl.
2. Starting with two mason jars, layer the burrito bowl. Put half of the brown rice that has been cooked at the bottom of **every** jar to start.
3. On top of the rice in **every** jar, layer half **every** of the black beans, corn, and cherry tomatoes.
4. Fill **every** container with half of the avocado salsa.
5. For the second half of the ingredients, repeat the layers in the same manner.

6. Before closing the jars, you might add a dollop of Greek yogurt to **every** mason jar burrito bowl.
7. Prior to serving, seal the Mason jars and place in the refrigerator.
8. Shake the contents of the jar to **combine** everything before serving the burrito bowl. After that, either serve the **Mixture** directly from the jar or onto a platter.

NUTRITION INFO (per serving):
Cals: 450 kcal **Carb**s: 65g Protein: 16g Fat: 17g Saturated Fat: 2g Cholesterol: 0mg Sodium: 140mg Fiber: 17g Sugar: 7g

210.Mason Jar Teriyaki Tofu with Veggies

Prep Time: 30 **min**s

Cook Time: 20 **min**s

Total Time: 50 **min**s

Servings: 2

Ingredients:

- 1 **cup of** extra-firm tofu, cubed
- 1/4 **cup of** teriyaki sauce
- 1 **cup of** broccoli florets, steamed
- 1 **cup of** bell peppers, **split**
- 1 **cup of** cooked quinoa
- 1/4 **cup of** green onions, **chop-up**
- 2 **tsp** sesame seeds
- 1 **tbsp** vegetable oil

Instructions:

1. For around 15 **min**s, marinate the cubed tofu in teriyaki sauce in a bowl.
2. The marinated tofu **Must** be sautéed in a pan with vegetable oil over medium heat **up to** it turns crispy and golden brown on all sides.
3. Start stacking the teriyaki tofu bowl using two mason jars. In **every** jar, start by placing half of the cooked quinoa at the bottom.
4. On top of the quinoa in **every** jar, distribute half of the sautéed teriyaki tofu, steamed broccoli florets, and thinly **split** bell peppers.
5. **Every** jar **Must** contain half of the **chop-up** green onions and sesame seeds.
6. For the second half of the ingredients, repeat the layers in the same manner.
7. Prior to serving, seal the Mason jars and place in the refrigerator.
8. Shake the contents of the jar to **combine** everything before serving the teriyaki tofu bowl. After that, either serve the **Mixture** directly from the jar or onto a platter.

NUTRITION INFO (per serving):
Cals: 420 kcal **Carb**s: 45g Protein: 20g Fat: 18g Saturated

Fat: 2g Cholesterol: 0mg Sodium: 750mg Fiber: 8g Sugar: 10g

211. Mason Jar Lemon Herb Chicken

Prep Time: 25 **min**s

Cook Time: 25 **min**s

Total Time: 50 **min**s

Servings: 2

Ingredients:

- 2 boneless, skinless chicken breasts
- 2 **tbsp** olive oil
- 2 cloves garlic, **chop-up**
- 1 lemon, juiced and zested
- 1 **tsp** dried oregano
- 1 **tsp** dried thyme
- 1/2 **tsp** salt
- 1/4 **tsp** black pepper
- 1 **cup of** cherry tomatoes, halved
- 1 **cup of** cucumber, diced
- 1/4 **cup of** red onion, thinly **split**
- 1/4 **cup of** feta cheese, **cut up**
- 2 **cups of** cooked quinoa

Instructions:

1. To make the marinade, **combine** the olive oil, crushed garlic, lemon juice, lemon zest, dried thyme, dried oregano, salt, and black pepper in a bowl.
2. The chicken breasts **Must** be added to the marinade and left to sit for approximately 15 **min**s.
3. The marinated chicken breasts **Must** be grilled **up to** fully done and have grill marks on both sides on a medium-hot grill or pan.
4. Before slicing the cooked chicken into thin strips, **let** it to rest for a few **min**s.
5. Start layering the lemon herb chicken dish in two mason jars. In **every** jar, start by placing half of the cooked quinoa at the bottom.
6. On top of the quinoa in **every** jar, place half of the thinly **split** lemon herb chicken, cherry tomatoes, diced cucumber, and thinly **split** red onion.
7. **Every** jar **Must** include half of the feta cheese **cut ups**.

8. For the second half of the ingredients, repeat the layers in the same manner.
9. Prior to serving, seal the Mason jars and place in the refrigerator.
10. Shake the contents of the jar to **combine** everything before serving the lemon herb chicken dish. After that, either serve the **Mixture** directly from the jar or onto a platter.

NUTRITION INFO (per serving):

Cals: 480 kcal **Carb**s: 43g Protein: 35g Fat: 19g Saturated Fat: 5g Cholesterol: 85mg Sodium: 660mg Fiber: 8g Sugar: 6g

212. Mason Jar Chili Lime Shrimp

Prep Time: 15 **min**s

Cook Time: 5 **min**s

Total Time: 20 **min**s

Servings: 2

Ingredients:

- 1 **lb Big** shrimp, **peel off** and deveined
- 2 **tbsp** olive oil
- 2 cloves garlic, **chop-up**
- 1 **tsp** chili powder
- 1/2 **tsp** cumin
- Zest and juice of 1 lime
- Salt and pepper **as needed**
- 1/4 **cup of chop-up** fresh cilantro
- 1/4 **cup of** diced red bell pepper
- 1/4 **cup of** diced green bell pepper
- 1/4 **cup of** diced red onion
- 1/4 **cup of** diced avocado

Instructions:

1. Olive oil, **chop-up** garlic, cumin, chili powder, lime juice, zest, and salt and pepper **Must** all be **combine**d in a bowl.
2. Toss the shrimp in the marinade after adding them to the bowl. Give it ten **min**s to rest.
3. The marinated shrimp are added to a skillet that is already heated to medium-high. Cook for two to three **min**s on **every** side, or **up to** they are opaque and pink.
4. Layer the cooked shrimp with the **chop-up** cilantro, bell pepper, red onion, and avocado in Mason jars.
5. Prior to serving, seal the jars and place them in the refrigerator. Before you eat, lightly shake.

Nutrition (per serving):

Cals: 280 kcal, **Carb**s: 6g, Protein: 25g

Fat: 17g, Saturated Fat: 2.5g, Cholesterol: 220mg

Fiber: 2g, Sugar: 1g, Sodium: 420mg

213. Mason Jar Pesto Shrimp with Pasta

Prep Time: 20 **min**s

Cook Time: 10 **min**s

Total Time: 30 **min**s

Servings: 2

Ingredients:
- 8 oz cooked pasta (e.g., spaghetti or penne)
- 1/2 **lb** cooked shrimp, **peel off** and deveined
- 1/4 **cup of** pesto sauce
- 1 **cup of** cherry tomatoes, halved
- 1/4 **cup of split** black olives
- 1/4 **cup of cut up** feta cheese
- Fresh basil leaves for garnish

Instructions:
1. Pasta **Must** be cooked as directed on the **box/pkg up to** it is al dente. Let it cool and then drain.
2. The cooked pasta, shrimp, pesto sauce, cherry tomatoes, and black olives **Must** all be **combine**d in a bowl.
3. Layer the spaghetti and shrimp **Mixture** in Mason jars, then top with feta cheese **cut up**s.
4. Fresh basil leaves are a nice garnish.
5. Prior to serving, seal the jars and place them in the refrigerator.

Nutrition (per serving):
Cals: 450 kcal, **Carb**s: 39g, Protein: 25g

Fat: 21g, Saturated Fat: 6g, Cholesterol: 170mg

Fiber: 4g, Sugar: 3g, Sodium: 530mg

214.Layered S'mores Dessert

Prep Time: 15 **min**s

Cook Time: 0 **min**s

Total Time: 15 **min**s

Servings: 2

Ingredients:
- 1 **cup of** graham cracker crumbs
- 1/4 **cup of dilute** butter
- 1 **cup of** chocolate pudding (store-bought or homemade)
- 1 **cup of** mini marshm**let**s
- 1/4 **cup of** chocolate chips
- 1/4 **cup of** crushed graham crackers for topping

Instructions:
1. Graham cracker crumbs and **dilute** butter **Must** be **combine**d in a bowl **up to** the crumbs are thoroughly covered.
2. Layer the graham cracker **Mixture**, chocolate pudding, miniature marshm**let**s, and chocolate chips in Mason jars.
3. Till the jars are full, keep adding layers.
4. Add crushed Graham crackers on top.
5. Keep chilled **up to** you're ready to serve.

Nutrition (per serving):
Cals: 400 kcal, **Carb**s: 55g

Protein: 3g, Fat: 20g, Saturated Fat: 12g

Cholesterol: 25mg, Fiber: 2g, Sugar: 36g

Sodium: 280mg

215.Mason Jar Banana Split Parfait

Prep Time: 15 **min**s

Cook Time: 0 **min**s

Total Time: 15 **min**s

Servings: 2

Ingredients:
- 2 ripe bananas, **split**
- 1 **cup of** vanilla yogurt
- 1/2 **cup of** diced fresh pineapple
- 1/2 **cup of split** fresh strawberries
- 1/4 **cup of** chocolate sauce
- 1/4 **cup of chop-up** nuts (e.g., walnuts or almonds)
- Whipped cream for topping
- Maraschino cherries for garnish

Instructions:
1. Layer the diced pineapple, strawberries, diced bananas, and vanilla yogurt in Mason jars.
2. Over the layers of fruit and yogurt, drizzle chocolate sauce.
3. Layer on some **chop-up** nuts.
4. Maraschino cherries are the finishing touch. Add whipped cream on top.
5. Serve right now or keep chilled **up to** you're ready to eat.

Nutrition (per serving):
Cals: 380 kcal, **Carb**s: 60g, Protein: 8g

Fat: 13g, Saturated Fat: 4g, Cholesterol: 15mg, Fiber: 6g

Sugar: 40g, Sodium: 80mg

216.Mason Jar Lemon Raspberry Trifle

Prep Time: 20 **min**s

Cook Time: 0 **min**s

Total Time: 20 **min**s

Servings: 2

Ingredients:
- 1 **cup of** lemon curd (store-bought or homemade)
- 1 **cup of** whipped cream
- 1 **cup of** fresh raspberries
- 1/2 **cup of** crushed shortbread cookies
- Lemon zest for garnish

Instructions:

1. Lemon curd, whipped cream, fresh raspberries, and shortbread biscuits **Must** all be layered in Mason jars.
2. Till the jars are full, keep adding layers.
3. Add lemon zest as a garnish.
4. Keep chilled **up to** you're ready to serve.

Nutrition (per serving

Cals: 480 kcal, **Carb**s: 53g, Protein: 4g

Fat: 28g, Saturated Fat: 16g, Cholesterol: 95mg

Fiber: 5g, Sugar: 36g, Sodium: 210mg

217.Layered Strawberry Cheesecake

Prep Time: 30 **min**s

Cook Time: 0 **min**s

Total Time: 4 **hr**s 30 **min**s (includes chilling time)

Servings: 4

Ingredients:

- 1 1/2 **cups of** graham cracker crumbs
- 1/4 **cup of** granulated sugar
- 1/2 **cup of** unsalted butter, **dilute**
- 1 **cup of** strawberries, hulled and **split**
- 16 oz cream cheese, **melted**
- 1 **cup of** powdered sugar
- 1 tsp vanilla extract
- 1 1/2 **cups of** heavy cream

Instructions:

1. Crumbs from Graham Crackers, Granulated Sugar, and **Dilute** Butter are **combine**d in a medium basin. **Combine** thoroughly.
2. To make an even crust layer, press the **Mixture** into the bottom of 4 mason jars.
3. Cream cheese, powdered sugar, and vanilla extract **Must** be **combine**d in a different basin and **combined** thoroughly.
4. Whip the heavy cream to stiff peaks in a separate dish.
5. Till everything is completely blended, gently fold the whipped cream into the cream cheese **Mixture**.
6. Repeat layering **up to** the cream cheese **Mixture** and **split** strawberries are on top of the crust in the mason jars.
7. To enable the flavors to mingle, cover the jars and place them in the refrigerator for at least 4 **hr**s or overnight.
8. Enjoy while serving chilled!

NUTRITION INFO (per serving):

Cals: 580 kcal, Fat: 45g, **Carb**s: 38g

Protein: 8g, Fiber: 2g

218. Mason Jar Tiramisu

Prep Time: 20 **min**s

Cook Time: 0 **min**s

Total Time: 2 **hr**s 20 **min**s (includes chilling time)

Servings: 4

Ingredients:

- 1 **cup of** heavy cream
- 1/2 **cup of** powdered sugar
- 8 oz mascarpone cheese
- 1 tsp vanilla extract
- 1 **cup of** strong brewed coffee, cooled
- 2 tbsp coffee liqueur (**non-compulsory**)
- 16 to 20 ladyfinger cookies
- Cocoa powder, for dusting

Instructions:

1. Whip the heavy cream and sugar **up to** soft peaks form in a big bowl.
2. The whipped cream **Must** be **combine**d with the mascarpone cheese and vanilla essence. Whip **up to** stiff peaks form.
3. Coffee liqueur (if using) and freshly made coffee **Must** be **combine**d in a **mini** dish.
4. To avoid soaking them too much, briefly dip **every** ladyfinger biscuit into the coffee **Mixture**.
5. **Every** Mason jar **Must** have a layer of dipped ladyfingers at the bottom.
6. On top of the ladyfingers, spoon a layer of the whipped cream **Mixture**.
7. Up **up to** the jars are full, add the ingredients again, finishing with a layer of whipped cream.
8. Using a fine strainer, sprinkle cocoa powder over the top.
9. Before serving, put the jars in the fridge for at least two **hr**s.
10. Enjoy while serving chilled!

NUTRITION INFO (per serving):

Cals: 540 kcal, Fat: 40g, **Carb**s: 35g

Protein: 6g, Fiber: 1g

219.Mason Jar Key Lime Pie

Prep Time: 20 **min**s

Cook Time: 12 **min**s

Total Time: 2 **hr**s 32 **min**s (includes chilling time)

Servings: 4

Ingredients:

- 1 1/2 **cups of** graham cracker crumbs
- 1/4 **cup of** granulated sugar
- 1/2 **cup of** unsalted butter, **dilute**
- 3/4 **cup of** key lime juice
- 2 tsp lime zest

- 14 oz sweetened condensed milk
- 1 **cup of** heavy cream
- 2 tbsp powdered sugar
- Lime slices and additional zest for garnish (**non-compulsory**)

Instructions:

1. Crumbs from Graham Crackers, Granulated Sugar, and **Dilute** Butter are **combine**d in a medium basin. **Combine** thoroughly.
2. To make an even crust layer, press the **Mixture** into the bottom of 4 mason jars.
3. **Combine** the key lime juice, lime zest, and sweetened condensed milk thoroughly in a another bowl.
4. The graham cracker crust in the mason jars **Must** be covered with the lime **Mixture**.
5. Whip the heavy cream and powdered sugar in a separate bowl **up to** stiff peaks form.
6. Create a top layer by spooning the whipped cream over the lime filling in the jars.
7. If desired, garnish with lime slices and more zest.
8. Before serving, put the jars in the fridge for at least two **hr**s.
9. Enjoy while serving chilled!

NUTRITION INFO (per serving):
Cals: 740 kcal, Fat: 50g, **Carb**s: 65g

Protein: 8g, Fiber: 1g

220.Layered Chocolate Mousse

Prep Time: 30 **min**s

Cook Time: 5 **min**s

Total Time: 2 **hr**s 35 **min**s (includes chilling time)

Servings: 4

Ingredients:

- 6 oz semisweet chocolate, **chop-up**
- 3 **cups of** heavy cream, **slice up**
- 1 tsp vanilla extract
- 2 tbsp powdered sugar
- 4 chocolate cookies, crushed
- Chocolate shavings, for garnish (**non-compulsory**)

Instructions:

1. The **chop-up** semisweet chocolate and 1 **cup of** of heavy cream **Must** be **dilute** in a microwave-safe basin while being stirred **up to** smooth. **Let** it to cool a little.
2. 2 **cups of** heavy cream, sugar, and vanilla extract **Must** be whipped in a another basin **up to** stiff peaks form.
3. Once the whipped cream and chocolate **Mixture** are thoroughly blended, gently fold them together.

4. Four Mason jars **Must every** have a layer of chocolate mousse in the bottom.
5. **Every** jar of mousse **Must** have a layer of crushed chocolate cookies on top.
6. The layers are repeated **up to** the jars are full, and then a layer of chocolate mousse is placed on top.
7. If desired, add chocolate shavings as a garnish.
8. Before serving, put the jars in the fridge for at least two **hr**s.
9. Enjoy while serving chilled!

NUTRITION INFO (per serving):
Cals: 770 kcal, Fat: 67g, **Carb**s: 41g

Protein: 6g, Fiber: 2g

221.Mason Jar Combined Berry Crisp

Prep Time: 15 **min**s

Cook Time: 25 **min**s

Total Time: 40 **min**s

Servings: 4

Ingredients:

- 2 **cups of combined** berries (strawberries, blueberries, raspberries, blackberries)
- 1 tbsp granulated sugar
- 1 tsp lemon juice
- 1/2 **cup of** all-purpose flour
- 1/4 **cup of** old-fashioned oats
- 1/4 **cup of** packed brown sugar
- 1/4 tsp ground cinnamon
- Pinch of salt
- 1/4 **cup of** unsalted butter, chilled and **slice** into **mini** pieces
- Whipped cream or vanilla ice cream, for serving (**non-compulsory**)

Instructions:

1. Set your oven's temperature to 375°F (190°C).
2. The **combined** berries **Must** be thoroughly covered with granulated sugar and lemon juice in a medium bowl.
3. Give **every** mason jar an equal amount of the berry **Mixture**.
4. **Combine** the all-purpose flour, oats, brown sugar, cinnamon, and salt in a different bowl.
5. Use your fingers to integrate the cooled butter chunks into the flour **Mixture up to** it resembles coarse crumbs.
6. The berries in the mason jars **Must** be covered with the crumb topping.
7. The jars **Must** be baked for 20 to 25 **min**s in the preheated oven, or **up to** the berries are bubbling and the topping is golden brown.
8. Take out of the oven, then **let** it cool somewhat.

9. If desired, serve warm with vanilla ice cream or whipped cream.

NUTRITION INFO *(per serving)*:

Cals: 310 kcal, Fat: 13g, **Carb**s: 47g

Protein: 3g, Fiber: 4g

222.Mason Jar Pumpkin Pie

Prep Time: 20 **min**s

Cook Time: 40 **min**s

Total Time: 1 **hr**

Servings: 4

Ingredients:

- 1 **cup of** pumpkin puree
- 1/2 **cup of** granulated sugar
- 1/2 **tsp** salt
- 1 **tsp** ground cinnamon
- 1/2 **tsp** ground ginger
- 1/4 **tsp** ground cloves
- 2 **Big** eggs
- 1 **cup of** evaporated milk
- 1 9-inch unbaked pie crust (store-bought or homemade)

Instructions:

1. Turn on the oven to 425 °F (220 °C).
2. Pumpkin puree, sugar, salt, cinnamon, ginger, and cloves **Must** all be **combine**d in a **combining** dish.
3. Add the eggs and **combine** thoroughly before adding the evaporated milk.
4. Roll out the pie dough and **slice** out circles that will fit within the Mason jar mouths using a jar lid or cookie **slice**ter.
5. In **every** Mason jar, firmly press the pie crust rounds into the bottom.
6. **Every** jar **Must** be about two-thirds full after being filled with the pumpkin filling.
7. On a baking sheet, arrange the filled jars and bake for 15 **min**s.
8. Bake the pie for a further 25 **min**s or **up to** the filling is set at 350°F (175°C) in the oven.
9. Before serving, take the pies out of the oven and let them cool fully.

NUTRITION INFO *(per serving)*:

Cals: 320 kcal, Fat: 14g, **Carb**s: 45g

Protein: 6g

223.Mason Jar Chocolate Chip Cookies

Prep Time: 15 **min**s

Cook Time: 12 **min**s

Total Time: 27 **min**s

Servings: 6

Ingredients:

- 1/2 **cup of** unsalted butter, **melted**
- 1/2 **cup of** granulated sugar
- 1/2 **cup of** brown sugar, packed
- 1 **Big** egg
- 1 **tsp** vanilla extract
- 1 1/2 **cups of** all-purpose flour
- 1/2 **tsp** baking soda
- 1/4 **tsp** salt
- 3/4 **cup of** chocolate chips

Instructions:

1. **Melted** butter, granulated sugar, and brown sugar **Must** be creamed **up to** light and fluffy in a **combining** dish.
2. **Combine** the egg and vanilla extract thoroughly before adding them.
3. **Combine** the salt, baking soda, and flour in a separate basin.
4. **Combine** just till **combined** after gradually incorporating the dry ingredients into the wet ones.
5. Add the chocolate chunks and stir.
6. Make six equal amounts of the cookie dough, and then roll **every** one into a ball.
7. **Every** cookie dough ball **Must** be pressed into the Mason jar's base.
8. The filled jars **Must** be placed on a baking sheet and baked for 12 **min**s, or **up to** the edges are golden brown, in a 350°F (175°C) preheated oven.
9. Before serving, let the cookies cool somewhat.

NUTRITION INFO *(per serving)*:

Cals: 420 kcal, Fat: 21g, **Carb**s: 55g

Protein: 5g

224.Layered Red Velvet Cake

Prep Time: 30 **min**s

Cook Time: 25 **min**s

Total Time: 55 **min**s

Servings: 12

Ingredients:

- 2 1/2 **cups of** all-purpose flour
- 1 1/2 **cups of** granulated sugar
- 1 **tsp** baking powder
- 1 **tsp** baking soda
- 1 **tsp** cocoa powder
- 1 **tsp** salt

- 1 1/2 **cups of** vegetable oil
- 1 **cup of** buttermilk
- 2 **Big** eggs
- 1 **tsp** vanilla extract
- 1 **tbsp** red food coloring
- 1 **tsp** white vinegar
- Cream cheese frosting
- Red velvet cake crumbs (for garnish, **non-compulsory**)

Instructions:

1. Turn on the oven to 350 °F (175 °C). Prepare three 8-inch cake pans with butter and flour.
2. **Combine** the flour, sugar, baking powder, baking soda, cocoa powder, and salt in a sizable **combining** basin.
3. **Combine** the vegetable oil, buttermilk, eggs, vanilla extract, red food coloring, and white vinegar in a separate basin.
4. **Combine up to** the batter is smooth, then gradually add the wet components to the dry ones.
5. Give **every** of the three prepared cake pans an equal amount of the batter.
6. A toothpick put into the center of the cakes **Must** come out clean after about 25 **min**s of baking.
7. The cakes **Must** cool in the pans for ten **min**s before being **take out**d to a wire rack to finish cooling.
8. Spread a substantial amount of cream cheese frosting between **every** layer when the cakes have completely cooled before assembling the layered cake.
9. More cream cheese frosting **Must** be used to coat the cake's top and sides. If preferred, red velvet cake crumbs can be used as a garnish.

NUTRITION INFO (per serving, cake only):
Cals: 480 kcal, Fat: 26g

Carbs: 58g

Protein: 6g

225.Mason Jar Carrot Cake

Prep Time: 20 **min**s

Cook Time: 25 **min**s

Total Time: 45 **min**s

Servings: 4

Ingredients:

- 1 **cup of** all-purpose flour
- 1 **tsp** baking powder
- 1/2 **tsp** baking soda
- 1/2 **tsp** ground cinnamon
- 1/4 **tsp** ground nutmeg
- 1/4 **tsp** salt

- 1/2 **cup of** vegetable oil
- 1/2 **cup of** granulated sugar
- 1/2 **cup of** brown sugar, packed
- 2 **Big** eggs
- 1 **tsp** vanilla extract
- 1 1/2 **cups of finely grated** carrots
- 1/2 **cup of** crushed pineapple, drained
- 1/4 **cup of chop-up** walnuts (**non-compulsory**)
- Cream cheese frosting (store-bought or homemade)

Instructions:

1. Turn on the oven to 350 °F (175 °C). Four 8-**oz** Mason jars **Must** have their interiors greased.
2. **Combine** the flour, baking powder, baking soda, cinnamon, nutmeg, and salt in a medium basin.
3. The vegetable oil, granulated sugar, brown sugar, eggs, and vanilla extract **Must** all be thoroughly blended in a different, sizable **combining** basin.
4. **Combine** just till **combined** after gradually incorporating the dry ingredients into the wet ones.
5. Add the **chop-up** walnuts (if using), crushed pineapple, and **finely grated** carrots.
6. Fill **every** Mason jar to about two-thirds full after evenly dividing the batter among the jars.
7. A toothpick put into the center of the cakes **Must** come out clean after about 25 **min**s of baking the filled jars on a baking sheet.
8. The cakes **Must** cool for a few **min**s inside the jars before being carefully **take out**d so they may finish cooling on a wire rack.
9. Spread cream cheese frosting over **every** cake after it has completely cooled.

NUTRITION INFO (per serving):
Cals: 600 kcal, Fat: 33g

Carbs: 70g

Protein: 7g

226.Mason Jar Blueberry Lemon Bread

Prep Time: 15 **min**s

Cook Time: 45 **min**s

Total Time: 1 **hr**

Servings: 8

Ingredients:

- 1 1/2 **cups of** all-purpose flour
- 1 **tsp** baking powder
- 1/4 **tsp** baking soda
- 1/4 **tsp** salt
- 1 **cup of** granulated sugar
- 2 **Big** eggs
- 1/2 **cup of** vegetable oil
- 1/2 **cup of** buttermilk

- 1 **tsp** vanilla extract
- Zest of 1 lemon
- 1 **cup of** fresh blueberries

Instructions:
1. Turn on the oven to 350 °F (175 °C). Grease eight 8-**oz** Mason jars on the inside.
2. **Combine** the flour, baking soda, baking powder, and salt in a medium bowl.
3. The sugar, eggs, vegetable oil, buttermilk, vanilla extract, and lemon zest **Must** all be thoroughly blended in a separate, **Big combining** basin.
4. **Combine** just till **combined** after gradually incorporating the dry ingredients into the wet ones.
5. Fold in the fresh blueberries gently.
6. Fill **every** Mason jar about halfway with the batter, and distribute evenly.
7. Bake the filled jars for about 45 **min**s, or **up to** a toothpick inserted into the center of the bread comes out clean. Place the filled jars on a baking sheet.
8. After letting the bread cool for a short while within the jars, carefully **take out** them so they may finish cooling on a wire rack.

NUTRITION INFO (per serving):
Cals: 320 kcal, Fat: 17g

Carbs: 39g

Protein: 4g

227. Mason Jar Oreo Cheesecake

Prep Time: 20 **min**s

Cook Time: No baking required

Total Time: 20 **min**s

Servings: 4

Ingredients:
- 1 **cup of** Oreo cookie crumbs
- 2 tbsp **dilute** butter
- 8 oz cream cheese, **melted**
- 1/4 **cup of** granulated sugar
- 1 tsp vanilla extract
- 1 **cup of** whipped cream
- 4 whole Oreo cookies for garnish

Instructions:
1. Crumbs from an Oreo cookie and **dilute** butter **Must** be thoroughly **combined** in a mini bowl.
2. Cream cheese, sugar, and vanilla extract **Must** be blended in a another basin.
3. Till the whipped cream is completely inte**finely grated**, gently fold it into the cream cheese **Mixture**.
4. Layer the Oreo cookie crumbs in the bottom of 4 Mason jars.

5. On top of the crumbs, spread a layer of the cream cheese **Mixture**.
6. The layers are repeated **up to** the jars are full, and then a layer of the cream cheese **Mixture** is added on top.
7. Give **every** container a complete Oreo cookie as a garnish.
8. Serve chilled at least two **hr**s prior.

Nutrition (per serving):
Cals: 380 kcal, Fat: 25g, **Carb**s: 33g

Protein: 5g

228. Layered Mango Coconut Pudding

Prep Time: 15 **min**s

Cook Time: No cooking required

Total Time: 15 **min**s

Servings: 4

Ingredients:
- 1 **Big** ripe mango, diced
- 1 **cup of** coconut milk
- 2 tbsp honey or sweetener of choice
- 1/2 **cup of** granola
- 1/4 **cup of** shredded coconut
- Fresh mint leaves for garnish

Instructions:
1. Mango dice, coconut milk, and honey **Must** all be blended together. **Up to** smooth, blend.
2. Layer the mango coconut **Mixture** in the bottom of four Mason jars.
3. The granola **Must** be placed on top of the mango **Mixture**.
4. The layers **Must** be repeated **up to** the jars are full, and then add a layer of granola to finish.
5. **Every** jar **Must** be topped with shredded coconut and fresh mint leaves.
6. Before serving, place in the fridge for at least one **hr**.

Nutrition (per serving):
Cals: 220 kcal, Fat: 10g, **Carb**s: 32g

Protein: 3g

229. Mason Jar Apple Cut up

Prep Time: 20 **min**s

Cook Time: 25 **min**s

Total Time: 45 **min**s

Servings: 4

Ingredients:
- 2 **cups of** apples, **peel off** and diced
- 2 tbsp lemon juice
- 2 tbsp granulated sugar

- 1/2 tsp ground cinnamon
- 1 **cup of** rolled oats
- 1/2 **cup of** all-purpose flour
- 1/4 **cup of** brown sugar
- 1/4 **cup of** unsalted butter, cold and cubed

Instructions:

1. Set the oven's temperature to 350°F (175°C).
2. **Combine** the diced apples with the sugar, cinnamon, and lemon juice in a bowl.
3. The rolled oats, all-purpose flour, brown sugar, and cubed butter **Must** be **combine**d in a different bowl. To **combine** it into coarse crumbs, use your fingers.
4. Divide the apple **Mixture** among the 4 Mason jars you have.
5. Over the apples in **every** jar, evenly distribute the oat **cut up Mixture**.
6. When the tops are brown and the apples are soft, place the jars on a baking sheet and bake in the preheated oven for 25 **min**s.
7. Before serving, take them out of the oven and **let** them to cool somewhat.

Nutrition (per serving):
Cals: 320 kcal, Fat: 14g, **Carb**s: 47g
Protein: 4g

230.Mason Jar Lemon Bars

Prep Time: 15 **min**s

Cook Time: 25 **min**s

Total Time: 40 **min**s

Servings: 4

Ingredients:

- 1 **cup of** graham cracker crumbs
- 1/4 **cup of** unsalted butter, **dilute**
- 1 **cup of** granulated sugar
- 2 **Big** eggs
- 1/4 **cup of** fresh lemon juice
- 1 tbsp lemon zest
- 2 tbsp all-purpose flour
- Powdered sugar for dusting

Instructions:

1. Set the oven's temperature to 350°F (175°C).
2. Graham cracker crumbs and **dilute** butter **Must** be thoroughly **combined** in a bowl.
3. To create the crust, press the graham cracker **Mixture** firmly into the bottom of 4 Mason jars.
4. The granulated sugar, eggs, lemon juice, lemon zest, and all-purpose flour **Must** be thoroughly **combine**d in a separate basin.
5. Divide the lemon **Mixture** evenly among the crusts in **every** jar.

6. The jars **Must** be baked for 25 **min**s, or **up to** the borders are set and the middle is somewhat jiggly, on a baking sheet in the preheated oven.
7. Take them out of the oven and **let** them to totally cool.
8. Before serving, sprinkle powdered sugar over the tops.

Nutrition (per serving):
Cals: 340 kcal, Fat: 15g, **Carb**s: 48g
Protein: 5g

231.Layered Caramel Brownie Trifle

Prep Time: 30 **min**s

Cook Time: 25 **min**s

Total Time: 55 **min**s

Servings: 4

Ingredients:

- 1 **box/pkg** brownie **combine** (+ required ingredients like eggs, oil, and water)
- 1 **cup of** caramel sauce
- 2 **cups of** whipped cream
- 1/2 **cup of chop-up** nuts (e.g., pecans, walnuts) for garnish

Instructions:

1. As directed by the brownie **combine**, preheat the oven.
2. According to the instructions on the **box/pkg**, prepare the brownie **combine**, and bake it in a baking dish for the allotted amount of time.
3. **Slice** the brownies into little squares after **let**ing them to cool fully.
4. Layer the trifle in 4 Mason jars, starting at the bottom of **every** with a layer of brownie squares.
5. Pour caramel sauce over **every** jar's layer of brownies.
6. On top of the caramel, spread a layer of whipped cream.
7. The layers are repeated **up to** the jars are full, and then a layer of whipped cream is added on top.
8. Add **chop-up** nuts to **every** jar as decoration.
9. Before serving, place in the fridge for at least 30 **min**s.

Nutrition (per serving):
Cals: 590 kcal, Fat: 30g
Carbs: 70g
Protein: 8g

232.Layered Cinnamon Streusel Coffee Cake

Prep Time: 20 **min**s

Cook Time: 40 **min**s

Total Time: 60 **min**s

Servings: 8

Ingredients:

- 2 **cups of** all-purpose flour
- 1 **cup of** granulated sugar
- 1/2 **cup of** unsalted butter, **melted**
- 1/2 **cup of** milk
- 2 **Big** eggs
- 2 **tsp** baking powder
- 1 **tsp** vanilla extract
- 1/2 **tsp** salt
- 1/4 **cup of** plain Greek yogurt
- For the Streusel:
- 1/2 **cup of** packed brown sugar
- 1/4 **cup of** all-purpose flour
- 1 **tsp** ground cinnamon
- 2 **tbsp** unsalted butter, **dilute**

Instructions:

1. Turn on the oven to 350 °F (175 °C). A 9-inch round cake pan **Must** be greased and floured.
2. The **melted** butter and granulated sugar **Must** be **combine**d and beaten **up to** light and fluffy in a **Big combining** basin. One at a time, add the eggs, beating thoroughly after **every** addition. Add the vanilla extract and stir.
3. **Combine** the salt, baking soda, and flour in a separate basin. Beginning and finishing with the flour combination, add this dry **Mixture** gradually to the wet ingredients, alternating with the milk. Add the Greek yogurt and **combine** thoroughly.
4. **Combine** the brown sugar, flour, and cinnamon in a **mini** bowl to make the streusel. Over the **Mixture**, drizzle the **dilute** butter and whisk **up to** the **Mixture** is crumbly.
5. In the prepared cake pan, distribute half of the cake batter. Over the batter, evenly distribute half of the streusel. With the remaining batter and streusel, repeat the layering.
6. For about 40 **min**s, or **up to** a toothpick inserted in the center of the coffee cake comes out clean, bake the cake in the preheated oven.
7. The cake **Must** cool in the pan for ten **min**s before being moved to a wire rack to finish cooling.

Nutrition (per serving):

Cals: 350 kcal, Fat: 14g, **Carb**s: 52g

Protein: 5g, Fiber: 1g, Sugar: 30g, Sodium: 200mg

233.Mason Jar Triple Chocolate Brownies

Prep Time: 15 **min**s

Cook Time: 25 **min**s

Total Time: 40 **min**s

Servings: 4

Ingredients:

- 1/2 **cup of** unsalted butter, **dilute**
- 1 **cup of** granulated sugar
- 2 **Big** eggs
- 1 **tsp** vanilla extract
- 1/3 **cup of** unsweetened cocoa powder
- 1/2 **cup of** all-purpose flour
- 1/4 **tsp** baking powder
- 1/4 **tsp** salt
- 1/2 **cup of** semisweet chocolate chips
- 1/2 **cup of** white chocolate chips
- 1/2 **cup of** milk chocolate chips

Instructions:

1. Turn on the oven to 350 °F (175 °C). A 9x9 baking dish **Must** be greased.
2. **Dilute** butter and granulated sugar **Must** be thoroughly **combined** in a **Big combining** dish. One at a time, add the eggs, stirring thoroughly after **every** addition. Add the vanilla extract and stir.
3. **Combine** the flour, baking soda, salt, and cocoa powder in a another basin. **Combine up to** just blended after gradually adding this dry **Mixture** to the wet ingredients.
4. The batter **Must** be incorporated with the semisweet, white, and milk chocolate chips.
5. Spread out the batter evenly as you pour it into the prepared baking pan.
6. For about 25 **min**s, or **up to** a toothpick inserted into the center of the brownies emerges with a few moist crumbs, bake the brownies in the preheated oven.
7. Before **Cutting** the brownies into squares and putting them in Mason jars for serving, let the brownies cool completely in the pan.

Nutrition (per serving):

Cals: 580 kcal, Fat: 30g, **Carb**s: 77g

Protein: 7g, Fiber: 4g, Sugar: 57g, Sodium: 230mg

234.Mason Jar Strawberry Shortcake

Prep Time: 20 **min**s

Cook Time: 15 **min**s

Total Time: 35 **min**s

Servings: 4

Ingredients:

- 2 **cups of** fresh strawberries, hulled and **split**
- 2 **tbsp** granulated sugar
- 2 **cups of** all-purpose flour
- 1/4 **cup of** granulated sugar
- 1 **tbsp** baking powder

- 1/2 **tsp** salt
- 1/2 **cup of** unsalted butter, cold and **slice** into **mini** pieces
- 3/4 **cup of** milk
- 1 **tsp** vanilla extract
- Whipped cream for topping

Instructions:

1. **Split** strawberries and 2 **tbsp** of sugar **Must** be combined in a bowl. To let the strawberries to release their juices, set aside.
2. Turn on the oven to 425 °F (220 °C). A baking sheet **Must** be greased or lined with parchment paper.
3. **Combine** the flour, 1/4 **cup of** sugar, baking soda, and salt in a sizable **combining** bowl. Use a pastry **slice**ter or your fingertips to incorporate the chilled butter **up to** the **Mixture** resembles coarse crumbs.
4. Stirring just **up to combined**, add the milk and vanilla extract to the flour **Mixture**. Watch out not to **combine** too much.
5. Lightly knead the dough on a floured surface, then pat it into a circle that is approximately 1 inch thick. **Slice** out shortcakes using a glass rim or a biscuit **slice**ter.
6. Shortcakes **Must** be baked for 12 to 15 **min**s, or **up to** golden brown, on the preheated baking sheet.
7. Before putting together the desserts in the Mason jars, let the shortcakes cool just a little.
8. Layer shortcake, macerated strawberries, and whipped cream in **every** Mason jar. Continue the layering, and then top it off with a dab of whipped cream.

Nutrition (per serving):

Cals: 460 kcal, Fat: 19g, **Carb**s: 67g

Protein: 6g, Fiber: 3g, Sugar: 23g, Sodium: 370mg

235.Layered Peanut Butter Cup of Parfait

Prep Time: 15 **min**s

Total Time: 15 **min**s

Servings: 2

Ingredients:

- 1 **cup of** creamy peanut butter
- 1/2 **cup of** powdered sugar
- 1 **cup of** heavy cream
- 2 **tbsp** granulated sugar
- 1 **tsp** vanilla extract
- 1 **cup of** crushed chocolate cookies
- 1/2 **cup of chop-up** peanut butter **cups of**

Instructions:

1. The creamy peanut butter and powdered sugar **Must** be thoroughly **combined** in a medium basin.
2. Whip the heavy cream, sugar, and vanilla extract in a separate dish **up to** stiff peaks form.
3. To create a light and fluffy peanut butter mousse, gently fold the whipped cream into the peanut butter **Mixture**.
4. Start arranging the dessert in two glasses for serving or Mason jars. Crushed chocolate cookies **Must** be the first layer you add.
5. Put a layer of the peanut butter mousse on top next.
6. On top of the mousse, scatter a layer of **chop-up** peanut butter **cups of**.
7. To fill the glasses to the appropriate level, keep adding layers.
8. Add some extra smashed chocolate cookies and **chop-up** peanut butter **cups of** as a garnish to finish.
9. Before serving, place the parfaits in the refrigerator for at least 30 **min**s to let the flavors to mingle.

Nutrition (per serving

Cals: 890 kcal, Fat: 63g, **Carb**s: 68g, Protein: 20g, Fiber: 5g, Sugar: 40g, Sodium: 490mg

236.Mason Jar Raspberry Almond Torte

Prep Time: 25 **min**s

Cook Time: 40 **min**s

Total Time: 1 **hr** 5 **min**s

Servings: 4

Ingredients:

- 1 **cup of** almond flour
- 1/2 **cup of** granulated sugar
- 1/2 **cup of** unsalted butter, **melted**
- 2 **Big** eggs
- 1 **tsp** almond extract
- 1/2 **cup of** fresh raspberries
- 1/4 **cup of split** almonds
- Powdered sugar for dusting

Instructions:

1. Turn on the oven to 350 °F (175 °C). Butter or cooking spray **Must** be used to grease four 8-**oz** Mason jars.
2. The **melted** butter and granulated sugar **Must** be **combined** in a sizable **combining** basin and creamed **up to** light and fluffy.
3. One at a time, add the eggs, beating thoroughly after **every** addition. Add the almond extract and stir.

4. After the almond flour has been thoroughly incorporated, gently fold it in.
5. Fill **every** Mason jar with about half of the batter after distributing it evenly among the greased jars.
6. In **every** jar, evenly distribute a few raspberries into the batter.
7. To completely encase the raspberries, add extra batter on top.
8. **Every** torte **Must** have the **split** almonds sprinkled on top.
9. The filled Mason jars **Must** be placed on a baking sheet, and the tortes **Must** be baked for 35 to 40 **min**s, or **up to** golden brown and a toothpick inserted into the center comes out clean.
10. Prior to serving and dusted with powdered sugar, let the tortes to cool slightly.

Nutrition (per serving):
Cals: 560 kcal, Fat: 41g, **Carbs**: 41g, Protein: 11g, Fiber: 5g, Sugar: 28g, Sodium: 25mg

237.Mason Jar S'mores Brownies

Prep Time: 15 **min**s

Cook Time: 25 **min**s

Total Time: 40 **min**s

Servings: 4

Ingredients:
- 1 **cup of** graham cracker crumbs
- 1 **cup of** brownie **combine**
- 1/2 **cup of** mini marshml**et**s
- 1/4 **cup of** chocolate chips
- 1/4 **cup of** vegetable oil
- 1/4 **cup of** water

Instructions:
1. **Combine** the brownie **combine**, water, and vegetable oil together in a bowl.
2. Place graham cracker crumbs, brownie batter, **mini** marshml**et**s, and chocolate chips in **every** mason jar.
3. The layers are repeated, and then a layer of **mini** marshml**et**s and chocolate chips is placed on top.
4. The mason jars **Must** be baked for 20 to 25 **min**s, or **up to** the brownies are thoroughly cooked, in a preheated oven set to 350°F (175°C).
5. Before serving, let them cool a little. Enjoy your mouthwatering S'mores Brownies from a Mason Jar!

Nutrition (per serving):
Cals: 400 kcal, Fat: 20g, **Carbs**: 55g, Protein: 4g
Fiber: 2g

238.Layered Chocolate Hazelnut Tiramisu

Prep Time: 30 **min**s

Cook Time: 0 **min**s (no-bake)

Total Time: 30 **min**s

Servings: 6

Ingredients:
- 1 **cup of** heavy cream
- 1/4 **cup of** powdered sugar
- 1 **tsp** vanilla extract
- 1 **cup of** mascarpone cheese
- 1/2 **cup of** chocolate hazelnut spread (e.g., Nutella)
- 1 **cup of** brewed coffee, cooled
- 24 ladyfinger cookies
- Cocoa powder, for dusting

Instructions:
1. Whip the heavy cream, sugar, and vanilla extract in a **combining** bowl **up to** stiff peaks form.
2. Mascarpone cheese and chocolate hazelnut spread **Must** be thoroughly **combine**d in a separate bowl.
3. Place a layer of the mascarpone-chocolate hazelnut **Mixture**, a layer of the ladyfinger cookies that have been soaked in coffee, and then a layer of whipped cream in **every** mason jar.
4. The layers are repeated, and the top layer is whipped cream.
5. Sprinkle chocolate powder on top.
6. Before serving, put the Mason jars in the fridge for at least two **hr**s. Your taste buds will be delighted by this layered chocolate hazelnut tiramisu!

Nutrition (per serving):
Cals: 450 kcal, Fat: 32g, **Carbs**: 35g
Protein: 6g, Fiber: 1g

239.Mason Jar Pevery Cobbler

Prep Time: 20 **min**s

Cook Time: 30 **min**s

Total Time: 50 **min**s

Servings: 4

Ingredients:
- 2 **cups of** peel off and **split** p**every**es
- 1/2 **cup of** all-purpose flour
- 1/2 **cup of** granulated sugar
- 1/2 **cup of** milk
- 1/4 **cup of** unsalted butter, **dilute**
- 1 **tsp** baking powder
- 1/2 **tsp** vanilla extract
- Pinch of salt
- Vanilla ice cream (**non-compulsory**, for serving)

Instructions:

1. Turn on the oven to 350 °F (175 °C).
2. **Combine** the flour, 1/4 **cup of** sugar, baking soda, and salt in a bowl.
3. When you **combine** the dry ingredients with the milk, **dilute** butter, and vanilla extract, the batter **Must** be smooth.
4. Layer **split** p**every**es in the bottom of **every** mason jar, then top with the remaining 1/4 **cup of** sugar.
5. Fill **every** jar to about two-thirds with p**every**es before pouring the batter over them.
6. The mason jars **Must** be placed on a baking sheet and baked for 25 to 30 **min**s, or **up to** the tops are golden brown and the p**every**es are bubbling, in a preheated oven.
7. Before serving, let them cool a little. For an added pleasure, top the p**every** cobbler in a mason jar with a scoop of vanilla ice cream.

Nutrition (per serving):

Cals: 300 kcal, Fat: 12g, **Carb**s: 45g

Protein: 4g, Fiber: 2g

240.Mason Jar Pineapple Upside-Down Cake

Prep Time: 20 **min**s

Cook Time: 25 **min**s

Total Time: 45 **min**s

Servings: 4

Ingredients:

- 1 can (20 oz) pineapple slices in juice, drained
- 1/4 **cup of** unsalted butter, **dilute**
- 1/2 **cup of** brown sugar
- 1/2 **cup of** all-purpose flour
- 1/4 **cup of** granulated sugar
- 1 **tsp** baking powder
- 1/4 **tsp** salt
- 1/4 **cup of** milk
- 1/2 **tsp** vanilla extract
- Maraschino cherries (**non-compulsory**, for garnish)

Instructions:

1. Turn on the oven to 350 °F (175 °C).
2. **Dilute** butter and brown sugar **Must** be thoroughly **combined** in a bowl.
3. Spread the butter-sugar **Mixture** at the bottom of **every** mason jar after evenly dividing it between them.
4. Top **every** jar's butter-sugar **Mixture** with a slice of pineapple. **Every** pineapple slice can **optionally** have a maraschino cherry placed in the middle of it.

5. **Combine** the flour, brown sugar, baking soda, and salt in a separate bowl.
6. When you have a smooth batter, **combine** the dry ingredients with the milk and vanilla essence.
7. The batter **Must** cover the pineapple slices in the mason jars to a depth of almost two-thirds.
8. For 20 to 25 **min**s, or **up to** a toothpick inserted into the center of the cakes comes out clean, bake the cakes in the mason jars in the preheated oven.
9. Before serving, let them cool a little. To serve, place the mason jars on a dish upside down with the pineapple on top. Enjoy your delicious pineapple upside-down cake made in a mason jar!

Nutrition (per serving):

Cals: 350 kcal, Fat: 12g, **Carb**s: 55g

Protein: 3g, Fiber: 2g

241.Layered Lemon Poppy Seed Cake

Prep Time: 25 **min**s

Cook Time: 30 **min**s

Total Time: 55 **min**s

Servings: 4

Ingredients:

- 1 **cup of** all-purpose flour
- 1/2 **cup of** granulated sugar
- 1 **tbsp** poppy seeds
- 1/2 **tsp** baking powder
- 1/4 **tsp** baking soda
- Pinch of salt
- 1/4 **cup of** unsalted butter, **dilute**
- 1/2 **cup of** buttermilk
- 1 **Big** egg
- Zest of 1 lemon
- 1 **tbsp** lemon juice
- 1/2 **tsp** vanilla extract
- Whipped cream or frosting of your choice (**non-compulsory**, for layering and topping)

Instructions:

1. Turn on the oven to 350 °F (175 °C).
2. **Combine** the flour, sugar, poppy seeds, baking powder, baking soda, and salt in a bowl.
3. **Dilute** butter, buttermilk, egg, lemon juice, lemon zest, and vanilla essence **Must** all be thoroughly blended in a separate basin.
4. When you have a smooth batter, **combine** the wet and dry ingredients and whisk **up to** **combine**d.
5. Divide the batter among the mason jars, filling **every** one about halfway, and lightly grease them.

6. For 25 to 30 **min**s, or **up to** a toothpick inserted into the center of the cakes comes out clean, bake the cakes in the mason jars in the preheated oven.
7. **Up to** they are totally cooled, let the layers to be assembled.
8. To assemble, put your preferred icing or whipped cream in between layers of cake in **every** mason jar.
9. If desired, you can garnish with little lemon zest or poppy seeds.
10. Enjoy your delicious lemon poppy seed cake with layers!

Nutrition (per serving):
Cals: 300 kcal, Fat: 12g, **Carb**s: 45g
Protein: 5g, Fiber: 1g

242.Layered Cannoli Dessert

Prep Time: 30 **min**s
Cook Time: 0 **min**s
Total Time: 30 **min**s
Servings: 4

Ingredients:
- 1 **cup of** ricotta cheese
- 1/2 **cup of** powdered sugar
- 1 **tsp** vanilla extract
- 1/4 **cup of** mini chocolate chips
- 1/4 **cup of chop-up** pistachios
- 8 cannoli shells, crushed

Instructions:
1. The ricotta cheese, powdered sugar, and vanilla essence **Must** all be **combined** in a **combining** dish. Well **combine up to** smooth.
2. Layer the crushed cannoli shells, a **tbsp** of the ricotta **Mixture**, a scattering of micro chocolate chips, and **chop-up** pistachios in **mini** glasses or dessert **cups of**.
3. Continue layering **up to** you r**every** the top of the glasses, then top with a garnish of **chop-up** pistachios and **mini** chocolate chips.
4. At least 10 **min**s **Must** pass before serving the dessert from the refrigerator.

Nutrition (per serving):
Cals: 280, Fat: 15g, **Carb**s: 30g
Protein: 7g, Fiber: 2g, Sugar: 18g

243.Mason Jar Chocolate Caramel Pretzel Pie

Prep Time: 20 **min**s
Cook Time: 10 **min**s
Total Time: 30 **min**s

Servings: 4

Ingredients:
- 1 1/2 **cups of** pretzel crumbs
- 1/4 **cup of** granulated sugar
- 1/2 **cup of** unsalted butter, **dilute**
- 1/2 **cup of** chocolate chips
- 1/4 **cup of** caramel sauce
- 1 **cup of** heavy cream
- 1 **tsp** vanilla extract

Instructions:
1. Pretzel crumbs, granulated sugar, and **dilute** butter **Must** all be thoroughly blended in a basin.
2. The pie crust is made by pressing the ingredients firmly into the bottom of **every** Mason jar.
3. Pour **dilute** chocolate chips over **every** jar's pretzel crust.
4. Over the chocolate coating, drizzle the caramel sauce.
5. Whip the heavy cream and vanilla extract in a separate dish **up to** stiff peaks form.
6. Add a big dollop of whipped cream to the top of **every** jar.
7. Add more caramel sauce if desired, then top with **cut up** pretzels.
8. Before serving, place in the fridge for at least one **hr**.

Nutrition (per serving):
Cals: 540, Fat: 38g, **Carb**s: 50g
Protein: 4g, Fiber: 2g, Sugar: 30g

244.Mason Jar Raspberry Lemonade

Prep Time: 10 **min**s
Cook Time: 0 **min**s
Total Time: 10 **min**s
Servings: 2

Ingredients:
- 1/2 **cup of** fresh raspberries
- 1/4 **cup of** fresh lemon juice
- 2 **tbsp** honey (adjust **as needed**)
- 1 1/2 **cups of** cold water
- Ice cubes
- Lemon slices and fresh raspberries for garnish

Instructions:
1. Fresh raspberries **Must** be pureed in a blender **up to** smooth.
2. Divide the raspberry puree evenly between the two Mason jars.
3. **Every** jar **Must** have fresh lemon juice and honey. Depending on the level of sweetness you desire, adjust the honey amount.

4. **Every** jar **Must** be filled with cold water, and the materials **Must** be thoroughly **combined**.
5. Garnish with lemon slices and fresh raspberries after adding ice cubes.
6. Serve right away or keep chilled **up to** you're ready to.

Nutrition (per serving):
Cals: 80, Fat: 0g, **Carbs**: 21g

Protein: 1g, Fiber: 3g, Sugar: 17g

245.Layered Watermelon and Cucumber Cooler

Prep Time: 15 **min**s

Cook Time: 0 **min**s

Total Time: 15 **min**s

Servings: 2

Ingredients:
- 2 **cups of** watermelon, diced
- 1 cucumber, **peel off** and **split**
- 10-12 fresh mint leaves
- 1 **tbsp** honey (**non-compulsory**, adjust **as needed**)
- 1 **cup of** cold water
- Ice cubes
- Watermelon slices and cucumber slices for garnish

Instructions:
1. Cucumber slices, **split** watermelon, and fresh mint leaves **Must** all be well blended in a blender.
2. To get rid of any pulp or seeds, you can **optionally** strain the **Mixture** through a fine-mesh screen.
3. If using, add honey to the drink to make it sweeter. To suit your tastes, adjust the sweetness.
4. Add ice cubes to two glasses or Mason jars.
5. Evenly distribute the watermelon-cucumber combination among the glasses.
6. Pour ice water into **every** glass, then whisk it thoroughly to blend.
7. Slices of cucumber, watermelon, and fresh mint leaves can be used as garnish.
8. Serve the chilled drink right away and savor it.

Nutrition (per serving):
Cals: 60, Fat: 0g, **Carbs**: 15g, Protein: 1g

Fiber: 1g, Sugar: 12g

246.Mason Jar Iced Green Tea with Honey and Mint

Prep Time: 5 **min**s

Cook Time: 5 **min**s (+ cooling time)

Total Time: 15 **min**s

Servings: 2

Ingredients:
- 2 green tea bags
- 2 **cups of** water
- 2 **tbsp** honey (adjust **as needed**)
- 1/4 **cup of** fresh mint leaves
- Ice cubes
- Lemon slices and mint sprigs for garnish

Instructions:
1. In a saucepan, bring the water to a boil. Add the green tea bags after removing from the heat.
2. Depending on the strength you want from your tea, let it steep for 3 to 4 **min**s.
3. While the tea is still warm, take out the tea bags and whisk in the honey, **let**ing it to dissolve.
4. Warm tea can be infused with fresh mint before being **let**ed to cool to room temperature.
5. Pour the tea into two Mason jars with ice after it has cooled.
6. Lemon slices and mint sprigs can be used as garnish.
7. You can put the jars in the fridge for a while to cool the tea even further.
8. Enjoy the iced green tea, which has been sweetened.

Nutrition (per serving):
Cals: 30, Fat: 0g, **Carbs**: 8g, Protein: 0g

Fiber: 0g, Sugar: 8g

247.Mason Jar Coconut Cream Pie

Prep Time: 20 **min**s

Cook Time: 10 **min**s

Total Time: 30 **min**s

Servings: 4

Ingredients:
- 1 1/2 **cups of** graham cracker crumbs
- 6 **tbsp** unsalted butter, **dilute**
- 1 **cup of** shredded coconut
- 1 **box/pkg** (3.4 **oz**s) instant coconut cream pudding **combine**
- 1 3/4 **cups of** cold milk
- 1 **cup of** heavy cream
- 2 **tbsp** powdered sugar
- 1/2 **tsp** vanilla extract
- 4 Mason jars (8-**oz** size)

Instructions:
1. The graham cracker crumbs and **dilute** butter **Must** be thoroughly **combined** in a medium basin. As you evenly distribute the **Mixture**

among the Mason jars, press **every** one to create the crust layer.
2. In a dry skillet over medium heat, softly brown the coconut shreds. Over **every** jar's crust, evenly distribute the toasted coconut.
3. Whisk the coconut cream pudding **combine** and chilled milk **up to** thickened in a different bowl. Over the coconut layer in **every** jar, pour the pudding.
4. Whip the heavy cream, powdered sugar, and vanilla extract **up to** firm peaks form in a chilled **combining** basin. In **every** jar, top the pudding layer with whipped cream.
5. Add extra toasted coconut as a garnish if desired. Mason jars **Must** be sealed with their lids and kept chilled **up to** serving time.

Nutrition (per serving):
Cals: 420 kcal, Fat: 30g, **Carb**s: 36g, Protein: 5g
Fiber: 3g

248. Mason Jar Black Forest Cake

Prep Time: 30 **min**s
Cook Time: 25 **min**s
Total Time: 55 **min**s
Servings: 4

Ingredients:
- 1 1/2 **cups of** all-purpose flour
- 1 1/2 **cups of** granulated sugar
- 1/2 **cup of** cocoa powder
- 1 **tsp** baking powder
- 1/2 **tsp** baking soda
- 1/2 **tsp** salt
- 1 **Big** egg
- 1/2 **cup of** whole milk
- 1/4 **cup of** vegetable oil
- 1 **tsp** vanilla extract
- 1/2 **cup of** boiling water
- 1 can (21 **oz**s) cherry pie filling
- 1 **cup of** heavy cream
- 2 **tbsp** powdered sugar
- 1/2 **tsp** almond extract
- 4 Mason jars (8-**oz** size)

Instructions:
1. Turn on the oven to 350 °F (175 °C). 4 8-**oz** Mason jars **Must** be floured and greased.
2. **Combine** the flour, sugar, baking soda, salt, baking powder, and cocoa powder in a sizable **combining** dish.
3. The dry components **Must** be **combine**d with the egg, milk, vegetable oil, and vanilla essence. Beat **up to** well blended at medium speed.

4. Once the batter is smooth, add the hot water and stir. It will be a thin batter.
5. Fill **every** Mason jar only halfway with the batter to **let** for rising. Then, pour the batter into the prepared Mason jars.
6. The jars **Must** bake for about 25 **min**s in a preheated oven, or **up to** a toothpick inserted in the center comes out clean. Place the jars on a baking sheet.
7. Let the cakes finish cooling. After the cake has cooled, spread cherry pie filling over **every** layer.
8. Whip the heavy cream, powdered sugar, and almond extract **up to** firm peaks form in a chilled **combining** basin. Place a dollop of whipped cream on top of **every** jar's cherry layer.
9. Add extra cherry pie filling or chocolate shavings as a garnish, if desired. Mason jars **Must** be sealed with their lids and kept chilled **up to** serving time.

Nutrition (per serving):
Cals: 590 kcal, Fat: 23g, **Carb**s: 92g, Protein: 7g
Fiber: 4g

249. Layered Pina Colada Trifle

Prep Time: 15 **min**s
Cook Time: No cooking required
Total Time: 15 **min**s
Servings: 4

Ingredients:
- 1 **box/pkg** (3.4 **oz**s) coconut cream pudding **combine**
- 1 3/4 **cups of** cold milk
- 1 can (20 **oz**s) crushed pineapple, drained
- 1 **cup of** shredded coconut
- 1 1/2 **cups of** whipped cream or whipped topping
- 1/4 **cup of** toasted coconut, for garnish (**non-compulsory**)
- 4 Mason jars (8-**oz** size)

Instructions:
1. Whisk the chilled milk and coconut cream pudding **combine** in a bowl **up to** the **Mixture** thickens. **Let** it to sit for a while so that it can solidify.
2. Put a spoonful of crushed pineapple, a layer of coconut cream pudding, a layer of shredded coconut, and a dollop of whipped cream in **every** Mason jar. The layers **Must** be repeated **up to** the jars are completely full.
3. To add texture and flavor, you might **optionally** sprinkle toasted coconut on top of **every** trifle.
4. Mason jars **Must** be sealed with their lids and kept chilled **up to** serving time.

Nutrition (per serving):
Cals: 320 kcal, Fat: 15g

Carbs: 43g, Protein: 5g

Fiber: 2g

250.Mason Jar Mint Chocolate Pudding

Prep Time: 15 **min**s

Cook Time: No cooking required

Total Time: 15 **min**s

Servings: 4

Ingredients:

- 2 **cups of** whole milk
- 1/3 **cup of** granulated sugar
- 2 **tbsp** cornstarch
- 1/4 **tsp** salt
- 1/4 **tsp** peppermint extract
- Green food coloring (**non-compulsory**)
- 1/2 **cup of** mini chocolate chips
- 1 **cup of** heavy cream
- 2 **tbsp** powdered sugar
- 1/2 **tsp** vanilla extract
- 4 Mason jars (8-**oz** size)

Instructions:

1. **Combine** the milk, cornstarch, salt, and granulated sugar in a medium saucepan. Stirring continuously, cook the **Mixture** over medium heat **up to** it thickens and begins to boil. Get rid of the heat.
2. To produce the appropriate mint color, stir in the green food coloring (if using) and peppermint extract.
3. Add the **mini** chocolate chips by blending.
4. Whip the heavy cream, powdered sugar, and vanilla extract **up to** firm peaks form in a chilled **combining** basin.
5. In the Mason jars, arrange the whipped cream and mint chocolate pudding in layers, starting with the whipped cream on the top and working your way down.
6. Top with extra chocolate chips or a sprig of fresh mint, if desired. Mason jars **Must** be sealed with their lids and kept chilled **up to** serving time.

Nutrition (per serving):
Cals: 500 kcal, Fat: 34g, **Carb**s: 43g

Protein: 6g, Fiber: 1g

251.Mason Jar Raspberry Cheesecake

Prep Time: 20 **min**s

Cook Time: No cooking required

Total Time: 20 **min**s

Servings: 4

Ingredients:

- 1 **cup of** graham cracker crumbs
- 4 **tbsp** unsalted butter, **dilute**
- 8 **oz**s cream cheese, **melted**
- 1/2 **cup of** powdered sugar
- 1 **tsp** vanilla extract
- 1 **cup of** fresh raspberries
- 1/4 **cup of** raspberry jam
- 1 **cup of** whipped cream or whipped topping
- Fresh raspberries, for garnish (**non-compulsory**)
- 4 Mason jars (8-**oz** size)

Instructions:

1. Graham cracker crumbs and **dilute** butter **Must** be thoroughly **combined** in a bowl. As you evenly distribute the **Mixture** among the Mason jars, press **every** one to create the crust layer.
2. Beat the cream cheese, powdered sugar, and vanilla extract **up to** they are smooth and creamy in a another bowl.
3. Starting with the cheesecake **Mixture** at the bottom and switching to raspberries, layer the cheesecake **Mixture** and fresh berries in the Mason jars.
4. To make the raspberry jam easier to drizzle, slightly warm it. Place a thin layer of raspberry jam on top of **every** cheesecake layer.
5. Add whipped cream to the top of **every** jar and, if preferred, fresh raspberries as a garnish.
6. Mason jars **Must** be sealed with their lids and kept chilled **up to** serving time.

Nutrition (per serving):
Cals: 450 kcal, Fat: 31g, **Carb**s: 36g

Protein: 5g, Fiber: 2g

252.Mason Jar Strawberry Lemon Infused Water

Prep Time: 5 **min**s

Total Time: 2 **hr**s 5 **min**s

Servings: 2

Ingredients:

- 1 **cup of** fresh strawberries, **split**
- 1 lemon, thinly **split**
- 4 **cups of** water
- Ice cubes

Instructions:

1. Strawberries and lemon slices **Must** be placed in a mason jar.
2. Add ice cubes and water to the jar.
3. To **let** the flavors to meld, seal the jar and place in the refrigerator for at least two **hr**s.
4. Before serving, stir, then indulge!

NUTRITION INFO *(per serving):*
Cals: 15 kcal, **Carb**s: 3g, Fiber: 1g

Sugars: 1g, Vitamin C: 40mg

253.Layered Blueberry Basil Lemonade

Prep Time: 10 **min**s

Total Time: 10 **min**s

Servings: 2

Ingredients:

- 1 **cup of** fresh blueberries
- 4-6 fresh basil leaves
- 1 lemon, juiced
- 2 **cups of** cold water
- 2 tbsp honey (adjust **as needed**)
- Ice cubes

Instructions:

1. Fresh blueberries, basil leaves, lemon juice, and water **Must** all be put in a blender. **Up to** smooth, blend.
2. Stir the blueberry-basil **Mixture** well after adding the honey.
3. Pour the lemonade **Mixture** over the ice in two mason jars, dividing it equally between them. Fill the jars with ice cubes.
4. If preferred, top with a few additional basil leaves and blueberries.
5. Serve right away and delight in!

NUTRITION INFO *(per serving):*
Cals: 60 kcal, **Carb**s: 16g, Fiber: 2g

Sugars: 12g, Vitamin C: 30mg

254. Mason Jar Pineapple Mango Smoothie

Prep Time: 8 **min**s

Total Time: 10 **min**s

Servings: 2

Ingredients:

- 1 **cup of** fresh pineapple chunks
- 1 **cup of** fresh mango chunks
- 1 **cup of** plain yogurt
- 1 **cup of** coconut milk
- 2 tbsp honey (adjust **as needed**)
- Ice cubes

Instructions:

1. Blend the mango and pineapple pieces with the coconut milk, honey, and plain yogurt. **Up to** smooth, blend.
2. Ice cubes **Must** be added to two Mason jars.
3. The smoothie **Mixture Must** be evenly distributed among the jars as you pour it in.
4. Jars **Must** be sealed. Serve right away or store in the fridge for later.

NUTRITION INFO *(per serving):*
Cals: 220 kcal, **Carb**s: 41g, Fiber: 3g

Sugars: 35g, Protein: 5g

255. Mason Jar Raspberry Lime Mojito

Prep Time: 10 **min**s

Total Time: 10 **min**s

Servings: 2

Ingredients:

- 1 **cup of** fresh raspberries
- 1 lime, juiced
- 10 fresh mint leaves
- 2 tbsp honey (adjust **as needed**)
- 1 **cup of** soda water
- Ice cubes

Instructions:

1. Fresh raspberries, lime juice, mint leaves, and honey **Must** be **combined** in a **mini** bowl to release their flavors.
2. Ice cubes **Must** be added to two Mason jars.
3. Distribute the blended **Mixture** among the jars.
4. Divide the **combined Mixture** evenly among the jars and then pour soda water over it.
5. To slowly meld all the flavors, stir.
6. If desired, add more raspberries and mint leaves as a garnish.
7. Serve right away and delight in!

NUTRITION INFO *(per serving):*
Cals: 60 kcal, **Carb**s: 14g, Fiber: 4g

Sugars: 9g, Vitamin C: 15mg

256. Layered Pevery and Ginger Iced Tea

Prep Time: 5 **min**s

Cook Time: 5 **min**s

Total Time: 2 **hrs** 10 **min**s

Servings: 2

Ingredients:

- 2 ripe p**every**es, **split**
- 1-inch fresh ginger, **split**
- 2 **cups of** hot water
- 2 black tea bags
- 2 tbsp honey (adjust **as needed**)
- Ice cubes
- Fresh mint leaves for garnish

Instructions:

1. Add the p**every** slices and ginger slices to a mason jar.
2. In **every** jar, put a black tea bag.
3. Pour boiling water evenly between the jars over the tea bags.

4. Give the tea about five **min**s to steep.
5. Take out the tea bags, then add honey to **every** jar while thoroughly combining.
6. Add ice cubes to the jars and **combine** once more.
7. To cool and enable the flavors to meld, seal the jars and place them in the refrigerator for at least two **hr**s.
8. Before serving, garnish with fresh mint leaves.
9. Before sipping on this cooling iced tea, stir!

NUTRITION INFO (per serving):
Cals: 70 kcal, **Carb**s: 18g, Fiber: 2g
Sugars: 16g, Vitamin C: 10mg

257.Mason Jar Cherry Almond Smoothie

Prep Time: 10 **min**s
Total Time: 10 **min**s
Servings: 2

Ingredients:
- 1 **cup of refrigerate** cherries
- 1 ripe banana
- 1 **cup of** almond milk
- 2 **tbsp** almond butter
- 1 **tbsp** honey (adjust **as needed**)
- 1/2 **tsp** vanilla extract
- 1/4 **cup of** rolled oats
- 1 **tbsp** chia seeds (**non-compulsory**)
- **Split** almonds and fresh cherries for garnish

Instructions:
1. **Refrigerate** cherries, banana, almond milk, almond butter, honey, vanilla extract, rolled oats, and chia seeds (if using) **Must** all be **combine**d in a blender.
2. Blend till creamy and smooth.
3. Place Mason jars with the smoothie inside.
4. Add fresh cherries and almond slices as a garnish.
5. Either serve right away or store in the fridge.

Nutrition (per serving):
Cals: 250 kcal, Protein: 6g, Fat: 12g, **Carb**s: 32g
Fiber: 5g, Sugar: 18g

258. Mason Jar Honeydew Cucumber Cooler

Prep Time: 15 **min**s
Cook Time: 0 **min**s Total
Time: 15 **min**s

Servings: 2

Ingredients:
- 2 **cups of** diced honeydew melon
- 1 cucumber, **peel off** and diced
- 10-12 fresh mint leaves
- 1 **tbsp** honey (adjust **as needed**)
- 1 lime, juiced
- 1 1/2 **cups of** water
- Ice cubes
- Mint sprigs and cucumber slices for garnish

Instructions:
1. The **split** honeydew melon, cucumber, mint, honey, lime juice, and water **Must** all be **combine**d in a blender.
2. Blend everything thoroughly **up to** it's smooth.
3. Ice cubes **Must** be added to mason jars.
4. In the mason jars, pour the honeydew cucumber cooler.
5. Add cucumber slices and mint sprigs as a garnish.
6. Serve the cool beverage right away and indulge.

Nutrition (per serving):
Cals: 70 kcal, Protein: 1g, Fat: 0.5g, **Carb**s: 18g
Fiber: 2g, Sugar: 15g

259. Layered Blackberry Mint Lemonade

Prep Time: 10 **min**s
Cook Time: 0 **min**s
Total Time: 10 **min**s
Servings: 2

Ingredients:
- 1 **cup of** fresh blackberries
- 1/4 **cup of** fresh mint leaves
- 2 **cups of** lemonade
- Ice cubes
- Lemon slices and blackberries for garnish

Instructions:
1. Fresh blackberries and mint leaves **Must** be pureed in a blender **up to** smooth.
2. Ice cubes **Must** be added to mason jars.
3. Fill **every** jar halfway with the lemonade by adding that much.
4. In order to create a tiered appearance, carefully pour the blackberry-mint puree over the lemonade in **every** container.
5. Lemon slices and blackberries make a nice garnish.
6. Just before enjoying, gently stir.

Nutrition (per serving):
Cals: 100 kcal, Protein: 1g, Fat: 0g
Carbs: 26g, Fiber: 3g, Sugar: 21g

260. Mason Jar Tropical Fruit Punch

Prep Time: 15 mins

Cook Time: 0 mins

Total Time: 15 mins

Servings: 2

Ingredients:

- 1 **cup of** pineapple chunks
- 1 **cup of** mango chunks
- 1/2 **cup of split** strawberries
- 1 lime, juiced
- 1 **tbsp** honey (adjust **as needed**)
- 1 1/2 **cups of** coconut water
- Ice cubes
- Pineapple wedges and mint leaves for garnish

Instructions:

1. **Split** strawberries, chunks of pineapple, chunks of mango, lime juice, honey, and coconut water **Must** all be **combine**d in a blender.
2. Blend **up to** well-**combine**d and smooth.
3. Ice cubes **Must** be added to mason jars.
4. Place the mason jars with the tropical fruit punch inside.
5. Slices of pineapple and mint are used as garnish.
6. Enjoy the goodness of the tropics as you gently stir.

Nutrition (per serving):

Cals: 180 kcal, Protein: 2g, Fat: 1g, **Carb**s: 43g

Fiber: 5g, Sugar: 33g

261. Mason Jar Spiced Apple Cider

Prep Time: 5 mins

Cook Time: 20 mins

Total Time: 25 mins

Servings: 2

Ingredients:

- 2 **cups of** apple cider
- 2 cinnamon sticks
- 4 whole cloves
- 1/4 **tsp** ground nutmeg
- 1/4 **tsp** ground ginger
- 1 **tbsp** maple syrup (**non-compulsory**, adjust **as needed**)
- Apple slices for garnish

Instructions:

1. Apple cider, cinnamon sticks, cloves, ground nutmeg, and ground ginger **Must** all be **combine**d in a pot.
2. Over medium heat, bring the **Mixture** to a simmer.
3. To **let** the flavors to fully meld, turn the heat down to low and simmer the **Mixture** for 15 to 20 mins.
4. Utilizing a sieve, **take out** the spices from the cider.
5. If using, stir in the maple syrup.
6. The spiced apple cider **Must** be put into mason jars.
7. Add apple slices as a garnish.
8. Serve hot and savor the comforting beverage.

Nutrition (per serving):

Cals: 120 kcal, Protein: 0g, Fat: 0g, **Carb**s: 30g

Fiber: 0g, Sugar: 26g

262.Layered Cranberry Orange Mocktail

Prep Time: 10 mins

Cook Time: 0 mins

Total Time: 10 mins

Servings: 1

Ingredients:

- 1/2 **cup of** cranberry juice
- 1/2 **cup of** orange juice
- 1/2 **cup of** sparkling water
- Ice cubes
- Orange slices and cranberries for garnish

Instructions:

1. Ice cubes **Must** be added to a glass.
2. Fill about one-third of the glass with cranberry juice by carefully pouring it over the ice.
3. Add sparkling water to the remaining third of the glass, gently pouring it over the cranberry juice.
4. To make the top layer, carefully pour orange juice over the sparkling water.
5. Orange and cranberry slices are used as garnish.
6. Serve right away and delight in!

Nutrition (per serving):

Cals: 100 kcal, **Carb**s: 24g, Sugars: 19g

Fiber: 1g, Vitamin C: 50mg

263.Mason Jar Sparkling Raspberry Lemonade

Prep Time: 15 mins

Cook Time: 0 mins

Total Time: 15 mins

Servings: 2

Ingredients:

- 1/2 **cup of** fresh raspberries

- 1/4 **cup of** freshly squeezed lemon juice
- 2 **tbsp** honey (adjust **as needed**)
- 1 **cup of** sparkling water
- Ice cubes
- Lemon slices and fresh raspberries for garnish

Instructions:

1. Use a fork to muddle the fresh raspberries in a glass or mason jar to release their juices.
2. The muddled raspberries **Must** be **combine**d with honey and freshly squeezed lemon juice. **Up to** the honey is dissolved, stir thoroughly.
3. Ice cubes **Must** be added to the Mason jar.
4. Over the ice and raspberry-lemon combination, pour sparkling water.
5. Lemon slices and fresh raspberries are garnishes.
6. Just before serving, stir lightly.
7. Enjoy your sparkling raspberry lemonade in a mason jar!

Nutrition (per serving):

Cals: 70 kcal, **Carb**s: 18g, Sugars: 14g

Fiber: 3g, Vitamin C: 30mg

264.Mason Jar Pevery Iced Tea

Prep Time: 5 **min**s

Cook Time: 5 **min**s

Total Time: 10 **min**s

Servings: 2

Ingredients:

- 2 **cups of** water
- 2 black tea bags
- 1 ripe p**every**, **split**
- 2 **tbsp** honey (adjust **as needed**)
- Ice cubes
- Fresh mint leaves for garnish

Instructions:

1. Bring the water to a boil in a little pan. Black tea bags are added after the heat is turned off. Give the tea about five **min**s to steep.
2. After removing the tea bags, add the honey and stir **up to** it is dissolved.
3. Wait **up to** the tea is at room temperature.
4. **Split** p**every**es **Must** be added to two mason jars or glasses, and they **Must** be lightly mushed to bring out their taste.
5. Add ice cubes to the jars.
6. Over the ice and p**every**es, pour the cooled tea.
7. Use fresh mint leaves as a garnish.
8. Give your Mason jar p**every** iced tea a good stir before serving.

Nutrition (per serving):

Cals: 50 kcal, **Carb**s: 14g, Sugars: 13g

Fiber: 1g, Vitamin C: 5mg

265.Layered Pomegranate Lime Spritzer

Prep Time: 5 **min**s

Cook Time: 0 **min**s

Total Time: 5 **min**s

Servings: 1

Ingredients:

- 1/2 **cup of** pomegranate juice
- 1/2 **cup of** limeade
- 1/2 **cup of** sparkling water
- Ice cubes
- Fresh pomegranate arils and lime slices for garnish

Instructions:

1. Ice cubes **Must** be added to a glass.
2. Slowly fill the glass with pomegranate juice **up to** about one-third of the way up.
3. Fill the remaining third of the glass with sparkling water before adding the pomegranate juice.
4. To produce the top layer, carefully pour limeade over the sparkling water.
5. Lime slices and fresh pomegranate arils can be used as garnish.
6. Enjoy your Layered Pomegranate Lime Spritzer right away!

Nutrition (per serving):

Cals: 90 kcal, **Carb**s: 23g, Sugars: 17g

Fiber: 1g, Vitamin C: 25mg

266.Mason Jar Blueberry Lemon Fizz

Prep Time: 10 **min**s

Cook Time: 0 **min**s

Total Time: 10 **min**s

Servings: 2

Ingredients:

- 1/2 **cup of** fresh blueberries
- 1/4 **cup of** freshly squeezed lemon juice
- 2 **tbsp** maple syrup (adjust **as needed**)
- 1 **cup of** club soda or sparkling water
- Ice cubes
- Lemon slices and fresh blueberries for garnish

Instructions:

1. Use a fork to muddle fresh blueberries in a glass or mason jar to release their juices.
2. Blueberries that have been mushed with maple syrup and freshly squeezed lemon juice. The maple syrup must be thoroughly dissolved.
3. Ice cubes **Must** be added to the Mason jar.
4. Add sparkling water or club soda to the ice cubes and blueberry-lemon combination.

5. Lemon slices and fresh blueberries are garnishes.
6. Just before serving, stir lightly.
7. Enjoy your delicious Blueberry Lemon Fizz in a Mason Jar!

Nutrition (per serving):

Cals: 60 kcal, **Carb**s: 15g, Sugars: 12g

Fiber: 2g, Vitamin C: 20mg

267. Mason Jar Orange Creamsicle Smoothie

Prep Time: 10 **min**s

Cook Time: 0 **min**s

Total Time: 10 **min**s

Servings: 2

Ingredients:

- 1 **Big** orange, **peel off** and segmented
- 1 ripe banana
- 1 **cup of** Greek yogurt
- 1/2 **cup of** almond milk (or any milk of your choice)
- 1 **tbsp** honey (adjust **as needed**)
- 1/2 **tsp** vanilla extract
- Ice cubes

Instructions:

1. Orange segments, bananas, Greek yogurt, almond milk, honey, and vanilla extract **Must** all be **combine**d in a blender.
2. Pour some ice cubes into the blender to create a cool, refreshing smoothie.
3. Blend the ingredients in a blender just **up to** the smoothie is smooth and well-**combine**d.
4. The smoothie **Must** be poured into Mason jars and served right away.

Nutrition (per serving):

Cals: 180 kcal, Protein: 8g, Fat: 2g, **Carb**s: 35g

Fiber: 3g, Sugar: 24g

268. Layered Watermelon Limeade

Prep Time: 15 **min**s

Cook Time: 0 **min**s

Total Time: 15 **min**s

Servings: 2

Ingredients:

- 2 **cups of** seedless watermelon, cubed
- 1 lime, juiced
- 2 **tbsp** honey (adjust **as needed**)
- 1 **cup of** sparkling water or club soda
- Ice cubes
- Fresh mint leaves for garnish

Instructions:

1. The seedless watermelon **Must** be pureed in a blender **up to** smooth.
2. Fill the remaining half of the mason jar with the watermelon puree.
3. To prepare the limeade, thoroughly blend the lime juice, honey, and water in a separate basin.
4. Over the watermelon puree in the Mason jar, pour the limeade.
5. To finish filling the jar, add some ice cubes and sparkling water or club soda.
6. To **combine** the layers, gently stir.
7. Serve immediately after adding fresh mint leaves as a garnish.

Nutrition (per serving):

Cals: 90 kcal, Protein: 1g, Fat: 0g, **Carb**s: 23g

Fiber: 1g, Sugar: 19g

269. Mason Jar Cucumber Mojito Mocktail

Prep Time: 10 **min**s

Cook Time: 0 **min**s

Total Time: 10 **min**s

Servings: 1

Ingredients:

- 1/2 cucumber, thinly **split**
- 6-8 fresh mint leaves
- 1 lime, juiced
- 2 **tbsp** agave syrup or simple syrup
- 1 **cup of** club soda or sparkling water
- Ice cubes

Instructions:

1. Use a muddler or the back of a spoon to **combine** the cucumber slices and mint leaves in a mason jar to unleash their flavors.
2. **Combine** the agave syrup and lime juice in the mason jar well.
3. Ice cubes **Must** be added to the jar before sparkling water or club soda.
4. Gently stir all the ingredients together.
5. Add a piece of cucumber and a few mint leaves as garnish.
6. Enjoy this revitalizing mocktail right away!

Nutrition (per serving):

Cals: 80 kcal, Protein: 0g, Fat: 0g

Carbs: 20g, Fiber: 1g

Sugar: 16g

270. Mason Jar Kiwi Strawberry Lemonade

Prep Time: 15 **min**s

Cook Time: 0 **min**s

Total Time: 15 **min**s

Servings: 2

Ingredients:

- 2 kiwis, **peel off** and **split**
- 1 **cup of** strawberries, hulled and **split**
- 1 lemon, juiced
- 2 **tbsp** honey (adjust **as needed**)
- 1 1/2 **cups of** water
- Ice cubes
- Lemon, strawberry, and kiwi slices as a garnish

Instructions:

1. Blend the strawberries and kiwis in a blender **up to** completely smooth.
2. Half-fill the mason jars with the fruit purée.
3. To create the lemonade, **combine** lemon juice, honey, and water in a separate basin.
4. Fill the remaining space in the mason jars with lemonade.
5. To blend the flavors, add ice cubes to **every** jar and gently **combine.**
6. Slices of kiwi, strawberry, and lemon can be used as garnish.
7. Serve this delicious lemonade right now and savor it!

Nutrition (per serving):
Cals: 120 kcal, Protein: 1g, Fat: 0g

Carbs: 30g, Fiber: 3g

Sugar: 24g

271. Layered Cherry Vanilla Smoothie

Prep Time: 10 **min**s

Cook Time: 0 **min**s

Total Time: 10 **min**s

Servings: 2

Ingredients:

- 1 **cup of refrigerate** cherries
- 1 ripe banana
- 1 **cup of** vanilla Greek yogurt
- 1/2 **cup of** milk of your choice
- 1 **tbsp** honey (adjust **as needed**)
- 1/2 **tsp** almond extract (**non-compulsory**)
- Ice cubes

Instructions:

1. The **refrigerate** cherries, banana, vanilla Greek yogurt, milk, honey, and almond extract (if used) **Must** all be **combine**d in a blender.
2. Blend all of the ingredients **up to** they are well-**combine**d and smooth.
3. Fill **every** mason jar halfway with **every** half of the cherry smoothie.
4. Fill **every** container with a few ice cubes.

5. To make the second layer, pour the leftover cherry smoothie into the jars.
6. Add a few fresh cherries as a garnish on top along with more ice cubes.
7. Enjoy this delicious cherry vanilla smoothie right away!

Nutrition (per serving):
Cals: 250 kcal, Protein: 10g, Fat: 2g, **Carb**s: 48g

Fiber: 4g, Sugar: 35g

272.Mason Jar Cranberry Ginger Fizz

Prep Time: 10 **min**s

Cook Time: 0 **min**s

Total Time: 10 **min**s

Servings: 2

Ingredients:

- 1 **cup of** cranberry juice
- 1 **cup of** ginger ale
- 2 **tbsp** fresh lime juice
- 1/4 **cup of** fresh cranberries
- 2 sprigs of fresh mint
- Ice cubes

Instructions:

1. Add ice cubes to a mason jar **up to** it is about three-quarters full.
2. Add the ginger ale and cranberry juice.
3. Add lime juice, then whisk it in slowly.
4. Add a sprig of mint and some fresh cranberries as a garnish.
5. Before serving, tightly screw the lid onto the mason jar.

Nutrition (per serving):
Cals: 90 kcal, **Carb**s: 23g, Fat: 0g, Protein: 0g

Fiber: 1g

273.Mason Jar Lavender Lemonade

Prep Time: 15 **min**s

Cook Time: 0 **min**s

Total Time: 15 **min**s

Servings: 2

Ingredients:

- 1/2 **cup of** fresh lemon juice
- 2 **cups of** water
- 1/4 **cup of** honey
- 1 **tbsp** dried lavender buds
- Ice cubes
- Lemon slices and fresh lavender sprigs for garnish

Instructions:

1. Heat the water and honey in a **mini** saucepan over low heat **up to** the honey dissolves.

2. Add the dried lavender buds after the heat is turned off. Steep it for 5 to 7 mins.
3. Place the water that has been infused with lavender in a mason jar and let it cool.
4. Add fresh lemon juice when the lavender water has cooled, and stir well.
5. Ice cubes **Must** be added to the Mason jar, which **Must** then be decorated with lemon and fresh lavender sprigs.
6. Before serving, tightly screw the lid onto the mason jar.

Nutrition (per serving):

Cals: 120 kcal, **Carb**s: 31g, Fat: 0g
Protein: 0g, Fiber: 1g

274.Layered Raspberry Pevery Iced Tea

Prep Time: 5 **min**s
Cook Time: 5 **min**s
Total Time: 10 **min**s
Servings: 2

Ingredients:

- 2 **cups of** brewed black tea, cooled
- 1/2 **cup of** raspberry juice or puree
- 1/2 **cup of** p**every** juice or puree
- 2 **tbsp** honey or simple syrup (adjust **as needed**)
- Fresh raspberries and p**every** slices for garnish
- Ice cubes

Instructions:

1. Add ice cubes to a mason jar **up to** it is about three-quarters full.
2. Over the ice, pour the cooled black tea **up to** the jar is halfway full.
3. Stir thoroughly after adding the honey or simple syrup.
4. Pour the raspberry juice or puree over the tea layer after combining it with honey or simple syrup in a different container.
5. Use the same procedure to layer the p**every** juice or puree in the mason jar.
6. P**every** slices and fresh raspberries make lovely garnishes.
7. Before serving, put the Mason jar's lid on securely and give it a gentle shake.

Nutrition (per serving):

Cals: 110 kcal, **Carb**s: 28g, Fat: 0g
Protein: 1g, Fiber: 2g

275.Mason Jar Honey Lavender Lemonade

Prep Time: 15 **min**s
Cook Time: 0 **min**s
Total Time: 15 **min**s
Servings: 2

Ingredients:

- 1/2 **cup of** fresh lemon juice
- 2 **cups of** water
- 1/4 **cup of** honey
- 1 **tbsp** dried lavender buds
- Ice cubes
- Lemon slices and fresh lavender sprigs for garnish

Instructions:

1. Heat the water and honey in a **mini** saucepan over low heat **up to** the honey dissolves.
2. Add the dried lavender buds after the heat is turned off. Steep it for 5 to 7 **min**s.
3. Place the water that has been infused with lavender in a mason jar and let it cool.
4. Add fresh lemon juice when the lavender water has cooled, and stir well.
5. Ice cubes **Must** be added to the Mason jar, which **Must** then be decorated with lemon and fresh lavender sprigs.
6. Before serving, tightly screw the lid onto the mason jar.

Nutrition (per serving):

Cals: 120 kcal, **Carb**s: 31g, Fat: 0g, Protein: 0g
Fiber: 1g

276.Mason Jar Hibiscus Cooler

Prep Time: 5 **min**s
Cook Time: 5 **min**s
Total Time: 10 **min**s
Servings: 2

Ingredients:

- 2 **cups of** water
- 2 hibiscus tea bags
- 1/4 **cup of** honey or agave syrup
- 1/2 **cup of** orange juice
- 1/2 **cup of** sparkling water
- Orange slices and mint leaves for garnish
- Ice cubes

Instructions:

1. Bring the water to a boil in a **mini** saucepan before adding the hibiscus tea bags.
2. **Take out** the tea bags after 4-5 **min**s of steeping the tea.
3. Once the honey or agave syrup has been

thoroughly incorporated, let the tea cool to room temperature.

4. Divide the cooled hibiscus tea between two mason jars.
5. **Every** jar **Must** have orange juice and sparkling water added.
6. Orange slices and mint leaves are added as decoration after adding ice cubes to the Mason jars.
7. Before serving, put the Mason jar's lid on securely and give it a gentle shake.

Nutrition (per serving):
Cals: 100 kcal, **Carb**s: 25g, Fat: 0g, Protein: 1g
Fiber: 1g

277.Layered Coconut Pineapple Smoothie

Prep Time: 10 **min**s

Cook Time: 0 **min**s

Total Time: 10 **min**s

Servings: 2

Ingredients:
- 1 **cup of** coconut milk
- 1 **cup of** fresh pineapple chunks
- 1 ripe banana
- 1/2 **cup of** Greek yogurt
- 1 **tbsp** honey
- 1/4 **tsp** vanilla extract
- Ice cubes (**non-compulsory**)
- Toasted coconut flakes for garnish

Instructions:
1. Blend together Greek yogurt, banana, coconut milk, pineapple pieces, honey, and vanilla extract. **Up to** smooth, blend. You can **combine** the smoothie again after adding some ice cubes if you desire a thicker consistency.
2. Pour a layer of the coconut-pineapple smoothie **Mixture** into a glass or Mason jar.
3. Over the top of the initial layer, scatter some toasted coconut flakes.
4. Alternate between the smoothie **Mixture** and the toasted coconut flakes to make additional layers.
5. Add additional pineapple pieces and coconut flakes as garnish.
6. Serve right away and delight in!

Nutrition (per serving):
Cals: 240 kcal, **Carb**s: 37g, Protein: 6g
Fat: 9g, Fiber: 4g, Sugar: 22g, Vitamin C: 60mg
Calcium: 92mg, Iron: 1mg

278. Mason Jar Mango Lassi

Prep Time: 5 **min**s

Cook Time: 0 **min**s

Total Time: 5 **min**s

Servings: 1

Ingredients:
- 1 **cup of** ripe mango, **peel off** and diced
- 1/2 **cup of** plain yogurt
- 1/4 **cup of** milk
- 1 **tbsp** honey (adjust **as needed**)
- 1/4 **tsp** ground cardamom
- **Split** mango and mint leaves for garnish

Instructions:
1. Mango chunks, plain yogurt, milk, honey, and ground cardamom are all **combine**d in a blender. Blend till creamy and smooth.
2. If necessary, taste and add more honey to the sweetness.
3. In a Mason jar, pour the mango lassi.
4. Add some mint leaves and some mango slices as a garnish.
5. Serve right away or chill **up to** you're ready to eat.

Nutrition (per serving):
Cals: 250 kcal, **Carb**s: 53g, Protein: 6g, Fat: 3g
Fiber: 3g, Sugar: 49g, Vitamin C: 60mg, Calcium: 180mg
Iron: 1mg

279.Mason Jar Strawberry Basil Lemonade

Prep Time: 10 **min**s

Cook Time: 0 **min**s

Total Time: 10 **min**s

Servings: 2

Ingredients:
- 1 **cup of** fresh strawberries, hulled and halved
- 8-10 fresh basil leaves
- 1/4 **cup of** freshly squeezed lemon juice
- 2 **tbsp** honey (adjust **as needed**)
- 2 **cups of** cold water
- Ice cubes
- Lemon slices and basil leaves for garnish

Instructions:
1. Blend fresh strawberries, basil leaves, honey, lemon juice, and a little bit of water in a blender. Blend basil and strawberries **up to** completely smooth.
2. A few ice cubes **Must** be placed in **every** Mason jar.
3. Evenly distribute the strawberry basil **Mixture** between the two jars.
4. Pour one **cup of** of cold water into **every** jar, then thoroughly whisk to **combine** the flavors.

5. Add a few basil leaves and some lemon slices as garnish.
6. Take a stir before sipping this revitalizing lemonade.

Nutrition (per serving):
Cals: 70 kcal, **Carb**s: 18g, Protein: 1g, Fat: 0g

Fiber: 2g, Sugar: 15g, Vitamin C: 58mg, Calcium: 30mg

Iron: 1mg

280. Layered Cantaloupe Mint Smoothie

Prep Time: 10 **min**s

Cook Time: 0 **min**s

Total Time: 10 **min**s

Servings: 2

Ingredients:
- 2 **cups of** ripe cantaloupe, **peel off** and cubed
- 1/2 **cup of** Greek yogurt
- 1/4 **cup of** fresh orange juice
- 1 **tbsp** honey (adjust **as needed**)
- 4-5 fresh mint leaves
- Ice cubes (**non-compulsory**)
- Mint sprigs for garnish

Instructions:
1. Blend ripe cantaloupe, Greek yogurt, orange juice, honey, and fresh mint leaves in a **mixer**. **Up to** smooth, blend. You can add a few ice cubes and **combine** the smoothie once more if you prefer it cooler.
2. Pour a portion of the cantaloupe mint smoothie **Mixture** into **every** glass or Mason jar, then top with a few mint leaves to create layers.
3. To add more layers, repeat the process.
4. Add a mint sprig as garnish to the top.
5. Serve right away and enjoy the delectable tastes!

Nutrition (per serving):
Cals: 120 kcal, **Carb**s: 26g, Protein: 5g

Fat: 1g, Fiber: 2g, Sugar: 24g, Vitamin C: 48mg, Calcium: 70mg, Iron: 1mg

281. Mason Jar Blueberry Lavender Lemonade

Prep Time: 15 **min**s

Cook Time: 5 **min**s

Total Time: 20 **min**s

Servings: 2

Ingredients:
- 1/2 **cup of** fresh blueberries
- 2 **tbsp** dried culinary lavender
- 1/4 **cup of** freshly squeezed lemon juice
- 2 **tbsp** honey (adjust **as needed**)

- 2 **cups of** water
- Ice cubes
- Fresh blueberries and lavender sprigs for garnish

Instructions:
1. Fresh blueberries, dried lavender, and honey are **combine**d with 1 **cup of** of water in a **mini** pot. Over low heat, bring to a simmer, and cook for about five **min**s, slightly crushing the blueberries to release their juices.
2. Turn off the heat and **let** the blueberry lavender combination to cool.
3. Discard the sediments after straining the blueberry lavender syrup into a dish.
4. A few ice cubes **Must** be placed in **every** Mason jar.
5. Pour half of the freshly squeezed lemon juice and half of the blueberry lavender syrup into **every** jar.
6. Pour one **cup of** of cold water into **every** jar, then thoroughly whisk to **combine** the flavors.
7. Add some fresh blueberries and a lavender sprig as garnish.
8. Enjoy the delicious flavor of this blueberry lavender lemonade after stirring it.

Nutrition (per serving):
Cals: 80 kcal, **Carb**s: 20g, Protein: 1g

Fat: 0g, Fiber: 2g, Sugar: 17g, Vitamin C: 30mg

Calcium: 30mg, Iron: 1mg

282. Mason Jar Green Apple Cinnamon Smoothie

Prep Time: 10 **min**s

Cook Time: 0 **min**s

Total Time: 10 **min**s

Servings: 2

Ingredients:
- 2 green apples, cored and **chop-up**
- 1 ripe banana
- 1 **cup of** baby spinach
- 1 **cup of** unsweetened almond milk
- 1/2 **cup of** plain Greek yogurt
- 1 **tbsp** honey or maple syrup
- 1/2 **tsp** ground cinnamon
- Ice cubes

Instructions:
1. Green apples, banana, baby spinach, almond milk, Greek yogurt, honey, maple syrup, and ground cinnamon **Must** all be blended together in a blender.
2. Blend till creamy and smooth. Add some ice

cubes and blend the smoothie again if it's too thick, **up to** you have the right consistency.

3. The smoothie **Must** be poured into Mason jars, garnished with some cinnamon, and served right away.

283.Layered Plum and Cardamom Iced Tea

Prep Time: 15 **min**s

Cook Time: 5 **min**s

Total Time: 20 **min**s

Servings: 4

Ingredients:

- 4 **cups of** water
- 4 black tea bags
- 2 ripe plums, pitted and thinly **split**
- 8 green cardamom pods, lightly crushed
- 4 **tbsp** honey or sugar, adjust **as needed**
- Ice cubes
- Fresh mint leaves for garnish

Instructions:

1. In a saucepan, bring the water to a boil. Black tea bags **Must** be added, and they **Must** steep for 5 **min**s. After brewing the tea, take the tea bags out and **let** it cool to room temperature.
2. Add a few slices of plum and a **mini** amount of cardamom to a Mason jar. Over the cardamom and plum slices, pour the cooled, made tea.
3. Add honey or sugar to the iced tea to achieve the desired level of sweetness.
4. The Mason jars **Must** be filled with ice, garnished with mint leaves, and served chilled.

284.Mason Jar Cherry Vanilla Lemonade

Prep Time: 10 **min**s

Cook Time: 0 **min**s

Total Time: 10 **min**s

Servings: 2

Ingredients:

- 1 **cup of** fresh or **refrigerate** cherries, pitted
- 1/2 **cup of** fresh lemon juice
- 2 **cups of** water
- 2 **tbsp** honey or agave syrup, adjust **as needed**
- 1 **tsp** vanilla extract
- Ice cubes
- Lemon slices and fresh cherries for garnish

Instructions:

1. The pitted cherries, fresh lemon juice, water, honey, agave syrup, and vanilla essence **Must** all be blended together.
2. Blend everything thoroughly and smoothly. If required, taste and adjust the sweetness.

3. Pour the cherry lemonade over the ice in Mason jars that have been filled with ice cubes.
4. Serve right away after garnishing with lemon slices and fresh cherries.

285.Mason Jar Raspberry Rosewater Lemonade

Prep Time: 10 **min**s

Cook Time: 0 **min**s

Total Time: 10 **min**s

Servings: 2

Ingredients:

- 1 **cup of** fresh or **refrigerate** raspberries
- 1/2 **cup of** fresh lemon juice
- 2 **cups of** water
- 2 **tbsp** honey or agave syrup, adjust **as needed**
- 1/2 **tsp** rosewater (**non-compulsory**)
- Ice cubes
- Fresh rose petals and lemon slices for garnish

Instructions:

1. Raspberries, fresh lemon juice, water, honey, agave syrup, and rosewater (if using) **Must** all be **combine**d in a blender.
2. Blend **up to** well-**combine**d and smooth. Adapt sweetness to your preferences.
3. Pour the raspberry rosewater lemonade over the ice in Mason jars after filling them with ice cubes.
4. Serve right away after garnishing with lemon slices and fresh rose petals.

286.Layered Apricot Mint Iced Tea

Prep Time: 15 **min**s

Cook Time: 5 **min**s

Total Time: 20 **min**s

Servings: 4

Ingredients:

- 4 **cups of** water
- 4 black tea bags
- 2 ripe apricots, pitted and thinly **split**
- 1/4 **cup of** fresh mint leaves
- 4 **tbsp** honey or sugar, adjust **as needed**
- Ice cubes
- Mint sprigs for garnish

Instructions:

1. In a saucepan, bring the water to a boil. Fresh mint leaves and black tea bags **Must** be added, and they **Must** steep for 5 **min**s. Once the tea has cooled to room temperature, take out the tea bags and mint leaves.
2. Add a couple apricot slices to a Mason jar. Over

the apricot slices, pour the brewed tea that has cooled.
3. Add honey or sugar to the iced tea to achieve the desired level of sweetness.
4. The Mason jars **Must** be filled with ice, garnished with mint sprigs, and served cold.

287.Layered Raspberry Lime Rickey

Prep Time: 10 **min**s

Cook Time: 0 **min**s

Total Time: 10 **min**s

Servings: 2

Ingredients:
- 1 **cup of** fresh raspberries
- 2 limes, juiced
- 2 **tbsp** honey or simple syrup
- 1 **cup of** sparkling water
- Ice cubes
- Fresh mint leaves for garnish

Instructions:
1. Fresh raspberries **Must** be pureed in a blender **up to** smooth. To **take out** the seeds, pass the raspberry puree through a fine-mesh sieve.
2. **Combine** honey or simple syrup with freshly squeezed lime juice in a **mini** bowl, adjusting the sweetness to your taste.
3. Ice cubes **Must** be distributed equally between the two glasses as they are filled.
4. Divide the raspberry puree in half and pour one half into **every** glass.
5. Pour the lime **Mixture** slowly, **let**ing it to stack on top of the raspberry puree in **every** glass.
6. Add sparkling water to the top of **every** glass.
7. Use fresh mint leaves as a garnish.
8. Before sipping, give the flavors a quick stir.

Nutrition (per serving):
Cals: 80 kcal, **Carb**s: 20g, Fiber: 5g,
Sugar: 12g, Fat: 0g, Protein: 1g, Vitamin C: 30mg

288. Mason Jar Pineapple Mint Agua Fresca

Prep Time: 15 **min**s

Cook Time: 0 **min**s

Total Time: 15 **min**s

Servings: 2

Ingredients:
- 2 **cups of** fresh pineapple chunks
- 10-12 fresh mint leaves
- 2 **tbsp** lime juice
- 2 **tbsp** honey or agave syrup
- 2 **cups of** water
- Ice cubes

- Pineapple slices and mint sprigs for garnish

Instructions:
1. Fresh pineapple chunks, mint leaves, lime juice, honey (or agave syrup), and a blender are all you need.
2. Blend the ingredients **up to** they are well **combine**d and the product is smooth.
3. Place equal amounts of ice cubes in **every** of the two Mason jars.
4. The pineapple-mint combination **Must** be poured into **every** Mason jar **up to** it is about halfway full.
5. Add 1 **cup of** of water to the top of **every** jar and **combine** thoroughly.
6. Slices of pineapple and a fresh mint sprig can be used as garnish.
7. To blend the flavors, tightly screw the lids onto the Mason jars and gently shake them.
8. To **let** the flavors to mingle, place in the refrigerator at least 30 **min**s before serving.

Nutrition (per serving):
Cals: 120 kcal, **Carb**s: 30g, Fiber: 3g
Sugar: 24g, Fat: 0g, Protein: 1g, Vitamin C: 60mg

289.Mason Jar Blackberry Sage Cooler

Prep Time: 10 **min**s

Cook Time: 5 **min**s

Total Time: 15 **min**s

Servings: 2

Ingredients:
- 1 **cup of** fresh blackberries
- 8-10 fresh sage leaves
- 2 **tbsp** honey
- 1 **cup of** water
- Ice cubes
- Sparkling water or club soda

Instructions:
1. **Combine** the blackberries, sage leaves, honey, and water in a **mini** saucepan. Over medium heat, bring the **Mixture** to a simmer.
2. In order to liberate the flavors of the blackberries, smash them with the back of a spoon while the **Mixture** simmers for around 5 **min**s.
3. Discarding the particles, turn off the heat and pour the liquid into a Mason jar.
4. In the refrigerator, let the blackberry-sage syrup cool completely.
5. Pour about 1/4 **cup of** of the blackberry-sage syrup over the ice in a Mason jar, then top with sparkling water or club soda to serve. Your preferred level of sweetness **Must** be used.

6. If desired, add more blackberries and sage leaves as a garnish after thoroughly stirring.

Nutrition (per serving):
Cals: 80 kcal, **Carbs**: 20g
Fiber: 5g, Sugars: 14g, Protein: 1g

290.Mason Jar Grapefruit Mint Spritzer

Prep Time: 5 **min**s

Cook Time: 0 **min**s

Total Time: 5 **min**s

Servings: 2

Ingredients:
- 1 **Big** grapefruit, juiced
- 6-8 fresh mint leaves
- 2 **tbsp** agave syrup or honey
- 1 **cup of** sparkling water or club soda
- Ice cubes
- Grapefruit slices and mint sprigs for garnish

Instructions:
1. Mint leaves **Must** be mushed with honey or agave syrup in a Mason jar to bring out their flavor.
2. Ice cubes **Must** be added to the jar before the freshly squeezed grapefruit juice is added.
3. Add more sparkling water or club soda to the container.
4. To thoroughly blend the flavors, stir well.
5. Slices of grapefruit and mint sprigs are garnishes.

Nutrition (per serving):
Cals: 60 kcal, **Carbs**: 15g, Fiber: 2g
Sugars: 12g, Protein: 1g

291.Layered Honeydew Mint Smoothie

Prep Time: 10 **min**s

Cook Time: 0 **min**s

Total Time: 10 **min**s

Servings: 2

Ingredients:
- 2 **cups of** ripe honeydew melon, diced
- 1 **cup of** Greek yogurt
- 1/4 **cup of** fresh mint leaves
- 1 **tbsp** honey
- 1/2 lime, juiced
- 1 **cup of** ice cubes

Instructions:
1. Greek yogurt, mint leaves, honey, lime juice, and **chop-up** honeydew melon **Must** all be **combine**d in a blender.
2. Blend till creamy and smooth.

3. Alternate layers of the honeydew mint smoothie and ice cubes **Must** be placed in **every** Mason jar.
4. Add a garnish of a mint sprig on top.

Nutrition (per serving):
Cals: 180 kcal, **Carbs**: 32g
Fiber: 2g, Sugars: 28g, Protein: 10g

292.Mason Jar Spiced Pear Cider

Prep Time: 5 **min**s

Cook Time: 15 **min**s

Total Time: 20 **min**s

Servings: 2

Ingredients:
- 2 ripe pears, **peel off** and diced
- 2 **cups of** apple cider
- 1 cinnamon stick
- 2-3 cloves
- 1/2-inch fresh ginger, **split**
- 1 **tbsp** maple syrup or honey
- Whipped cream (**non-compulsory**)
- Ground cinnamon (for garnish)

Instructions:
1. The diced pears, apple cider, cinnamon stick, cloves, and ginger slices **Must** all be **combine**d in a pot.
2. Over medium heat, bring the **Mixture** to a soft simmer and cook it for roughly 15 **min**s to let the flavors merge.
3. Add the honey or maple syrup after turning off the stove.
4. Pour the spiced pear cider into Mason jars after it has had a chance to cool slightly.
5. Add some whipped cream and ground cinnamon to the top, if you want.

Nutrition (per serving):
Cals: 150 kcal, **Carbs**: 38g, Fiber: 5g
Sugars: 28g, Protein: 1g

293.Mason Jar Lemon Lavender Infused Water

Prep Time: 5 **min**s

Cook Time: 0 **min**s

Total Time: 5 **min**s

Servings: 2

Ingredients:
- 1 lemon, thinly **split**
- 2-3 sprigs of fresh lavender
- 1 **tbsp** honey (**non-compulsory**, for added sweetness)
- Ice cubes

- Water

Instructions:

1. Put a couple lemon slices and a sprig of fresh lavender in **every** Mason jar.
2. To **every** jar, add a **tbsp** of honey for a sweeter beverage.
3. Add ice cubes to the jars.
4. Fill the jars with water, then gently **combine** the ingredients together.
5. Prior to serving, give the flavors some time to meld.

Nutrition (per serving):

Cals: 10 kcal, **Carb**s: 3g, Fiber: 1g

Sugars: 2g, Protein: 0g

294.Mason Jar Blueberry Chamomile Lemonade:

Prep Time: 10 **min**s

Cook Time: 5 **min**s

Total Time: 15 **min**s

Servings: 2

Ingredients:

- 2 **cups of** water
- 2 chamomile tea bags
- 1/4 **cup of** fresh blueberries
- 1/4 **cup of** freshly squeezed lemon juice
- 2 **tbsp** honey (adjust **as needed**)
- Ice cubes
- Lemon slices and extra blueberries for garnish

Instructions:

1. Bring the water to a boil in a **mini** saucepan before adding the chamomile tea bags. **Take out** the tea bags after 5 **min**s of steeping, and let the tea to cool to room temperature.
2. To liberate their juices, **combine** some fresh blueberries in a mason jar.
3. The cooled chamomile tea, honey, and freshly squeezed lemon juice **Must** all be added to the mason jar. The honey **Must** be thoroughly **combine**d and dissolved.
4. Ice cubes **Must** be added to the Mason jar, and extra blueberries and lemon slices **Must** be garnished.
5. Dispense and savor!

NUTRITION INFO (per serving):

Cals: 70, Fat: 0g, **Carb**s: 19g

Fiber: 1g, Protein: 0g

295.Layered Pevery Basil Iced Tea:

Prep Time: 10 **min**s

Cook Time: 5 **min**s

Total Time: 15 **min**s

Servings: 2

Ingredients:

- 2 **cups of** water
- 2 black tea bags
- 1 ripe p**every**, thinly **split**
- 4-6 fresh basil leaves
- 1 **tbsp** honey (adjust **as needed**)
- Ice cubes

Instructions:

1. Bring the water to a boil in a **mini** saucepan before adding the black tea bags. **Take out** the tea bags after 5 **min**s of steeping, and let the tea to cool to room temperature.
2. Put a layer of thinly **split** p**every**es and a few basil leaves in the bottom of a mason jar.
3. Pour half of the cooled black tea and half of the honey into the mason jar.
4. Ice cubes **Must** be placed on top of the tea layer.
5. The remaining p**every**es, basil leaves, black tea, and honey **Must** be used in the same manner.
6. Stir it just enough to **combine** the flavors.
7. Dispense and savor!

NUTRITION INFO (per serving):

Cals: 40, Fat: 0g, **Carb**s: 10g

Fiber: 1g, Protein: 0g

296.Mason Jar Watermelon Hibiscus Cooler:

Prep Time: 15 **min**s

Cook Time: 0 **min**s

Total Time: 15 **min**s

Servings: 2

Ingredients:

- 2 **cups of** cubed watermelon (seeds **take out**d)
- 1 **cup of** hibiscus tea, cooled
- 1 **tbsp** honey (adjust **as needed**)
- 1 lime, juiced
- Fresh mint leaves
- Ice cubes

Instructions:

1. Cubed watermelon **Must** be pureed in a blender **up to** smooth. Pour the watermelon juice into a basin after passing it through a fine mesh sieve.
2. Add some ice cubes and some fresh mint leaves to a mason jar.

3. Add half of the watermelon juice to the mason jar after adding half of the hibiscus tea.
4. Add half of the lime juice and half of the honey, then taste to find the right amount of sweetness.
5. Apply the same method to the second Mason jar.
6. Stir it just enough to **combine** the flavors.
7. Dispense and savor!

NUTRITION INFO (per serving):
Cals: 70, **Fat**: 0g, **Carb**s: 18g

Fiber: 1g, Protein: 1g

297.Mason Jar Mango Ginger Smoothie:

Prep Time: 10 **min**s

Cook Time: 0 **min**s

Total Time: 10 **min**s

Servings: 2

Ingredients:
- 1 ripe mango, **peel off** and **chop-up**
- 1 **cup of** plain Greek yogurt
- 1 **cup of** unsweetened almond milk
- 1 **tbsp** honey (adjust **as needed**)
- 1/2-inch piece of fresh ginger, **finely grated**
- 1/2 **tsp** vanilla extract
- Ice cubes

Instructions:
1. Mango chunks, Greek yogurt, almond milk, honey, ginger, and vanilla essence **Must** all be **combine**d in a blender.
2. Blend till creamy and smooth. **Must** the smoothie be too thick, add more almond milk.
3. Add a couple ice cubes to the mason jar.
4. In the Mason jar, pour the mango-ginger smoothie.
5. Garnish with a few slices of fresh mango and some **finely grated** ginger, if desired.
6. Dispense and savor!

NUTRITION INFO (per serving):
Cals: 190, **Fat**: 3g, **Carb**s: 30g

Fiber: 3g, Protein: 11g

298.Layered Kiwi Passion Fruit Lemonade:

Prep Time: 15 **min**s

Cook Time: 0 **min**s

Total Time: 15 **min**s

Servings: 2

Ingredients:
- 2 ripe kiwis, **peel off** and **split**
- 1/2 **cup of** passion fruit juice
- 1/4 **cup of** freshly squeezed lemon juice
- 2 **tbsp** honey (adjust **as needed**)

- Ice cubes

Instructions:
1. The **peel off** kiwis **Must** be puréed in a blender **up to** smooth. Use a fine mesh sieve to pour the kiwi puree into a bowl.
2. Add a couple ice cubes to the mason jar.
3. Pour half of the passion fruit juice, half of the kiwi puree, and half of the freshly squeezed lemon juice into the mason jar.
4. Add half of the honey and stir, adjusting the sweetness to your liking.
5. Apply the same method to the second Mason jar.
6. Stir it just enough to **combine** the flavors.
7. Dispense and savor!

NUTRITION INFO (per serving):
Cals: 120, **Fat**: 1g, **Carb**s: 30g

Fiber: 3g, Protein: 2g

299.Salsa de Pimienta (Pepper Sauce)

Prep Time: 5 **min**s

Cook Time: 15 **min**s

Total Time: 20 **min**s

Servings: 4

Ingredients:
- 1 **tbsp** butter
- 1 **tbsp** all-purpose flour
- 1 **cup of** beef or vegetable broth
- 1/2 **cup of** heavy cream
- 1 **tbsp** cracked black pepper
- Salt **as needed**

Instructions:
1. Melt the butter in a saucepan over medium heat.
2. To create a roux, stir in the flour and heat it for one **min**.
3. Stir in the broth gradually, then bring to a simmer.
4. Cook while continuously stirring **up to** the sauce thickens.
5. Add the black pepper and heavy cream after lowering the heat.
6. Cook for a further five **min**s, stirring now and then.
7. **As needed**, add salt to the dish.
8. Serve over steak or roasted veggies after being taken off the heat.

NUTRITION INFO (per serving):
Cals: 120, **Fat**: 10g, **Carb**s: 5g

Protein: 2g

300.Torta de Maracuyá (Passionfruit Cake)

Prep Time: 20 **min**s

Cook Time: 40 **min**s

Total Time: 1 **hr**

Servings: 8

Ingredients:

- 2 **cups of** all-purpose flour
- 1 1/2 **tsp** baking powder
- 1/2 **tsp** baking soda
- 1/4 **tsp** salt
- 1/2 **cup of** unsalted butter, **melted**
- 1 **cup of** granulated sugar
- 2 **Big** eggs
- 1 **tsp** vanilla extract
- 1 **cup of** passionfruit pulp (about 8-10 passionfruits)
- 1/2 **cup of** buttermilk

Instructions:

1. Set the oven's temperature to 350°F (175°C). A 9-inch round cake pan **Must** be greased and floured.
2. **Combine** the flour, baking soda, baking powder, and salt in a medium bowl.
3. Cream the butter and sugar in a different, big bowl **up to** they are light and creamy.
4. Add the vanilla essence next, then add the eggs one at a time.
5. Add the passionfruit pulp and stir.
6. Beginning and finishing with the dry ingredients, add the wet elements to the dry ingredients gradually, alternating with the buttermilk.
7. After smoothing the top, pour the batter into the prepared cake pan.
8. Bake for 35 to 40 **min**s in a preheated oven, or **up to** a toothpick inserted in the center of the cake comes out clean.
9. After the cake has cooled in the pan for ten **min**s, move it to a wire rack to finish cooling.

NUTRITION INFO (per serving):

Cals: 310, Fat: 12g

Carbs: 47g

Protein: 4g

Made in United States
Orlando, FL
13 December 2024

55557808R00061